ABOUT BUTTONS

A Collector's Guide

150 A.D. to the Present

Peggy Ann Osborne

Schiffer Publishing Ltd

77 Lower Valley Road, Atglen, PA 19310

Dedication

With love to the two people I most admire in the world, my parents, Mary Louise and Les VandeBerg.

A plated-brass button, ca. 1960s.

Printed in America.
ISBN: 0-88740-555-X

Published by Schiffer Publishing, Ltd.
77 Lower Valley Road
Atglen, PA 19310
Please write for a free catalog.
This book may be purchased from the publisher.
Please include $2.95 postage.
Try your bookstore first.

We are interested in hearing from authors
with book ideas on related subjects.

Note: Whenever possible, the buttons in this book are pictured at actual size; when they are not, their true size is stated in the caption, although there will be no doubt be accidental exceptions.

Acknowledgements

I would like to acknowledge the following collectors for generously allowing me to photograph some of their buttons: Marion Roche, Mary Louise VandeBerg, M.W. (Freddie) Speights, Ann Wilson, Bruce and Jane Beck, Charles and Jacklyn Beck, Judy Wehner, Orville Magoon, Lucille Weingarten, Robert Selman, Martha Breen, Joann Wyman, Ron Cole, Mary C. Johnson, Laurel Brown, Florence Dieckmann, Kate McDermid, Debra Hill, Lynette Parmer, Joan Cress, Polly Kirlin, Colleen Farevaag, and the late Christine Harrison.

For their enthusiastic kindness in sharing knowledge, advice, and practical assistance, I offer my thanks to Tessie Yustak, Jean Speights, Camille VandeBerg, Carol Freitag, Rose Peschke, Florence Bubser, Sam Gassman, Barbara Johnson, Art Wood, Joyce Lowry, Roy Teuber, Patricia Ward, George Theofiles, Mike Brooks, Stuart and Beverly Denenberg, Patrick Kelly (of Park Forest, IL), Fred Fallin, Ted Hake of Hake's Americana and Collectibles, Steve King at WGN Radio in Chicago, Mike Woshner, Professor Edmund Sullivan, and the staff and reference department at Grande Prairie Library in Hazel Crest, Illinois.

For their sharing of manufacturing information and anecdotes, insights, and/or buttons, a sincere and grateful thank-you to David Rector at Blue Moon Button Art, Diana Epstein and Millicent Safro of Tender Buttons, Judi Danforth and Peggy Zilinsky at Danforth Pewterers, Daniel Baughman at Bergamot Brass Works, Robert Prenner at Ben Silver, Glenna Bennett at JHB International, Chris at Buttons n' Things, the Tadema Gallery in London, Debra Hill at Britex Fabrics, Druscilla White at Duttons for Buttons (England), Kirk Stanfield, Dave Smith at The Walt Disney Corporation, Mr. Frietag at Blumenthal Buttons, David Schoenfarber at Streamline Industries, Bjorn Amelund in Paris for the Patrick Kelly estate, Susan Train of Paris Vogue, Michael Kearney for Todd Oldham, and Patti Fontanini at Hanna-Barbera Productions.

For their inspiration, heartfelt advice and support, I send my fondest personal gratitude to Robert Johnston, Sandra Dieckmann, Ilya Nykin, Claire Garrity, Louis Wamble, David Wilson, Barbara and David Berger, and Jake Bernstein.

At Schiffer Publishing, I would like to acknowledge the advice, constant encouragement, and aid from the entire staff, and especially thank Leslie Bockol for her wit and wordsmithing capabilities, Douglas Congdon-Martin, my photographic mentor, for his practical lessons and able advice, and Sue Taylor, for her daily smile and talented art design, and Betty Brooks, for the much-needed hugs and help. There are no words possible to properly thank two people I am now fortunate enough to be able to call, in the best sense of the word, my friends: my editor, Nancy Schiffer, who has been unflaggingly enthusiastic about this project and whose command of the language has greatly benefited the book, and my publisher, Peter Schiffer, for whom this book has been both a personal triumph and nightmare!

The hand was a favorite sentimental theme in Victorian design. The buttons include, from the top: molded black glass, dyed brass with inset pearls, brass with celluloid background, 'Austrian Tiny' made of tin, brass 'picture' button, incised black glass, a 'steel cup' with brass, a larger steel cup with brass and a wooden background, small mother-of-pearl with brass, pierced brass, iridescent pearl with silver, silver-lustered and molded black glass, a large iridescent grey mother-of-pearl button with a brass-banded carved-pearl hand, and a small oval carnelian and gold button. All ca. 1860-1890. 1/2" to 1 2/3".

Foreward

A very unusual one-piece brass button with a bitingly satirical scene: an aristocratic gentleman sits, reading a large gazette balanced on the back of a crouching servant. Probably English, ca. 1810-1825. Its actual size is 2/3".

When i was asked to write something to introduce this book, I realized that it was important to intoduce the author, who happens to also be my daughter, as well as the book. She and buttons have something in common: the more you know of them, the more there is to learn.

Peggy is intrigued by life and is in turn intriguing herself. Her enthusiasm and her novel ways of approach have always fascinated those around her, whatever field she was presently pursuing. Her joy in her subjects and her ability to convey it is often addictive: it was she who brought me into the button world, not the other way around—I became a collector, as have many others, because her enthusiasm made it impossible not to.

She has alway been a researcher, delving into any subject that piques her interest. For many years she has had a special love for art and design and has combined that with a study of history and explorations of various cultures.

When Peggy became a button collector she naturally was drawn to them as art objects and was fascinated by their detail and craftsmanship; in keeping with her predilictions, she became intensely involved with not only collecting them but with studying them. She likes to ferret out the unusual, search for the rare, find the unique. Her interest in buttons has not been based on their value as collectibles but on their workmanship and place in history whether ancient or brand new.

In this book, her second one about buttons, she offers us a unique approach, inviting us to see buttons as she does. The book is serious yet humorous, a broad study as well a very specific one—she shows us the world through its buttons. She presents buttons as chroniclers of time and events, buttons as reflections of the society around them, buttons as windows on fashions and fads; she delves into button design as a bridge between manufacture and art, takes us on a journey through three centuries of art history, and finally, invites us to view a gallery where all of the works of art on display are buttons.

Here is a new way of looking at buttons, of grouping and displaying buttons, and of appreciating buttons. May it open your eyes, your heart, and your mind to the pleasures of button collecting.

Contents

A very rare plique-à-jour enamel button, a floral design, molded of brass with transparent enameling, ca. 1880s-90s.

PART TWO
Buttons as a Reflection of Art

PART ONE

Buttons as a Reflection of Culture

Introduction

For more than two centuries, clothing buttons have reflected the world around them. They have graphically illuminated social mores; pictured current trends in sports, hobbies, decor, politics, fashion, and art; celebrated innumerable events, fairs, wars, and movements.

Buttons continue to be among the most visible of consumer accessories, and are growing just as rapidly as collectibles. Although there have been button collectors' organizations since 1938, the present focus on buttons in fashion, combined with several new books on the subject, has made them one of today's most popular collectibles.

In the United States, the National Button Society publishes its own magazine and sponsers annual conventions, as do many individual state button organizations. The British Button Society also publishes a bulletin for its members. Dozens of dedicated button dealers have been joined by countless general antiques dealers in carrying collector's buttons, and retail stores specializing in antique or collectible buttons can be found in New York City, Chicago, New Orleans, London, Paris, San Francisco, Freeport (Maine), and many other places.

This book delves into the cultural connections behind button design; its purpose is to focus attention on the 'look' of a button—not from a collector's viewpoint in terms of materials and competitive categories, but from the original concept of the makers. More often than not, button design was far from serendipitous; it was, instead, inspired: manufacturers *reacted* to changes around them by producing buttons whose designs *reflected* those changes. To understand buttons from this perspective, their origins and places in time must be considered.

The many eighteenth-century buttons that still exist are wonderful examples of the influence that contemporary life had on the design of such supposedly prosaic items. These buttons were actually social commentaries in a sometimes dangerous age, a fashionable and a silent way to preach, satirize, sympathize, lament, or boast. Such buttons were worn by gentlemen of means during the last quarter of the eighteenth century and were the finest ever made, in terms of workmanship and beauty. (All references in this book refer to the fashions and buttons of the western world unless other areas are specified.) The women of the eighteenth century wore few buttons of any kind—and those few were smaller and far simpler than were the men's.

Of all of the eighteenth century's socially relevant buttons, none were more reflective than those made in France throughout the years of the Revolution (1788-1795). The French Revolution can be traced event by event, beginning to end, through buttons. Every change in the political structure, each sway in public opinion, the dramatic battles, and the subtle philosophical shifts all were documented on the buttons worn by the men of the time.

By the mid-nineteenth century, the fashions of both men and women were ornamented with a great variety of buttons. As men's clothing became more sedate during the final decades of the nineteenth century, their buttons began to shrink in size and variety, while women's accessories did the opposite. The designs on this era's 'picture buttons' (almost always 2-piece metal buttons with pressed brass fronts and painted-tin backs) were invariably connected with every aspect of the surrounding culture and social trends.

During the twentieth century, buttons have continued, for women's and children's wear, to be bellwethers of social and political trends. Buttons have had their ups and downs in fashion, though, with two periods of button-mania, in terms of their scope and popularity: the mid 1930s through the 1940s, and the mid-1980s to the present day. There is a worldwide renaissance of interest which, now going into its second decade, shows no sign of abating.

New button companies have sprung up in the wake of this fervor and buttons of surprising variety are presently being produced in almost every country. Not only are they rife with reflections of the world around them, some of these brand new buttons are more socially relevant in their designs than buttons have been since the eighteenth century.

Chapter 1. Eighteenth Century

During the last half of the eighteenth century, buttons were quite a bit larger — averaging about 1 1/2" in diameter—than they have been at any other time. They were made in sets with anywhere from six through fifteen related images. (It is very unusual to find a complete set—most were broken up long ago and dispersed into private collections.) Sometimes the era's button-makers offered stock sets with popular themes, but the majority of eighteenth-century buttons were custom-ordered and designed.

There was little that happened in late-eighteenth-century society that escaped the gaze of button-makers: almost any social trend or newsworthy event was fair game: new hobbies, sports, fads, hairstyles, fashions, and inventions quickly showed up on buttons, which were as much almanacs of their times as they were fasteners.

Button manufacture was then centered in England, Austria, France, and colonial America, but the epitome of artistry—the under-glass button—was a type almost exclusively associated with France.

Under-glass buttons were hand-crafted works of fine art. The backs—usually of iron—and the glass fronts were tightly banded together with a metal rim. Under the glass were any number of decorations or objects: sometimes there were actual flowers, grains, or even insects inside the buttons; others had tiny ivory or wax sculptures of figures or scenes.

Occassionally the decor consisted of a painting on the reverse of the glass itself, but the majority of these buttons contained prints, engravings, drawings, or paintings. The miniature paintings, on ivory, vellum, or paper, were protected by the glass covers. Miniatures used in buttons were most commonly done by now-anonymous artists, but there are examples signed by some of the leading painters of the day.

Glass-enamel paints were used on porcelain or metal bases. These painted-enamels were not as much in need of protection from the elements and thus were not set under glass.

Some of the other materials used for buttons at this time were embroidered fabrics, assorted metals, mother-of-pearl, glass, porcelain, and pottery.

Porcelain and pottery buttons were made by almost every one of the famed European potteries during the eighteenth and into the nineteenth century, including Copenhagen, Chantilly, Sèvres, Crown Staffordshire, Minton, Coalport, Meissen, Battersea, Bow, Derby, and Delft, but the most coveted are those made by Wedgwood.

A mid-eighteenth century set of rebus buttons from France, signed with a crown and cross on the reverse; heavy, one-piece engraved silver, these were used on a gentleman's overcoat. 1 1/2" in diameter.

A rebus is a riddle made up of letters, words and pictures that, combined, form a sentence, phrase, or name. Their origin is uncertain, but they do appear in ancient Chinese, Egyptian, and Syrian texts. In fifteenth-century France, they were quite the rage, with whole publications dedicated to them; by mid-eighteenth century, they had again returned to great popularity in France.

From the top, the riddles on these buttons mean:

Elle a vaincu (She has conquered)
Elle m'aime (She loves me)
Elle aime sans détour (She loves me without varying)
Elle m'a cédé (She has yielded to me)
Elle est sans coeur (She has no heart)
Tu est sans ami(s) (You are without friends)

A very unusual set of engraved ivory buttons featuring the champion English pugilists of the late-eighteenth century. 1 1/2".

This extremely unusual copper-rimmed iron button from the 1760-80 era features a paper doll under a protective glass cover. Inspired by the mid-eighteenth century French mania for the jointed paper-dolls known as *pantins*, the doll in the button has articulated paper legs ands arms that dance freely about, a paper head with hand-drawn face, and a fabric dress.

A rage among the aristocracy, who hung them on sticks and carried them about town, pantins appeared to dance when properly manipulated. They originated in France, by 1850 were introduced in England and became popular there. Both men and women played with these little dolls, which were sometimes drawn or painted by very well-known artists. Pantins—which could be very expensive—became an addiction for many, and they literally went broke buying them. Finally, the French king tried to outlaw them; too many of his courtiers were under their spell. Others were also railing against the fad: a contemporary French doctor published an article attacking pantins, stating that the incessant jiggling of these dolls would cause pregnant women who saw them to give birth to jerking and deformed children!

A ticket of admission to a "flying boat and grand air balloon" ascension in Dover, England, in 1784.

Opposite page:
One of the most desirable sets of buttons known, these are water-color paintings under glass of hot-air balloons, made at the time of the balloons' invention. They are rather comical and more than a bit satirical in nature; the bottom button says *La Folie du Siècle*, "The Joke of the Century." *Courtesy of M. W. Speights*

Set under glass and rimmed in copper, a genuine Japanese rose-beetle sits, preserved through the centuries, on dried wheat. Buttons of this type, made in reaction to the eighteenth century's naturalism movement, are called 'habitats'. *Courtesy of M. W. Speights*

Eighteenth-century under-glass habitat button enclosing a moth on a linen-like background. Rimmed in copper. *Courtesy of Bruce and Jane Beck*

Reverse-painting on the underside of the glass: an insect, very detailed, on a branch. Iron back, copper rim, with an ivory background. *Courtesy of Bruce and Jane Beck*

Very rare, beautifully-carved ivory scene set under glass on blue painted vellum. The detail and three-dimensionality is quite amazing. The silhouette-like scene is of an old woman with a girl behind her, talking to a fashionably-attired young lady. This reflects the Neo-Classic trend in garden design during the eighteenth century. (Note the pillared structure and fence, and see Chapter 6, on gardens.) *Courtesy of Bruce and Jane Beck*

A very high convex glass covers this floral design formed of woven fabric and twisted gold-wire stems. Tooled copper rim. *Courtesy of M. W. Speights*

Two Neo-Classical Greek figures, nude. Hand-drawn and colored, black and white ink on silk. The man is Hermes with winged hat, carrying a caduceus. This button has an unusual setting: the back is an ivory disc with a shank screwed into it. The silk sits atop the ivory, and glass atop it, all held tightly together with the copper rim. *Courtesy of Bruce and Jane Beck*

Painted-enamel on oval porcelain, set in heavy silver. A mother and her son. Late eighteenth century.

An aristocratic French lady, probably a portrait miniature done for a private individual, although she may have been a well-known figure of the court. Some buttons of this sort were not actual portraits, but commentaries on various new hairstyles, millinery modes, and fashions. Ivory miniature, set under-glass, iron back, brass rim, ca. 1770-1790. *Courtesy of Bruce and Jane Beck*

Portrait of a woman, enamel paint on porcelain, set in copper, iron back.

Man hiking with stick; a beautifully-done gouàche painting, with fine detail on face and clothing. The scene includes a moon high above and church in back-ground to right. Set under glass, copper rim, iron back. *Courtesy of Bruce and Jane Beck*

A high convex disc of Staffordshire porcelain, set in and rimmed with silver. The scene in painted enamel is of a hunter and his dog, ca. eighteenth century. Very rare. *Courtesy of Bruce and Jane Beck*

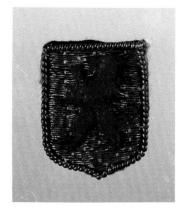

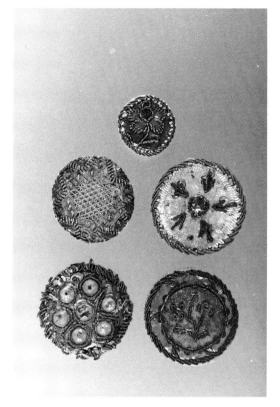

Very unusual heraldic buttons made of fabric, from the eighteenth century. The lion was first padded, then embroidered in heavy red silk. The gold-wire wrapped thread used to border and define the shield is copied from a very early Indian technique, and is called a purl. Purl was made by flattening a silver wire, coating it with gold, and wrapping the flattened, ribbon-like piece around a silk thread. Pure gold was also flattened, and then wrapped around silk this way, but very rarely.

During the eighteenth century, men wore silk or satin frock coats of incredible fussiness, covered with embroidered details, trims and great numbers of matching buttons. These buttons typify this style. The star-designed gold-wire embroidered button has a heavy cotton thread back, and has an embroidered flower at the center and a gold foil background. The others have sequins, foils, pastes, and gold-wire wrapped silk roping.

Eighteenth-century fabric buttons were not often pictorial. These examples include a very rare fan design, embroidered on satin tightly gathered around a wooden disc and trimmed with tiny cut-steel beads around the edge. The rose is embroidered with four colors on silk brocade. The black-velvet button is a very rare type: a multi-shaded woven ribbon was folded and embroidered for the rose and buds; the stems and leaves are simply embroidered with green silk thread. 1" – 1 1/2".

Cut-steel and steel-disc buttons of the type made by Matthew Boulton, in England, during the 1770-1800 period. Boulton did not invent the cut-steel technique, but popularized it for jewelry. He made many buttons, with these being rather typical: heavy steel bodies with large, facet-cut steels riveted to them. One has a cup-set paste 'diamond' in the center-this is a double-imitation button, for cut-steels were intended to 'imitate' diamonds.

During the last decades of the eighteenth century, the crystal chandelier had come into style, and with it came a desire to 'glitter' under the lights. All manner of cut marcasites, steel, and paste suddenly became popular as never before. Contemporary cartoons show men wearing cut-steel buttons and blinding people with the glare!

Metal buttons with 'shell-construction' were made in France and England from about 1750-1810. Most of them were military buttons, but these two were men's frock-coat buttons. The left is copper, featuring an English symbol. The right, brass with the fleur-de-lis of the French court, ca. 1770-1790.

Metal-shell buttons consisted of a bone or ivory disc tightly covered with a thin sheath of die-stamped metal. Instead of a loop shank, catgut cording was wound around the backs and tied in a criss-cross pattern before the metal shell was crimped over the edge of the disc. 1 1/8".

Assorted types of non-pictorial mother-of-pearl buttons from the late 1700s. The top button is rimmed with brass and is set with paste 'gems'. Early pearl buttons like these tend to be very thick and have heavy, metal-loop shanks. 1"–1 2/3".

Engraved and pigmented mother-of-pearl buttons with hunting scenes, from a set of 10. These are mid- to late-eighteenth-century rarities. 1 1/2".

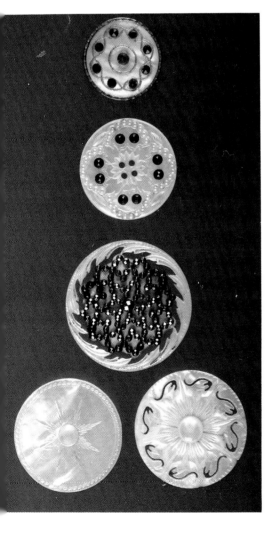

A lovely floral design on an eighteenth-century Sheffield silver button (rolled silver over copper). True Sheffield buttons are very rare. This one is signed on the bottom of the rim.

Coaching scene engraved and pigmented, on a very thick mother-of-pearl button. Coach buttons were generally used in England, worn on the heavy overcoats of the men who drove the coaches portrayed. They tend to be very thick and over-sized, so that their gloved hands could handle the task of buttoning and unbuttoning them in the cold.
Courtesy of Bruce and Jane Beck

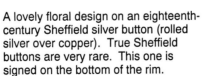

Glass-sulphide medallion on blue ground under a highly-convex glass cover, framed in brass. This portrays an eighteenth-century hunting dog. The name 'Jake Heed' is written on the banner. *Courtesy of Bruce and Jane Beck*

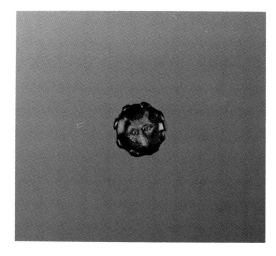

A small, very early glass-sulphide fox head, a breeches or vest button, mounted in heavy brass. Sulphides are coveted by button and glass collectors alike; eighteenth century examples are few and far between and quite valuable.

A 'Tassie Gem'. This button is a rare example of the first type of molded glass-paste cameo, made by James Tassie who invented the technique of molding glass into cameos from casts he took from genuine hardstone cameo carvings in the mid-eighteenth century. The brown background was applied by hand using a water-based paint. He travelled to Italy and Venice to make hundreds of such castings from the famous collections of ancient hard-stone cameos. One of his biggest customers was his friend and fellow-Britisher, the potter Josiah Wedgwood, who purchased molds from Tassie to make his own medallions.

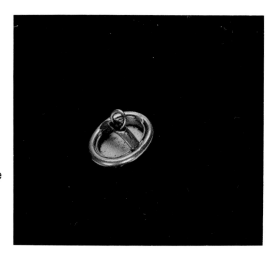

Reverse of the Tassie button, showing its white glass body, and heavy silver mounting.

The young Benjamin Franklin, American printer, publisher, philosopher, inventor, scientist, and diplomat to King Louis XVI's court. A very rare subject and an equally rare technique: an *en cliché* medallion set under-glass. 1 1/2". *Courtesy of M.W. Speights*

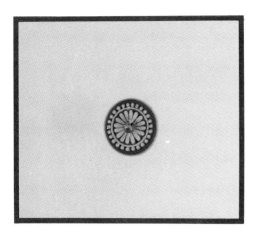

Very seldom found, these small, one-holed shirt buttons were only made by the Wedgwood firm and can be safely attributed to them. They were attached by guiding thread up the hole, through a separate tiny gold bead at the top, and back down through the same hole, ca. 1775-1780s.

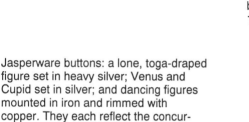

Jasperware buttons: a lone, toga-draped figure set in heavy silver; Venus and Cupid set in silver; and dancing figures mounted in iron and rimmed with copper. They each reflect the concurrent, late-eighteenth-century mania for Neo-Classic art and decor.

Wedgwood

The eighteenth-century English potter Josiah Wedgwood was a perfect blend of creativity, business sense, and perfectionism. His firm made buttons from the late 1770s to the early 1800s, and any of these Wedgwood buttons (or an early copy by one of his competitors) is a great find for a collector today.

Buttons that can be positively identified as Wedgwood creations are few and far between; there was always an incised 'WEDGWOOD' mark on the back of the clay medallions, but the buttons were usually set in metal and and the backmark—if there is one—cannot be seen. It is best to simply call them 'Wedgwood-types', or the term that Josiah Wedgwood himself used, 'jasperware'.

Wedgwood experimented a great deal with his molded-cameo plaques and medallions, changing the color several times. All-black bodies were the earliest, produced in 1769. During the next five years, the firm made solid-colored cameos in white, cream, and terra-cotta. In 1774, the first two-toned cameos were produced: molded in one piece, the background color in these early cameos was painted on by hand; needless to say, this proved too labor-intensive. Wedgwood quickly found a more efficient method, still used today—the medallions are separately formed, attached to colored bases, and fired.

Most Wedgwood-type buttons have white figures on dark or light blue backgrounds, but buttons were also made with black, yellow, sage-green, and lilac bases. Extremely rare examples of tri-colored buttons exist as well.

The great majority of jasperware buttons were mounted in silver, gilded brass, copper, or steel frames with heavy metal shanks and iron backs. Some of the rarest had the clay medallions mounted on flat iron buttons or were set under glass. Matthew Boulton—famous for his steel buttons and jewelry—was the source of many of Wedgwood's metal mountings.

Wedgwood stopped producing buttons in the early years of the nineteenth century. The only Wedgwood buttons made since were two designs produced by the firm in 1951—a woman's head and a seated figure. Made in limited numbers, they are not mounted in metal, have self-shanks, and are incised 'Wedgwood'.

The only Wedgwood buttons made since were two designs produced by the firm in 1951–the woman's head seen here, and a seated figure. Made in limited numbers, they were not mounted in metal, were self-shanked, and incised 'Wedgwood'.

Because the aristocracy and bourgeoisie wore most of the buttons produced during the eighteenth century, various aspects of *their* comfortable world were portrayed: elegant landscapes, well-tended animals and flowers, classically-designed buildings and objects. Little vignettes of the upper classes' gracious daily life appeared, and, most commonly, portraits of their loved ones or social peers.

Some of the most intriguing buttons of the eighteenth century were not only decorative and socially *au courant*, they were a form of communication: they editorialized about the world around them. This is particularly apparent in buttons with political references and war themes.

Such buttons advertised one's affiliations and beliefs, extolled the virtues of some and lambasted others. There were buttons celebrating the politics and rulers in England and the new United States, but the most extensive and intriguing group of buttons to ever reflect a historic event were those crafted throughout the years of the French Revolution.

Gorgeous ivory-miniature landscape: a palace and its grounds, deer grazing in foreground—one is an albino deer. Set under-glass, with a copper rim and iron back. *Courtesy of Bruce and Jane Beck*

This button has an unusual glass cover with scalloped bevels on the edges, a brass rim, and heavy brass base. The scene, painted on ivory, is of a formally coiffed and dressed lady sitting on a chaise reading a book, with her feet up on a pillow. Who knows if the man in knee britches, carrying a cane and hat in hand, is a suitor or supplicant? *Courtesy of Bruce and Jane Beck*

Ivory miniature, painted with opaque oils, of flowers; under-glass, iron back, copper rim. *Courtesy of Bruce and Jane Beck*

Portrait miniature of the young French Marquis de Lafayette, whose exploits during the American Revolution made him a hero in America; a watercolor on paper, set in iron, with a brass rim and high convex glass cover, ca. 1780. *Courtesy of Bruce and Jane Beck*

A lovely portrait, hand-painted on silk, said to be Marie Theresa of Austria, mother of Marie Antoinette. Set under glass, with a silver rim and back. Very rare, ca. 1775-1790, 1 2/3".

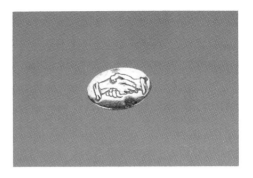

One-piece heavy brass breeches or waist-coat button, engraved with shaking hands, a symbol of several solidarity and political groups in the American colonies.

Enamel portrait miniature of the Marquis de Lafayette, a dear friend of George Washington—his children actually lived with the Washington family for several years. Upon his death, earth was sent from America to cover his casket in France, thus ensuring that he would be 'buried' in both countries. This button set in iron with a wide brass rim is extremely rare, very desirable in spite of the broken area of enamel, ca. 1780s, 2" in diameter. *Courtesy of Bruce and Jane Beck*

Beautifully engraved, heavy one-piece copper button; English, with rampant royal lion and crown. It says *Libertas. Pro. Patria. Courtesy of Bruce and Jane Beck*

Buttons made with 'secret society' symbols on them are rare; they were not commercially attractive to manufacturers because of their small audience. Most of these societies had roots in Christianity but had evolved into secular social organizations. This is an extremely rare eighteenth-century brass Masonic button, embossed with the various symbols of the society.

Engraved tombac, commemorating the American Revolution. Tombac was a greyish metal in common use for buttons during the eighteenth century, but rarely since. This is a 'colonial', a collector's term for heavy, one-piece metal buttons made in colonial America, although American and European-made metal buttons of the time are usually too similar to differentiate, ca. 1776, 1 1/8". *Courtesy of Bruce and Jane Beck*

A Federal eagle, symbol of the brand new United States of America, was engraved on this one-piece brass 'roach back', an oval-shaped breeches- button, ca. 1770s to 1780s.

Chapter 2. The French Revolution

The cockade, symbol of the Revolution in France, made of ribbon and worn by partisans. The wording is *Vive la république une et indivisible la liberté ou la morte* (Long live the Republic, one and indivisible, liberty or death). Painted on heavy paper, set in iron, under glass, and rimmed with copper, ca. 1791-92. *Courtesy of M. W. Speights*

The French Revolution was a violent social and political movement that crushed the *ancien regime* and brought about the formation of the first French Republic, but once set in motion it continued to rage on. Radical anarchists seized control and the fledgling Republic descended into a nightmarish 'Reign of Terror', all concepts of liberty and justice forgotten. A reactionary counter-revolution ensued and the period finally ended with the establishment of a moderate new government, the *Directoire*.

The Revolution left a rich legacy of buttons, mute testimony to the forces that tore the country apart. Far more than quaint trimmings from old French fashions, these are tangible reflections of history, fragments from the epicenter of a shattering culture.

It is difficult in our electronic age to understand what such buttons meant to the people of those turbulent times: there were no weekly news magazines, no T.V. editorials or radio commentaries; sporadic gazettes printed often contradictory and confusing accounts of the latest events, and gossip and rumor abounded. Even the churches and *academies*, once important centers of information, were under attack. Nevertheless, men found other ways to communicate: debates in private salons, speeches at legislative assemblies, handbills in public squares, and with conspicuous buttons designed to recap current events or commemorate past ones.

The buttons of the Revolution pictured the royalty, politicians, aristocrats, peasants, terrorists, angry mobs, the clergy, and sometimes even entire platoons of lilliputian soldiers.

While buttons with hand-painted portraits made before the French Revolution were usually sentimental tokens worn by loved ones, buttons that were made during the years of the conflict were almost always propaganda in favor of, or excoriating, the luminaries portrayed, or were memorials to the 'martyrs' of the Revolution. Many such buttons were molded in metal or had etchings or drawings under the glass rather than actual paintings, thus being more readily and rapidly available for general sale. Underglass buttons with scenic or allegorical designs were still most often custom-ordered and hand-painted.

The buttons of the Revolution actually form a precise chronicle—a timeline—of events. By understanding the various slogans and symbols, one can date the buttons quite precisely. The changes in designs, sometimes quite subtle, were always tied to current events: each shift in the political climate generated new buttons, and the previous ones not only became instantly obsolete, but dangerously 'politically incorrect'.

An ivory miniature of King Louis XVI, very unusual for its subject and its oval shape. Set under glass, rimmed with brass and faceted, riveted cut-steels, iron back, ca. 1780-1789, 1 1/4".

Jacques Necker, Finance Minister of France under Louis XVI. Sheffield silver (on copper) with the Sheffield-style rolled edge apparent at back. The wording is: *Necker Louis déta Gloire Les Hommes Commencent Ate Connoitre,* referring to a quote from Necker about Louis—"From your glory men are beginning to know you." *Courtesy of Bruce and Jane Beck*

Charlotte Corday, who gained lasting fame by assassinating the radical Jean Paul Marat in his bathtub in 1793. A lovely painting on ivory, set under glass, rimmed in brass and enclosed by a fancy cut-steel openwork border. *Courtesy of M. W. Speights*

Two under-glass buttons, copper framed, ink drawings on silk. Dated 1788, the wording *Potius mori quam Foedari* is Latin for "better to die than to live without honor." The reference to the Bastille prison has to do with its generally hated status, not to the later storming and battles. These buttons from the very early Revolutionary times, show the rising feelings of frustration and rebellion, ca. late 1788. *Courtesy of Bruce and Jane Beck.*

Pre-revolutionary France was an absolute monarchy before unrest and financial collapse forced King Louis XVI, in 1789, to institute the 'Estates General', a congress made up of appointed representatives from the Three Estates: the clergy, the nobility, and the common man.

L'Etat, c'est Moi, or, *I Am the State*, had been a simple statement of fact for generations, but now, for the first time, the King was no longer the sole embodiment of France but was part of a governing system.

It quickly became apparent that the nobility and clergy would always vote together, with the commoners having no hope of ever winning a vote; when they protested, these disenfranchised members were literally locked out of the meetings.

Having been frozen out of the Assembly, the ousted commoners from the legislature gathered at a nearby tennis court and swore to remain there, stubborn and unyielding, until a new constitution was written. The King reacted by ordering the feuding members of the Three Estates into joint session, and announced his intention to permanently disband the congress. When the 'public estate' legislators refused to go and threatened violence, several members of the noble and clerical estates joined them. King Louis capitulated. The Assembly remained in tact, and began work on a constitution.

The Revolution had begun when this hand-hammered Sheffield silver (plated-copper) button was made, between February and May of 1789; the precise dating is possible because the design is so clear in its symbolism: figures of the 'Three Estates'—nobility, clergy and commoners—stand hand-in-hand in solidarity behind a crown set atop a pillowed pedastal. The new congressmen still optimistically expected to work not only with the King but with one another. *Courtesy of Bruce and Jane Beck*

This 'Three Estates' button—a hand-colored etching, under glass, rimmed in copper—also came from the Revolutionary fervor of May to June of 1889. It features a bitter allegorical scene: the King in a carriage being pulled by a soldier and a cleric, pushed along by a nobleman. A commoner is being crushed under the wheels. The writing says *Patience. . . , ça ira*, "Patience. . . . it will be alright," a reference to the brewing unrest, ca. late 1788. *Courtesy of M. W. Speights*

A hand-colored allegorical etching of the Three Estates—the clergy and nobility joining to keep a commoner bent under the weight of the world—set under-glass in a copper-rimmed button. This dates between late April of 1789 (when the disillusionment about working together had set in) and the rebellion on June 20, 1789. *Courtesy of M. W. Speights*

The French people, however, were beset with uncertainties and within days, on July 14th, 1789, acting on a rumor of military action against them, Parisians stormed a fortified prison where the munitions were kept—the Bastille—and seized it.

Afterwards, the city returned to a state of mild discontent, and for the next year, King Louis ruled in tandem with the legislature. Many of the revolutionary leaders intended to get rid of him, but the people still felt some small measure of loyalty to the King and wanted a limited royal presence.

One-piece pressed-brass button with Revolutionary symbols including a *bonnet rouge* or liberty cap atop a pike, crossed swords, and oak leaves. The swords represent the nobility; the pike, the people; and the wording—*Vive la Nation, Vive le Roi, et La Liberte* (Long live the nation, the King, and Freedom)—the new reality of the royal position in 1790.

The King would never have been part of a list like this before the Revolution: after all, he *was* the nation. After the legislature was established in 1789, he shared billing with 'the nation' for the first time, but would still have been listed first. After the constitution was written in 1791, the king dropped to third place, behind both 'the nation' and 'the law'. 1 1/4". *Courtesy of Bruce and Jane Beck*

Brass 'shell-type' uniform buttons impressed with both royal and republican slogans. The thin metal is crimped tightly around bone discs; the sewing attachment at the back is made of crossed cords of catgut. Made for various town militias and guards in France, these buttons also featured the symbols of the Revolution, all of which were taken from the ancient Romans:

1) the fasces, Roman symbol of law and power, depicted as a cylindrical bundle of rods (the power to discipline) with a protruding axe-head (the power to punish).

2) the red cap of liberty, signifying freedom from slavery, "held aloft at ceremonies and rituals and hoisted on poles and liberty trees as a symbol of the new age in human freedom."[1]

3) the pike, a symbol of battle from the Roman javelin, but battle at the hands of the people: pikes were home-made weapons. (Having no munitions, the public was encouraged by radical leaders to make pikes "To your pikes . . . sharpen them up to exterminate aristocrats."[2]

4) a wreath of oak leaves, representing honor, from Roman laurel crowns.

The storming and fall of the Bastille, the hated prison-fortress in Paris where the munition were stored, hand-painted on ivory. The under-glass button has an iron back, ca. 1789. *Courtesy of M. W. Speights*

A post-Bastille reverse-painting done on the back of the glass, copper rimmed, iron back: '*Liberte*', cannons, flags, and the fasces, ca. 1789.

Patriot Palloy

Patriot Palloy was one of history's most interesting characters! An opportunist and entrepreneur, Palloy was so adept as self-promotion that he can be favorably compared with America's showman P.T.Barnum. After the Bastille had been stormed, its future was the subject of some debate; Palloy was perhaps the loudest voice arguing in favor of the building's destruction. Once the leaders of the revolution had agreed to it, Palloy himself sought and received the contract to do the job. He brought the building down with a crew of more than a thousand stonemasons, laborers, carpenters, and iron-smelters—a six month project.

He did this not out of patriotic hatred for the old symbol, but because he had every intention of turning the old Bastille into his new business. While his crew was tearing it down, "Palloy's energies went into promoting the cult of the Bastille as a political tourist attraction, complete with guided tours, historical lectures and accounts" and into producing a theatrical exhibit to "recapitulate both the horrors of the Bastille and the euphoria of its fall so that successive waves of visiting patriots could be recruited for revolutionary enthusiasm."[3]

Ever thinking of new angles, Palloy soon devised a plan to bring the reality of the Bastille to the multitudes of Frenchmen outside of Paris for whom it had been a remote event: he began to assemble a travelling-Revolution kit—a sort of educational display and 'museum store' to be carried through France by dramatically-costumed 'Apostles of Liberty'.

To fill the travelling-kits' trunks, he created "every conceivable kind of item from the debris of the Bastille that remained to him. Inkwells had been made from 'fetters' and other items of ironwork", paper fans were fashioned from miscellaneous documents found in the ruins, and he had his masons sculpt models, book-ends, and "paperweights from its stones in the shape of little Bastilles."[4]

The road show was short-lived: Diogenes Palloy, the man who actually named himself "Patriot Republican," ended up in prison, a victim of the mercurial path of the Revolution. He did not, however, lose his head!

One-piece stamped-iron button, 1 1/2", rimmed with a copper band. This is an extremely rare example, and although not at all attractive—in fact, it's dreary looking—it is also my favorite button. In just 22 words it sums up the hopes of the early revolutionists, exuding the joy and exhilaration of their newfound freedom, before anarchy dashed them. The translation is:

Legislators
This metal is made from the chains of your bondage
which your speech on June 23rd caused to break on the following July 14th
+ By Patriot Palloy+

The button is a true relic—it really was fashioned from the iron chains found during the demolition of the despised prison, and was a gift from Patriot Palloy to members of the National Assembly. It refers to the 'Tennis-Court Oath' on June 23, one of the pivotal moments of western history (often called the spark which triggered the Revolution), and to the day the Bastille was stormed (July 14, 1789).

An impressed brass *Vivre Libre ou Mourir* with pike, liberty cap, and fasces, ca. 1791.

It is recorded in a contemporary memoir that when the royal family was caught fleeing the country, arrested, and escorted back to Paris, one of their guards used the newly fashionable buttons on his own coat to frighten the six-year-old *Dauphin* (Crown Prince); he forced the child to "demonstrate what a good reader he was by repeating out loud the newly fashionable motto inscribed on his buttons: '*Vivre Libre ou Mourir*' (Live Free or Die)."[6]

In 1790, the Assembly completed writing its constitution and Louis became a 'constitutional monarch', ruling only by the will of the people. Henceforth he was known as the *king of the French*—a title which implies a postion of state, like president of the United States, as opposed to *King Louis of France*, a statement of regal birthright. The favorite slogan now became *La Nation, La Loi, et Le Roi* (The Nation, The Law, and The King); it would have been unthinkable before this time to have him ranked third, but he was now on shaky ground, ruling by appointment, not by Divine Right.

Unhappy and frightened, in July, 1991, the Royal family fled Paris only to be caught and returned. The attempted escape enraged the populace and "signified the annihilation of the royal mystique".[5] For the next fourteen months, the entire family was kept under house arrest, humiliated and scorned. Louis was forced to publicly rubberstamp all of the new legislation, but it was just a symbolic gesture.

By June of 1792 the French army had lost a war with Austria, people were burdened with new taxes, and many were nearly starving. The king and the queen both became the focus of anger, rebellions broke out in the countryside, and marches began in Paris. The royal residence was attacked in a bloody uprising in August, the family thrown into prison, and the monarchy abolished.

Year One of the French Republic began in September of 1792. Within days, Paris was torn apart as thousands of political prisoners and aristocrats were massacred by incensed mobs. Even the execution of Louis XVI (now known as the citizen Louis Capet) in 1793, followed by that of Marie Antoinette several months later, did not end the drama.

Another engraved and punched tombac button, dated 1792 with *Vive la Republique* (Long live the Republic).

The rarest group of buttons from the French Revolution, as distinguished by material, are those made by Wedgwood in England; it may seem odd that a member of the English gentry would have supplied the revolutionaries with buttons, but until they actually overthrew the monarchy in 1792, Wedgwood supported their cause.

This small (1") button—a brass-rimmed pottery medallion mounted in iron—says *Vivre Libre ou Mourir*, "Live Free or Die," and features a fleur-de-lis, symbol of the Bourbon kings of France. This combination of symbol and wording dates it from late 1790 through the first half of 1791: the King still reigned, but was in a threatened position. *Courtesy of M. W. Speights*

Tombac, a sturdy, silver-colored metal, commonly used for buttons during the late eighteenth century, and not since, was almost always just engraved or punched with simple designs. This 1792 example celebrates Year One of the French Republic, declared in September 1792, following the overthrow of the king.

The man-faced lion engraved on this heavy brass button is a chilling symbol of the execution of Louis XVI in early 1793. Seen impaled by a liberty-cap topped pike, the lion is a double entendre: the king of the beasts with the face of the king of men. Lions were, in fact, so symbolically identified with royalty that a genuine lion, a very old one that had resided in the menagerie at Versailles, was actually put under 'house-arrest' after the uprising. The pathetic old thing was spat upon, poked at, generally abused, and finally, shamefully neglected. (Amazingly, he did survive the turmoil to see happier times.)[7] This is a very rare button, ca. 1793.

After the attack on the palace in August of 1992, Louis was deposed—the newest buttons now said only *La Nation et La Loi* (The Nation and The Law). Buttons such as this small brass one with 'The King' (*Le Roi*) furiously scratched out are thought to have belonged to impassioned patriots with neither the patience to wait for the new design, or, perhaps, the funds to purchase them. This is, in effect, a recycled button!

Le Chant du Depart, "The Song of the Dead," a now-forgotten, bloodthirsty little ditty, was immortalized on this rare brass button. In 1792, this song was was popular as was *La Marseillaise*. Actual size, 1 1/8".

The entire first verse and the refrain of the French National Anthem *La Marseillaise* was embossed on this brass button, only 1 1/8" in diameter, and quite rare. The anthem was written early in 1792 and was wildly popular.

For two years pandemonium and fear had ruled France, but the worst was yet to come: in the summer of 1794, the 49 days known as the 'Great Terror' were directed—if one can say that about a nightmare raging wildly out of control—by the National Inquisitor, Robespierre.

His new law denied any legal consul to an accused person, allowing ..."judgement by 'moral proof' rather than tangible evidence. Only one penalty remained—death. The psychological effect was chilling. Justice and humanity were banished...Crimes against the Revolution were defined so vaguely...that men and women accused of diverse offenses were tried by the Revolutionary Tribunal in batches of fifty at a time."[8] During this short, ghastly period, more than two hundred people a week were beheaded.

Political beliefs and station in society did not determine who was executed. The pendulem swung in both directions: the patriots of one week were counter-revolutionaries the next; 'heroines of the people' became condemned traitors overnight. "Rich and poor, noble and peasant, duchess and flowerseller were conveyed to the guillotine..."[9]

An extremely rare under-glass button rimmed in brass with a serrated steel inner-rim. The hand-colored print shows a well-attended execution; the victim lying on the platform is about to be beheaded by a sword-wielding executioner while a priest holding a cross shrinks back to the side. *Courtesy of M. W. Speights*

Heavy one-piece brass button with embossed *Liberté-Egalité* (Liberty-Equality) and oak branches. During the 1794 Reign of Terror, oak leaves, and the oak trees themselves, underwent a period of great popularity with the average citizen, as a non-threatening symbol of justice recalling the earlier, idealistic days of the Revolution. Because the terrorists who had taken control did not take well to anything that could be seen as criticism, a safe symbol such as this one was a way of expressing longing for better times while simultaneously expressing solidarity with the cause.

No one was safe: Robespierre himself was one of the final victims of his own reign of terror. Without him, the inquisitions ended. But Paris was still wracked with uprisings and street battles for several months—a power struggle between the radical anarchists and the counter-revolutionaries.

Finally, in 1795, under the popular young general Louis Napoleon (just back from fighting abroad), French army troops attacked the insurrectionists, and ended the fighting. A new ruling body—the five-man council known as the *Directoire*—took charge and the country settled into an uneasy calm. The French Revolution was over.

This small, copper-rimmed under-glass button features a tinted print of the young General Napoleon Bonaparte, ca. 1795 *Courtesy of M. W. Speights*

The end of the Revolution, 1795. A stunning under-glass button with an allegorical scene—doves perched atop the fasces (symbolizing peace having conquered power)—painted on a mother-of-pearl background. Both its subject and the pearl background make this a very unusual button. *Courtesy of M. W. Speights*

Water-color paintings on paper, set under-glass in copper-rimmed iron backs. Such sets were sold late in the Revolution for the same sentimental reason as was the button at right, and were not custom-ordered but marketed; the quality of the paintings is hurried rather than fine. The idealistic fantasy-like scenes employ a cupid-like figure to represent the participants and recall the events of the 1789-1792 period. 1 1/2" .

Heavy engraved-brass button celebrating the conclusion of the Revolution, with a cornucopia (symbolic of plenty and contentment), a pike with liberty cap atop, and a laurel branch. On the banner above are the words *Liberte*, and below, *abondance-paix* (abundance-peace), ca. 1795 *Courtesy of Bruce and Jane Beck*

Chapter 3.
Aftereffects of the French Revolution

The French Revolution had far-reaching aftereffects on both world politics and culture. Almost every revolution since has been modeled on it. Dress, manners, and social class restrictions were changed. Modern language still reflects the Revolution with much present civic terminology stemming from it, including 'terror,' 'bureaucrat,' 'aristocrat,' 'anarchy,' and 'reactionary'; even the political terms 'left' and 'right' were first used to describe radicals and reactionaries seated on either side of the President of the National Assembly in 1790.[1]

The same long-term influence applies to button design. The buttons made during the Revolution are not the only ones inspired by the event; many were produced in later years to commemorate the people and events of the revolutionary period.

France was left so de-stabilized after the Revolution that for the next seventy-five years the country experienced revolts eight more times, and an assortment of governments and monarchs were overthrown.

The Directoire ran the nation from 1795 to 1799. General Napoleon Bonaparte, with great popular support thanks to his long record of successful military campaigns all over Europe, overthrew the Directoire and became the First Consul.

In 1804, his ego unchecked, he crowned himself Napoleon I, Emperor of France. Although Napoleon codified many of the administrative, economic, and legal reforms of the Revolution (Napoleonic Law still is the basis of the French legal system), many of the hard-fought freedoms "perished at his hands...The Rights of Man were turned on their head as discipline, hierarchy and authoritarianism replaced the revolutionary device of liberty, equality and fraternity. Under his rule, France passed into the hands of an autocrat with far more absolute power than Louis XVI had ever enjoyed."[2]

Blind to the growing financial woes of the nation, he embarked on the Napoleonic Wars, attacking countries all over Europe. Eventually his army was defeated and Napoleon was forced to abdicate. In 1814 he was sent into rather comfortable exile on the Mediterranean island of Elba.

Napoleon Bonaparte as Emperor, a rare subject. The quality of this beautifully detailed, painted-enamel with foil trim is unusually high. It is set in an ornate pierced-brass frame, ca. 1800-1815. *Courtesy of M. W. Speights*

Once he had crowned himself Emperor of the French, Napoleon had need of a royal cypher, and it became the bee (for Bonaparte). The royal bee was used everywhere: this dress-trim was one of many embroidered on his cloaks. Gold-wire and silk, ca. 1800-1815.

This lovely portrait of the Empress Josephine is a rare example of an *en grissaille* painting on glass, set in a copper button mount. Josephine almost always wore white, and is seen here in a Greco/Roman gown known as a chiton, a look Napoleon strongly encouraged, ca. 1800.

This pair is not Caesar and his Empress, but Napoleon Bonaparte and his first wife Josephine, depicted as the Roman royals. The carved mother-of-pearl cameos are set in embossed brass frames with acorn and oak-leaf borders, also an aspect of the Neo-Classic symbolism of the times, ca. 1800.

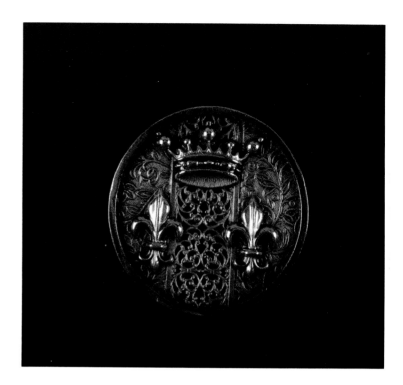

This dates from the time of the first restoration of the monarchy in France, from 1814 to 1824. A heavy one-piece pierced brass button with a separate rim, it features the fleur-de-lis and crown.

The wives of Napoleon Bonaparte: Josephine and Marie Louise. Napoleon divorced Josephine, his nearly obsessive love-match, because she was unable to bear him an heir, and married Marie Louise. The bottom button, made of pressure-molded black horn, depicts Josephine. The others are of Marie Louise: black horn, carved shaded-pearl cameo, and one-piece pressed brass with a laurel-leaf border. Her daily hairstyle, as shown on the top button was Grecian and held with one or more filets—narrow gold bands. The swept-back hairstyle, diadem, and high-collared gowns seen in the two center buttons were those worn for her wedding and state occassions. 2/3" to 1 1/4", ca. 1810 to 1815.

French uniform buttons from the 1814 to 1824 period. The sun-face symbol is not from the so-called 'Sun King', Louis XIV, but from the guard uniforms of Louis the XVIII, brother of the guillotined Louis XVI. The button at right is cast pewter; at left, two-piece plated brass.

The crowned, flaming salamander, symbol of Francis I of France. It doesn't date from his reign during the sixteenth century of course, but was a popular sentimental design when the monarchy had been restored in the nineteenth century. A 'steel-cup' with a very detailed, molded brass attachment. 2/3".

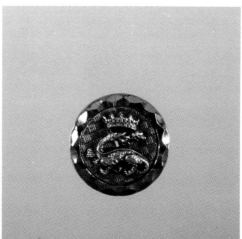

Surprisingly, the next man chosen to lead France was a king, Louis XVIII, brother of the guillotined former monarch. His rule had barely begun when he was forced to flee, chased away by the unexpected arrival of the armed and determined former Emperor Bonaparte, who recaptured the crown.

The second reign of Bonaparte was short-lived; after only three months he was again deposed and banished to a permanent and far less hospitable exile on St. Helena, a desolate island off the west coast of Africa.

Re-instated as king, Louis XVIII managed to remain in power until his death in 1824, but his successor, King Charles I, was forced to abdicate in 1830 in favor of a constitutional choice, the 'Citizen King', Louis Phillipe.

Yet another revolt dethroned Louis Phillipe in 1848 and a president was chosen instead: Prince Louis Napoleon, nephew of Bonaparte. After four years, true to his Napoleonic heritage, he proclaimed himself Emperor Napoleon III in 1852 and the republic became an empire for the second time.

Following its defeat in the Franco-Prussian War, the country overthrew Napoleon III in 1870, and proclaimed itself, for the third time, a free Republic. This was the horrible period of The Commune, when in 1871 the people of Paris seized the city and held control for two months. The right-wing republic that took over after ousting Napoleon, and the radical Communards fought in the streets in the most violent period France has ever known; in just sixty-one days, over 25,000 people died.

By the 1880s Paris had again settled down to become the social and fashion center of the world. The times seemed idyllic.

A man's waistcoat button, inlaid glass mounted in brass, profile of Napoleon III, Emperor of France from 1852-1870. He was the nephew of Napoleon I (Bonaparte). Rare, ca. 1850s to 1860s.

A tri-colored enamel on brass (colors of the French flag) with the royal cypher of Napoleon III: the fleur-de-lis and "N," ca. 1860 to 1870.

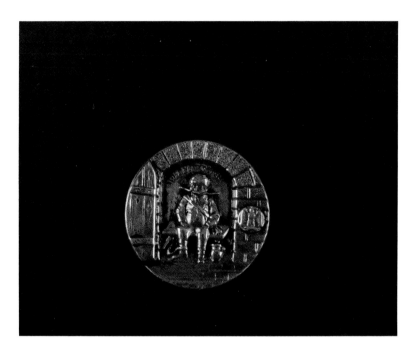

Brass two-piece 'picture button'. A caricature of Napoleon III sitting in prison after being deposed, his handle-bar mustache at a ridiculous length, a shackle on his right leg, and a chamber pot to his left, ca. early 1870s.

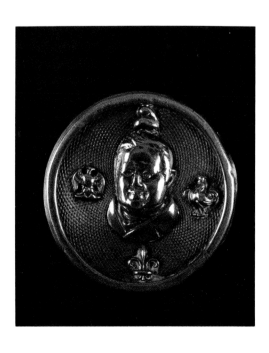

A rare portrait of Adolphe Thiers, the man whose leadership helped put an end to the Commune and the Seige of Paris; President of the French Republic, 1871 to 1873. A silver-plated copper propaganda piece with the various symbols of France: the liberty cap, the cock, the fleur-de-lis, and imperial eagle, ca. 1871.

An entire genre of buttons picture a quasi-political group called the *jeunesse doreé,* "gilded youth," that arose late in 1794 following the Reign of Terror. By mid-1795, crushed by the military, the group was gone, but during this short time they were the most public part of the counter-revolutionary movement trying to bring back a more moderate, democratic rule.

Particular favorites of collectors, these buttons are known as the 'fops' and date from various times throughout the nineteenth century. They were manufactured in a variety of materials including steel, pearl, wood, lithographs, and brass; some of the most beautiful were enameled.

The term 'fop', used long before the Revolution in France, disparagingly describes a certain type of aristocratic dandy, a staple of court life for generations, and is not an accurate name for this unique and far different group. Collectors should instead use the French terms for the men—*Incroyable,* "incredible"—and the women—*Merveilleuse,* "marvelous"—used not in admiration but in dismayed astonishment.

Although the 'gilded youth' appeared to be frivolous in dress, action, and speech, and had a predilection to singing strange songs and dancing in the streets, they were violent reactionaries who led attacks on terrorists and engaged in constant street fights. They actually helped shift the political balance; as it became more acceptable to criticize the radical anarchists who had taken control of the once-popular Revolution, the public finally rose against them.

During the chaotic times of the Terror, it had been dangerous to dress in formal style; by appearing in public as caricatures of the fops—the most despised stereotype of 'useless' aristocrats—the *jeunesse doreé* were showing their fearless commitment to a free society, even for former nobles.

The *Incroyable* were pictured on the majority of the buttons. They sometimes appear together with their female counterparts, but the *Merveilleuse* are seldom pictured alone. The 'gilded youth' wore bicorne hats with white cockades (symbol of the counter-revolution), short satin britches with bows around the knees, and long-tailed frock coats one size too small. Huge cravats covered their necks from chest to chin.

The *Incroyable* invariably carried a stick to aid in their frequent street fights, and even their hairdo was symbolic—rather than the officially encouraged short and straight hairstyle of the 'patriots', they wore their powdered hair braided and be-ribboned at the back, as had the former aristocracy, but in a parody; the *Incroyable* left the long hair at the sides loose and disheveled.

The *Merveilleuse* often wore scarlet ribbons around their necks, a flippant homage to the fate of the guillotined, and dressed in the new look from the mid-1790s—unfettered, Neo-Classic Grecian-styled white muslin gowns (the forerunner of the classic Empire look of the Napoleonic era). In fact, some of what collectors call fop buttons do not have the poorly-fitted weird look, disheveled hair, or walking sticks appropriate to this rebellious style, and are really just depictions of normally-dressed people of the 1805 to 1825 period.

So-called 'fop' buttons, made during the Revolution's centennial period, in the 1890s. They picture the *'jeunesse d'oreé* of the late eighteenth century. From upper left, they include: pressed brass, steel cup with brass Eiffel Tower insert over a pearl backbround, mother-of-pearl with brass escutcheon, a lovely painted enamel (the rarest and by far the best example shown of a true *merveilleuse and incroyable* couple), painted enamel on brass, *champlevé* enamel on brass, steel-cup with brass inset, one-piece engraved and molded brass, two-piece brass 'picture button', steel based-button with added pierced-brass border and brass figures, and molded brass. 3/4" to 1 1/2".

America's Statue of Liberty has appeared sporadically on buttons of many different materials since being installed in New York Harbor in 1886. A gift to the United States from the people of France, it was created during the French Centennial fervor to commemorate the revolutions of the two countries. "For France, without any question," it has been said, "the Revolution began in America."[3] The French were solidly behind the American Revolution, which occurred barely a decade before their own conflict began; they found hope for their own future in the founding of the young republic across the Atlantic. Some of the American leaders, most notably Benjamin Franklin, actually reached cult status in Paris.

Officially named "Liberty Enlightening the World" and designed by French sculptor Auguste Bartholdi, 'The Lady' was formed with huge copper sheeting over an iron frame engineered by Gustave Eiffel (creator of the Tower in Paris). At the tremendous celebration on the day of its unveiling, bands played *La Marseillaise* and the French flag was as prevalent on the streets of New York as was the Stars and Stripes.

This two-piece pressed brass picture button is very hard to find; it was manufactured at the time of the unveiling ceremonies for the Statue of Liberty. The rope-like border design complements the scene of New York Harbor, boats, and bridge. *Courtesy of M. W. Speights*

The Statue of Liberty, a gift from the people of France in anticipation and celebration of their Revolution's centennial, presented to the United States in recognition of the American Revolution's inspiration. This very unusual and beautiful button was made in France in the 1880s of cameo-carved smoky pearl in a brass collet rimmed with a star-cut steel border. *Courtesy of Bruce and Jane Beck*

Made as a souvenir of the U. S. Sesquicentennial Celebration. The detail and rough-textured background helps distinguish this from later versions.

Additional Statue of Liberty buttons include two of gilded Burwood (pressed wood composition), three small sleeve buttons issued for the 75th and the 100th anniversary celebrations, and pierced plastic.

The Eiffel Tower was built for the Paris Universal Exposition of 1889, the huge fair celebrating the Centennial. Designed by Gustav Eiffel, the 984-foot tall, latticed-iron structure symbolized the fair and was immediately popular with tourists, nearly two million of whom visited it the first year. Parisians themselves, however, were not so quick to love it.

I have heard collectors remark that it is impossible for a fop, a character of the late eighteenth century, to have visited the Eiffel Tower, built a century later, as is depicted on several buttons. That is true, but it was not intended as reality; it is symbolic. Fops were a product of both the city of Paris and the Revolution; the Tower, the most identifiable symbol of Paris, was a product of its Centennial celebration.

Another large group of buttons directly influenced by the Revolution was made around the time of its 1889 Centennial celebration. Large fêtes took place and the French people were feeling very sentimental about the Revolution. Late-nineteenth-century buttons reflected this and often favored a newly romanticized view of the old aristocracy; even the unfortunate Louis XVI and Marie Antoinette, her friends—the beautiful and tragic Princesse de Lamballe and the devoted young Swedish Count von Ferson—and many others were sympathetically portrayed, as were revolutionaries like Jean-Paul Marat's assasin, Charlotte Corday.

Many of these buttons were colored lithographs set in metal, celluloid, or very rarely in pearl. A few were rimmed with paste jewels. The public must have just loved them because large numbers of these buttons still exist.

Portraits of some figures were transfer-applied or hand painted on porcelain buttons during the 1890s, but the rarest of the commemorative portraits were small hand-painted minatures made for the 'carriage trade.' They are not much easier to find than the painted-ivory, under-glass buttons of the eighteenth century.

Button-makers produced many other commemoratives during the 1890s Centennial period, including enameled buttons with typical Revolutionary themes or symbols. These are rare.

Eiffel Tower buttons, at top of molded composition and at bottom of aluminum with a painted background, both ca. 1890. The Eiffel Tower, designed by Gustave Eiffel, was commissioned for the Paris Universal Exposition of 1889, a huge world's fair celebrating the Centennial of the French Revolution. The monument was intended to symbolize the fair for all of its vistors, an idea which seems unremarkable now, but was then a brand new concept—one which has been used by every world's fair since.

Centennial set of painted-enamel on copper French Revolution commemoratives. This set nearly duplicates a well-known eighteenth-century set of painted under-glass buttons. (These are pictured under Chapter 2, French Revolution.) In the 1950s, yet another, lighter-weight version of this set was offered, in limited numbers, to American button collectors. *Courtesy of Robert Selman*

A lovely painted-enamel portrait of excellent quality on a *champlevé* enameled brass button. This elegant lady is fashionably dressed and coiffed in the manner of a late-eighteenth-century French aristocrat, ca. 1890s.

A very pretty painted-enamel portrait of an aristocratic French lady of the late eighteenth century, in the center of a *cloisonnè* enamelled brass button, ca. late nineteenth century.

Under-glass miniature painted on ivory mounted in a brass rim with an added border of scalloped brass and diamonds. The painting is similar to one of Marie Antoinette. Under-glass painted buttons are far rarer from this era than from the eighteenth century, though not quite as valuable. Shown actual size, ca. 1890s.

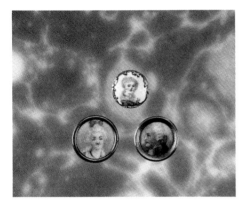

At top, a tiny painted enamel of Marie Antoinette and below, two lithographs mounted in brass glove buttons.

Lithography was first developed early in the nineteenth century, as a process for the mass-printing of pictures. The early designs were etched on stone and the prints were taken off the stone. Other materials, most commonly textured metal plates, were later used in place of the etched stones, as the process developed and refined throughout the century. It revolutionized the entire printing field, giving rise to a huge graphic arts industry. For the first time, 'art' became affordable and available to the common man. Such printers as the famed business team Currier and Ives supplied a never-ending variety of pictures to the seemingly insatiable public. Advertising also quickly became a huge outlet for the process as manufacturers issued thousands of ligthographed trade cards, and so on.

The earliest lithography processes were in black and white. The advent of colored lithography later in the century was enough to cause a near mania among the populace, who snapped up, and saved, every bit of colorful lithographed paper they could find. All of this was hardly lost on button makers, who, from the earliest days of the invention, set small black and white lithographs—protected only with a coating of clear varnish—into assorted button frames. Later in the 1800s, the buttons with lithographs had clear glass or celluloid covers over the colored-paper inserts.

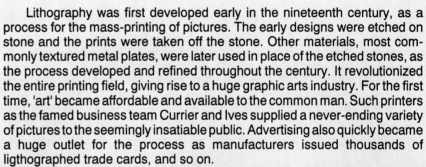

A lithograph in a rare, large mother-of-pearl setting with an inner border of smoky-pearl held in place with cut-steel rivets.

This is an extremely fancy lithograph button, set under-glass in the manner of an eighteenth-century button, and rimmed with paste 'diamonds'. The picture is of the Revolution's Charlotte Corday, who assassinated radical leader Jean Marat while he soaked in his tub. *Courtesy of M. W. Speights*

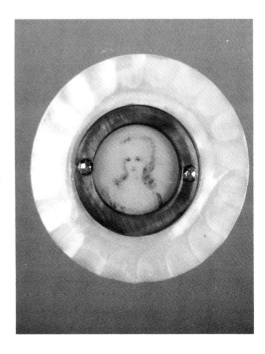

Another button depicting Louis XVI as the young Dauphin (prince) of France in 18.. A transfer on porcelain, it is a far more unusual button than are the many lithographed examples with the same likeness. Ca. late 1890s.

Three lithographs mounted in small brass button frames, ca. late 1890s. These buttons have been (mis)identified since the 1940s as depictions of Marie Antoinette's friend, the Swedish Count Axel von Fersen; they actually represent her husband, the doomed King Louis XVI, as a young prince. The Fersen identity stems from an early collector's enthusiasm for the sometimes-heard romantic tale that the Queen and the Count were lovers, a bit of gossip disputed by historians. There was no other reason for these identities—contemporary written descriptions of the Count don't match at all.

During the late 1800s, when these buttons were made, the French went through a period of intense sentimentality about their Revolution, one that included romanticized and forgiving views of the executed royal couple, Louis and Marie Antoinette. Among the many items manufactured at that time was a set of lithographed paper dolls depicting the kings and queens from European history, as children, published by Frederick Stokes in 1896. The set included a doll identified as Louis XVI, Dauphin, with the exact same lithographed portrait that is seen in the largest button at the center below.

The three small buttons here are among the multitude that have been found picturing the same face, hair, and clothing as is seen on the paper doll, but from slightly different angles—these different poses were on the advertising and packaging for the doll set.

These lithographed buttons are set in a variety of brass and white-metal frames. All depict French aristocrats and royals from the Revolutionary period. At the top left, top center, and bottom center is Marie Antoinette. The center button is Louis XVI as a boy, as discussed above (this is the exact lithograph used for the paper doll).

The button at lower left probably does represent the tragic Count von Fersen, for it closely matches his curly blond description: he did not wear his hair powdered and beribboned as does the boy shown in the many lithographs known as Fersen buttons. In addition, the count was not famous as a child, but as a young man—the age of the one shown in this particular print. Only the Dauphin of France, the future king, had fame enough as a child to justify manufacturers' use of such an image.

Commemorative buttons reproduced in the 1950s showing Napoleon I in exile on Ile Ste. Helene, and Napoleon standing atop the world, above the clouds. Plated white metal.

Fleur-de-lis buttons were made in profusion off and on throughout the nineteenth century during various displays of patriotic fervor. This group includes pierced brass, at center, and four silver buttons, two of which are enameled.

Fleurs-de-lis on nineteenth century buttons in a multitude of materials, ranging in size from 1" to 2" in diameter.
Left row, top to bottom: *champlevé* enamel on brass; enameled brass mounted in heavy grey pearl; molded black glass; a silver heraldic crest; enamelled brass.
Center row: pierced brass; engraved and painted copper with fancy cut and pierced steel trim (the oldest button shown, ca. 1810); brass with steel trim; steel-cup with brass center; and a lovely scallop-edged enamel with gold and silver foil, on copper.
Right row: Pierced and filligreed brass with riveted cut-steel trim; brass with iridescent mother-of-pearl back ground; pierced brass; high quality *bleu de roi* enamel with foil trim; molded and gilded brass.

As far back as George Washington's first term as president, American men wore buttons on their clothing that broadcast their political preferences. Political pin-back buttons celebrating or commemorating various presidents and candidates are very popular collectibles today, but for the first 100 years of American history (until the 1896 invention of 'pin-backs') political buttons were true clothing buttons.

None of these early political buttons are common; many are exceedingly rare. The ones made later, in the twentieth century, are certainly easier to find, but not at all the norm, being outshadowed by the many more pin-backs that exist.

Political buttons break down into three categories, by their purpose: celebratory and commemorative pieces, memorials, and campaign items.

The Washington political buttons were of course not campaign buttons—Washington did not campaign for the office—but were commemoratives, issued to those who attended his first ceremony. Although very valuable and rare, numbers of them still exist, for the attendees each received a full set of coat buttons that were cherished by the recipients and carefully preserved by their heirs. A reported twenty-seven different designs exist, all made of brass or copper. (Modern reproductions exist, so be cautious if offered one for sale. The original Washington inaugural buttons have somewhat unfinished edges, hand-soldered shanks, and were never cast, but stamped from sheets of very thin metal.)

A "G.W." (as collectors call these buttons), heavy copper. This is the linked-states design, one of the many patterns of George Washington inaugural buttons, with the 13 original colonies represented by initials in the encircling border. This button, and other Washington inaugurals have been reproduced throughout the years. 1 1/2". *Courtesy of Bruce and Jane Beck*

Five types of George Washington inaugural buttons, heavy brass, punched and engraved. Very valuable buttons, and although rare, by no means one-of-a-kind: their value lies in their historical significance, ca. 1789, 3/4" to 1 1/2".

Andrew Jackson's campaigns of 1826 and 1830 generated some interesting buttons that were quite subtle. Plain-faced, heavy, one-piece gilded brass, they have embossed backmarks reading "Jackson Huzza, Jackson's Victory, Andrew Jackson/ Mar 4, 1829." These are celebratory, not campaign, buttons.

The first election with political-campaign clothing buttons was that of 1834. The new party, the Whigs, ran Henry Clay, who lost, but buttons of both the party itself and of Clay were made.

The 1840 campaign of William Henry Harrison, the first Whig to be elected president, "was without a doubt the wildest, the most exciting, colorful, and nonsensical of all political campaigns in American history...Genteel politics had given way to hard campaigning: parades and rallies were numerous, and often culminated in the emptying of several barrels of hard cider...".[1]

The first election to have had political *campaign* buttons was also the first election for the new party, the Whigs, in 1834. This heavy, one-piece brass button features a liberty cap, the Whig party emblem.

Henry Clay was the Whig candidate for the 1834 elections. Although he lost, his image does appear in these small molded-glass and brass waistcoat buttons. Actual size, less than 1/2".

Gilded brass commemorative buttons of George Washington and General LaFayette. These stem from the Marquis de LaFayette's triumphant return to America in 1824. On this visit he was represented with a set of solid gold buttons with this picture of Washington on them. The public was in turn offered gilded brass buttons with LaFayette pictured on them; they were such a hit that they were reproduced many more times; the Washington button was issued soon after; in gilded brass of course, not solid gold, for general sale.

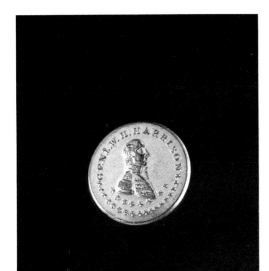

The profile on this copper-covered, faced- brass button from the 1840 campaign is that of General William Henry Harrison. The backmark reads "Scovil and co (sic) Waterbury."

Harrison Log Cabin button, cider barrel on porch. The earlier Whig campaigns used a liberty-cap as their emblem, with at least six different variations in buttons known. But Whig buttons from 1840 (in more than sixty variations) show the new Whig party emblem—a log cabin with a cider barrel out front, , symbolizing the supposedly humble birth of W.H. Harrison, a true man of the people. Ironically, he was not only a non-drinker, but was actually a high-born British subject, the last American president to have been one. Buttons showing Harrison on horseback, or the profile head seen at left, are far more unusual than those with log cabins. Brass with tin back, marked "E. Pritchard, Waterbury, Conn," ca. 1840.

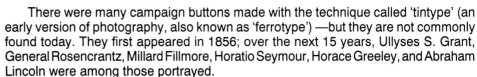

There were many campaign buttons made with the technique called 'tintype' (an early version of photography, also known as 'ferrotype') —but they are not commonly found today. They first appeared in 1856; over the next 15 years, Ullyses S. Grant, General Rosencrantz, Millard Fillmore, Horatio Seymour, Horace Greeley, and Abraham Lincoln were among those portrayed.

The Republican Party was founded by defecting Whigs in 1856. Abraham Lincoln, their first candiate, won the election. He led the country into and out of The Civl War, but soon after he was re-elected in 1864, he became the first American president to be assassinated.

Highly convex two-piece brass campaign button from 1848 with an embossed profile bust of Zachary Taylor, the 12th American president and his slogan, 'Rough and Ready'. There were also buttons featuring him on horseback. *Courtesy of Bruce and Jane Beck*

Molded black-horn button commemorating Abraham Lincoln's death: it has busts of Washington and Lincoln, their names on the ribbons encircling them, and 'Liberty' at the top. This is among the rarest of all of the molded-horn buttons. *Courtesy of Bruce and Jane Beck*

A political campaign clothing-button picturing Lewis Cass, American presidential candidate in the 1850s. This tintype waistcoat button may be unique; no other clothing buttons of any type picturing Cass have been reported.

A pad-backed (fabric shank) fabric button with a molded black glass center that says 'UNION'. The Civil War was about to split the country when this button was made in the middle of the nineteenth century. *Courtesy of Bruce and Jane Beck*

A man's waistcoat button with a very rare tintype photograph of Mary Todd Lincoln; following her husband's death, she became the second most famous widow of the nineteenth century, after Queen Victoria.

Goodyear Rubber

In 1868 hard-rubber temporarily became the new material of choice for campaign buttons.

Goodyear rubber buttons are pure Americana—the only major type of button made solely by manufacturers in the United States. All of the marked Goodyear rubber buttons were made between 1855 and 1875 by just two companies: the India Rubber Comb Company and the Novelty Rubber Company. 'Goodyears' may look dull at first, but are a complex category enjoyed by many collectors.

Not particularly popular during their own time—the buttons were said to give off an unpleasant odor when damp or warm, and the designs flattened under heat or pressure—they failed completely as an export product.

Charles Goodyear first discovered vulcanization (setting) of rubber in 1839. He eventually received over sixty different patents for rubber and its uses; the patent of 1851 is the one which dealt with the button-making process. The legal costs of defending all these patents kept him a poor man—he spent more than one term in debtor's prison—and he died, broke, in 1860.

Goodyear button backs are marked "Patent" (on small sizes it was abbreviated "P = T"), often the name "Goodyear" and a date, usually "1851," along with the name or initials of the maker. The rarest mark is "1849-51." A few have the exact patent date—"May 6, 1851;" these have nothing to do with the date of manufacture, only with the patent.

Extremely unusual Goodyears were combined with additional decorations: a brass escutcheon shaped like a woman's head, an inlaid steel star, a brass cross, a glass bead, or a disc of mother-of-pearl. These are so rare as to be nearly one-of-a-kind. One otherwise-plain button rimmed in brass has also been reported.

From 1/4" to 1 3/4" in diameter, most of the Goodyears are plain-faced or have simple pressed patterns. Pictorials are more interesting and include flowers, two different fruits, two lady's heads, the Liberty head, a wasp, a beetle, stars, crosses, birds, three animal heads, a dog in a hoop, a scarce dancing-frog duo and the very rare Falcon Huntress.

Advertising collectors look for the rare examples made for the Gail Borden Milk Company uniforms, and a handful of similar others; they have the companies' names on the fronts of the buttons.

The most valuable Goodyears are two campaign buttons from 1868, showing the victorious Ulysses S. Grant and Schuyler Colfax, and the defeated Horatio Seymour and Francis P. Blair. Known as 'jugates'—items with both the presidential and vice-presidential candidates pictured—the buttons are very expensive and nearly unobtainable. The dancing-frogs design is also political—a reference to the 'Greenback' free-currency movement, also from 1868.

A few U.S. uniform buttons were Goodyears: two were navy designs, others featured the general service eagle. The rarest is a Civil War infantry button with an 'I' in a sunken center, used by 'Berdan's Sharpshooters' in the Civil War. This crack Union troop wore dark green clothing with black rubber buttons to avoid detection from the sun's glint reflecting off the standard-issue shiny brass buttons.

Goodyears aren't always black. A limited number are brown, many less are dull red or black-specked orange, and a very few are tan. Shapes include squares, scalloped, ovals, ruffled-edges, cones, and two different two-piece buttons: the ball-in-a-saucer is easier to find than the other, shaped something like a top-hat.

Except for the fore-mentioned rarities, Goodyear rubber buttons are inexpensive. Examples often turn up in old button boxes. (I found my Grant and Colfax political button—worth upwards of $350.00—in a huge jar of junky buttons purchased for twenty-five cents at a flea market. It pays to keep looking!)

The very rare Goodyear Rubber 'jugate' campaign button of Republicans Ulysses Grant and Schuyler Colfax, who won the national election over Democrats Horatio Seymour and Francis Blair in 1868.

Dancing frogs. A marked Goodyear political button referring to the 'Greenback' free-currency movement of the 1868 campaign.

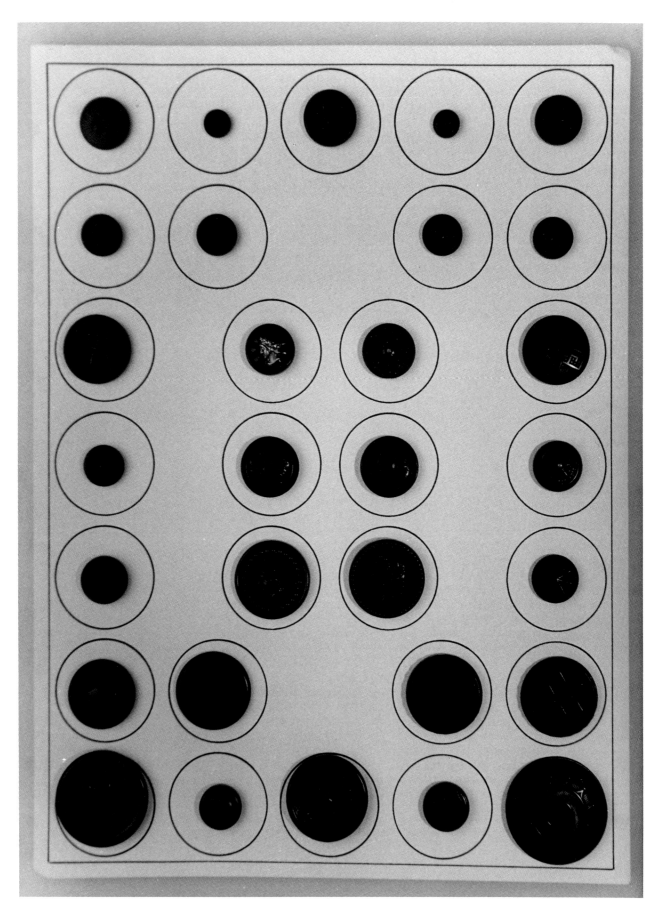

An assortment of Goodyear rubber
buttons, ca. 1855-1875.

In 1880, an otherwise-plain two-piece brass button with the embossed names of the presidential and vice-presidential candidates James A. Garfield and Chester Arthur, and losers Hancock and English appeared. This simple style of button design must have been a hit with the public: the manufacturers repeated the same design in 1884 for Grover Cleveland and Thomas A. Hendricks, and four years later for the Cleveland and Thurman Democratic ticket and the winning Harrison and Morton Republican team.

By this time, campaign lapel-studs were outnumbering political clothing buttons. Then, in 1896, a new invention became a grand success, celluloid-covered pin-back buttons. From then on, the manufacture of these 'pin-backs' vastly outnumbered clothing buttons, studs, and all other types of political memorabilia.

James Blaine ran as the Republican presidential candidate in 1876, 1880, and 1884. A phrase from the speech nominating him in the 1876 election became his slogan: "like an armed warrior, like a plumed knight, he rode into the halls of congress and threw his shiny lance. . . against the brazen forehead of every traitor to his country. " The moniker 'plumed knight' stuck. By the 1884 election, a plumed knight was used as the emblem for the entire Republican party. Shown is a two-piece brass button from this election bearing a knight with a sword.

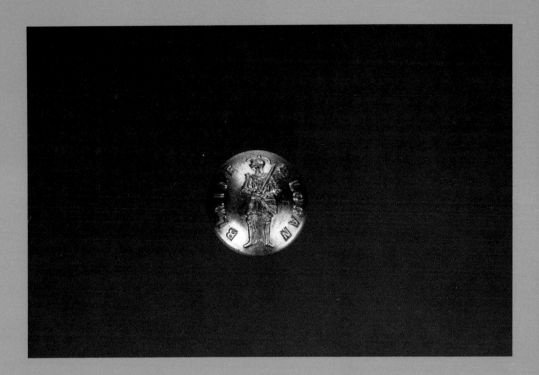

A very plain, convex, two-piece brass button with the names of the 1884 Democratic candidates, Cleveland and Hendricks, embossed on it.

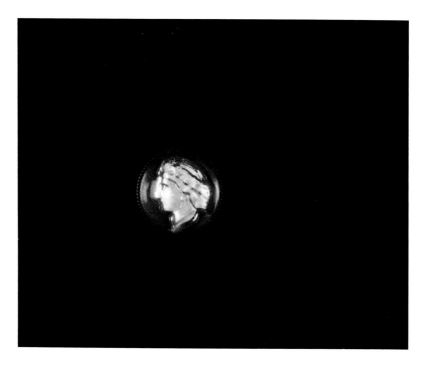

A rare glass sulphide of the Liberty Head symbol, set in brass. This button dates from the 1876 American Centennial. Old sulphides are all very collectible, but in button form they are particularly coveted!

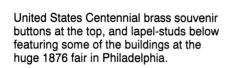

United States Centennial brass souvenir buttons at the top, and lapel-studs below featuring some of the buildings at the huge 1876 fair in Philadelphia.

These lapel studs are American Centennial commemoratives, made of tortoiseshell with silver inlay. The symbolic British lion attacks the American eagle on the stud marked 1776; on the other, dated 1876, the two creatures co-exist. *Courtesy of Bruce and Jane Beck*

Chapter 5. England's Queen Victoria: A Personal Life

England's Queen Victoria succeeded to the throne in 1837 at the age of 18, and ruled for 64 years until her death in 1901. It could almost be said that she defined the nineteenth century in England, a period which in good measure is known as the Victorian Age. (In it's arts, beliefs, and formalities, the Georgian period of rule, up to 1836, was more a manifestation of the eighteenth century.)

Contrary to widely held beliefs, Queen Victoria's influence on fashion was quite limited. She was not one of the era's trendsetters, except in her effect on the jewelry industry: she did popularize 'Scotch-pebble' (agate) brooches, and certain forms of carved cameos, painted miniatures in lockets, and other sentimental accessories. But her real influence was on the mourning industry, particularly its jewelry.

She had married a minor German prince who was actually her cousin, Albert of Saxe-Coburg-Gotha, for love—an unusual match in royal terms. Never crowned king due to the British parliament's refusal to consider it, he and Victoria were married in February,1840. Exactly nine months later, the Princess Royal, Victoria ('Vicky') was born. She was followed by Albert Edward ('Bertie') (1841), Alice (1843), Alfred (1844), Helena (1846), Louise (1848), Arthur (1850), Leopold (1853), and finally, Beatrice (1857). Albert died in 1861, when he and Victoria were both only 42. The queen went into a lifelong mourning period, considered an extremely excessive and exaggerated period of time even by the people of that era.

The relationship between Victoria and her oldest son was ever after strained; Victoria blamed Bertie (the future King Edward) for his father's death, since Albert had caught cold while on a mission to clear up a scandal the ever-womanizing young man had caused at school. Albert never recovered his strength, finally succumbing to typhoid fever.

Queen Victoria shown on buttons of pressed brass and molded red-dyed horn. These all date from the time of her coronation in 1838.

Prince Albert, consort of Queen Victoria. This silk weaving framed in brass is a rare example of a Stevengraph button. *Courtesy of M. W. Speights*

This brass escutcheon attached to a mother-of-pearl base is of a middle-aged Queen Victoria, perhaps the most realistic version of her to appear on buttons. She was seldom portrayed by artists in a realistic fashion, for the Queen was not a particularly attractive woman, ca. 1840s-50s.

Brass uniform button from Victoria's personal guard.

In 1876, Victoria was proclaimed Empress of India, a cause for great celebration in England and British India. Many souvenirs, including buttons, were produced.

As far as cultural influence was concerned, the nineteenth century belonged to England, and Victoria *was* England. The Italians, French, Portugese, and Dutch had pulled out of their colonies almost completely, but England remained a colonial power, ruling nearly a third of the world: India, Australia, Egypt, Canada, Scotland, Ireland, many Far Eastern and African nations and coastal African, Caribbean, and Pacific Islands. Victoria's soldiers were everywhere. Her civil servants ran governments and businesses across the globe; her industries were ranked above all others and financial matters worldwide were based on the British standard. England imported any number and variety of items from her colonies and protectorates, but exported only two things: her sports (golf, tennis, hunting, cricket, etc.) and her strictly defined manners and morality.

Queen Victoria's Diamond Jubilee in 1897, celebrating sixty years of rule, was a time of national celebration and produced many sentimental souvenir buttons.

Although Victoria's influence had already waned, her presence was still psychologically stabilizing. Her death, just three weeks after the turn of the twentieth century, seemed eerily symbolic of the beginning of a new age.

'V' for Victoria. There were two periods when buttons were rife with 'V' designs: first during Victoria's reign, and later at the end of World War II when the 'V' stood for Victory. Those shown here date from the nineteenth century. Included are pressed, engraved and gilded brass buttons; dyed, engraved, and cameo-cut pearls; molded black glass; inlays in composition and tortoiseshell; and a wooden button. 1/2"- 1 1/2". *Courtesy of the 'V' for Vande Berg Collection.*

Scotland was not only important to Great Britain, but to Victoria personally: her castle at Balmoral was a favorite family destination and she delighted in the music, jewelry, fabrics, and culture of the Scots. These buttons feature the lamb of the Order of the Golden Fleece —seal of the city of *Glasgow*—and the thistle—symbol of Scotland. The lamb is molded from black glass; the thistles, from left, are sterling silver, pressed brass, and painted brass with tin, ca. mid-nineteenth century.

Ireland inspired its share of buttons, including these with clover-leaf designs, ca. mid- to late-nineteenth century.

A pressed brass button with an odd rendition of Victoria made after 1876 when she became 'Empress of India'. A palm frond is the background for a tiny 'framed' portrait of the Queen sitting under a native throne-like canopy, reminiscent of some in India and Singapore.

A mother-of-pearl button with a paisley transfer design, hand painted. Paisley designs were incredibly popular during the middle and late Victorian era; the patterns originated on woven Kashmiri shawls that were brought to England from India. There are also great similarities to the colors and patterns of the loomed carpets from the Caucasus, Persia, India, Pakistan, and Turkey. The expensive imported shawls were soon copied by the thousands by Scottish weavers in the town of Paisley, hence the name.

This button is an excellent example of a true, very ornate and colorful paisley pattern. Paisley designs that originated in the west tended to emphasize only the comma-shaped 'pine' typically found in paisley patterns, and many collectors erroneously think that paisley refers to that shape as opposed to an overall look; paisley patterns—which came in great variety—typically have many elements to them.

Paisley buttons. Top row: four champlevé enamels, center: tôle and painted glass; bottom: steel cup with brass, dyed, and painted brass, ca. 1850-1890.

Opposite page:

Paisley buttons made of glass, brass, engraved and molded luster-coated black glass, mother-of-pearl, and inlaid tesserae. While the 'pine' shape is a symbol of fertility in the East, Victorian women who wore these buttons were probably quite unaware of it! Ca. 1860s-1900. 3/4" to 1 1/2".

Both the Queen and Albert were great fans of the new invention of photography; many tintype photographs were taken of the family's members. Tiny tintypes often were set as buttons, and it is known that Victoria was also a customer for these.

The Queen appears herself, as a child, in some of the tinype buttons of the era; since tintypes had not yet been invented in Victoria's childhood, this seems impossible, but the photos were actually shots taken of old lithographs and paintings of her. Such tintypes were not just personal accessories made exclusively for the Queen's family to wear, but were available for public sale.

Old drawings and paintings also were the basis of the tintype buttons picturing Victoria's eldest child, the Princess Royal. (This princess, her mother's namesake, married the King of Prussia, Frederick, and became the mother of Kaiser Wilhelm II, whose grandiose ambitions led to the start of World War I in 1914.

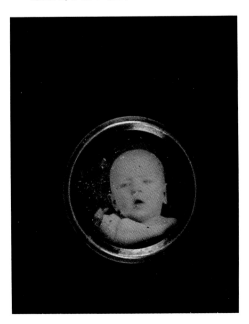

A daguerreotype mounted in a heavy brass button frame, the only example I have ever seen in a button. Daguerreotype photographs on glass were popular from the 1840s to the 1860s, but were supplanted by the newer tintypes, even though the tintype process gave far less detail. *Courtesy of Polly Kirlin*

This tintype of the Queen as a young Princess wearing a tartan plaid sash is mounted in a very ornate brass frame with an additional inner scalloped-brass border. Not a true photograph from life— the camera had not yet been invented when Victoria was this age–this is an example of a tintype taken from a print. Actual size, 1 1/4".

Another view of Queen Victoria as a child, taken from a painting.

Three tintype buttons with Victoria as a young woman, none of them shot from life: left, a contemporary engraved photograph from a print of the Queen and Albert at a party; middle, the young Queen in a riding habit; and right, Queen Victoria from a watercolor portrait done in 1855 by F. Winterhalter.

Tintype button of Victoria, the Princess Royal, on her wedding day, January 25, 1858, taken from the official portrait painted for that event. 3/4".

The Princess Royal, Victoria's eldest child, who was named after her mother and called Vicky. This tintype is mounted in an unusually fancy brass frame. 3/4".

Tintype buttons with prints that may portray Queen Victoria's three youngest daughters; from left, the Princess Alice, Beatrice (the youngest and favorite child) and Helena. 1/2" each.

Prince Alfred, Victoria's second son. Tintype photography was quite new when this picture of the twelve-year-old Prince was taken, from life, about 1856. 1/2".

The most famous ballerina of the middle decades of the nineteenth century was the Italian star Maria Taglioni, who found her greatest success in England. She became the young Queen Victoria's dancing teacher, and they remained lifetime friends. Taglioni's youthful likeness on this man's waistcoat button from the 1860s is a tintype photograph, shot from an earlier lithograph.

This tintype picture, taken from a print, shows the Empress Josephine of France.

A tintype button showing a Currier and Ives print, thus incorporating two of the nineteenth century's most sweeping innovations: lithography and photography.

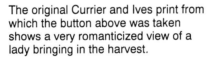

The original Currier and Ives print from which the button above was taken shows a very romanticized view of a lady bringing in the harvest.

The photograph of this unknown gentleman was taken from life. Such buttons were ordered for loved ones to wear and were known as 'gem' tintypes, a name stemming from their small size, ca. 1855-1900.

Tintypes

Photography was never actually 'invented', but was developed in a series of steps throughout the nineteenth century. Although many had tried various methods of affixing an image to a surface, it wasn't until 1827 that the theory actually met with success: a Frenchman, Joseph Niepce, managed to fix an image to glass. Daguerreotypes, used from 1835 to 1860, were an enhancement of this process. This technique was supplanted by the tintype.

Tintypes (or ferrotypes) are photographs done on a 'japanned' (black-lacquered) sheet of thin iron, which was then varnished. First invented in 1853, they were popular from the mid-1850s through about the 1890s. The small photos were shot with a multi-lens camera and therefore were affixed as multiple images on the metal sheets. These could then be cut apart, and the individual images set into button mountings, jewelry frames, or put into tiny albums. Because of their small size, tintypes are often called 'gem photos'. Tintype buttons are almost all small brass-rimmed men's waistcoat (vest) buttons; the far-fewer larger ones were worn on women's dresses.

Royal, military, and political leaders of the era frequently posed for tintypes that were then reproduced on a grand scale for admirers to wear. Almost every American politician of the 1860s era appeared on tintype campaign buttons, although they are now quite hard to find. Political collectors value these highly, but they were so fragile few have survived. Tintypes are easily scratched, faded, and destroyed; the surfaces should never be exposed to sunlight, touched, or cleaned.

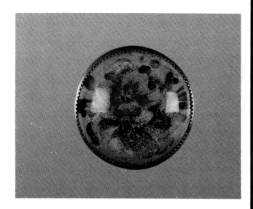

A cut-out lithographed paper 'scrap' pasted to the reverse of the glass cover documents a very popular hobby known as 'decalomania', but it is quite unusual to find one in a button. The new process of colored lithography was so new and thrilling that people collected any piece of it that came their way, often pasting ads, trade cards, etc. into 'scrap' books. (Scraps were small, colored lithographs, bits of paper printed by the thousands just to satisfy the mania for collecting them.) The button is rimmed in brass with a loop shank attached to a bar across the open back.

Tintypes were inexpensive, allowing the average citizen the privilege of owning a loved one's portrait, something previously available only to those who could afford to have a painted portrait done. These photographs were often taken by traveling tintypists who circled the countryside, or at tourist attractions, fairs, and beach resorts.

On close examination of the buttons, however, it becomes evident that not all tintypes were shot from live models. A large number of the images on these buttons were photographed from lithographed, painted or etched portraits, and in these cases, the person portrayed on the button was generally not an ordinary family member, but was a person of some note to the citizens of the mid-nineteenth century. For instance, a tintype portrait button of Caroline Columbier has previously been labelled as a photograph of a "typical Civil War soldier's sweetheart"—when in fact she was Napoleon Bonaparte's first true love. The tintype was shot not directly from her but from a painting of her done in the late eighteenth century, fifty years before the invention of the tintype.

This levels an interesting challenge to button collectors. When I realized that many of my tintypes were of famous people, and that the tintypes had been photographed from other sources, I began searching old portrait archives and art prints to try to identify some of my tintype buttons. I was able to identify an amazing number of them—twenty-three from a collection of thirty! I encourage others to continue this fascinating search themselves.

A collodian photograph of Queen Victoria, mounted in a brass button, from her Diamond Jubilee celebration in 1897. A widow for nearly 40 years, the Queen was finally persuaded to join her subjects in public and to wear something other than straight black, although she still bore this solemn appearance.

An assortment of buttons featuring colored lithographs printed on paper and on celluloid. The large black celluloid button with the bluebird is the most attractive lithograph I have seen on a button. Scenes are far less usual on lithographed buttons than are flowers and people, ca. 1860s to 1900.

There was no item too prosaic for Victorian button design! Here are pins, on buttons of molded black horn, brass, and black glass.

Fans, assorted, on nineteenth-century buttons including, top row: pewter, silver inlaid in horn, brass with a 'screen-back', molded black glass, engraved and pigmented mother-of-pearl, black glass, and a carved iridescent pearl. Middle: black glass, brass with white metal, pewter with black finish, and brass. Bottom: carved shaded pearl, and black glass.

Fans were quite popular throughout the nineteenth century. This lovely button is brass with a separate brass center and attached faceted steel fan.

Buttons decorated with objects of all kinds appealed to the fashion-conscious women of the late Victorian era, including these with (left) anchors, (center) door-knockers, and (right) keys, feathers, shells, and torches.

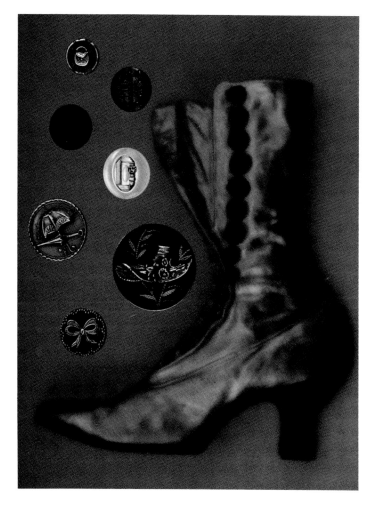

A high-button shoe complements ladies accessories on Victorian-era buttons, including purses, buckles, umbrellas, a hat, and a bow. A buckle shown on a button has always struck me as very funny, but there are enough of them to actually gather a large specialized collection of them! 3/4" to 1 1/2".

Chapter 6. Cultural Reflections: 1775-1885

There is hardly an aspect of culture that has not been reflected in the buttons of various societies: whatever was in the news, whatever was of personal or political importance to people, and certainly the latest social trends, were all fair game to button designers.

1 Religions

Religion may seem an odd subject for button design, but there have been so many religious designs on buttons manufactured over the years that some collectors actually specialize in them. The vast majority of buttons with religious themes or symbolism are of Christian influence, but with a more diligent search, one can find buttons relating to all of the major world religions.

Christian subjects on buttons usually relate to the stories of various saints or Bible passages; images of the Madonna are mysteriously few and far between, and the image of Christ is almost never seen.

Buddha images that were actually religious in intent are rare on buttons: most Buddha buttons are modern western items, and purely decorative.

The Hindu, Moslem, and Judaic symbols are much harder to find, in part due to the lesser number of clothing buttons used in cultures where these religions have been based.

A solid gold vest button, probably early twentieth century, picturing a Roman Catholic communion chalice. 1/2".

Christian religious scenes and stories on pressed brass 'picture buttons', including, clockwise, the Madonna and Child (copied from Raphael), the Angel of Peace , the Angel Gabriel, Michael the Archangel slaying a dragon, and Charlemagne and the Warning Angel, ca. late 1800s.

Assorted Christian scenes, from top, clockwise: German monks, drinking; Moses in the Bullrushes (copied from Delaroche's *Finding of Moses*), St. Joan of Arc, a religious crusader at the Fall of Granada; St. Joseph and the Christ-child; St. Christopher with a faux wood painted background; and Rebecca and Eliezer at the well. All are late-nineteenth-century brass 'picture buttons'.

Button collectors have always enjoyed finding religious meaning in buttons; these brass (and upper right, molded glass) buttons have been given names relating to Bible stories, but it is more likely they are simply depictions of life in the Middle East, ca. late nineteenth century.

Two versions of St. George slaying the dragon: from left, brass with cut-out top and painted background, and copper rimmed in tinted tin, ca. 1870s to 1880s.

An unusual scene on a one-piece cast pewter button: a European village woman worshipping at a way-side shrine.

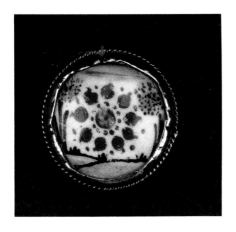

A rare Turkish silver button—niello metal-working technique with the Arabic script known as Naskhi engraved in very high, sharp relief; the toggle-piece attached by a short chain is the Islamic crescent and star symbol. Niello is made by engraving a design into silver, then coating the entire piece with an amalgam of lead, sulpher, and borax. When polished, the black mixture remains in the depressed areas, leaving the higher silver area shining.

Hindu symbolism—a god-sign between earth and sky; hand-painted porcelain disc set in a hand-hammered, heavy silver frame. This is a very old button.

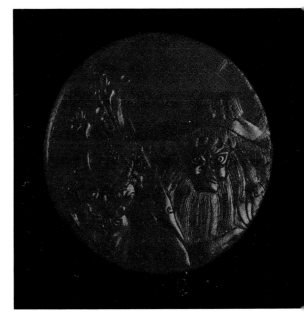

Molded and dyed wooden button from Japan showing an *oni*, a type of demon, and an old man, possibly one of the Immortals, no doubt from a parable, myth, or traditional tale.

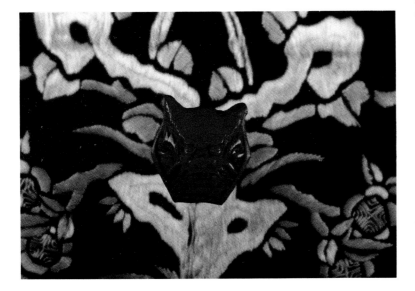

A Chinese demon carved from the red lacquer known as cinnabar. It is very unusual to find a cinnabar button in a realistic shape, and this subject is very rare as well.

From Norse mythology, Odin, the leading god of Valhalla. At left, a silver escutcheon on grey pearl; at right, molded black horn.

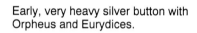

Early, very heavy silver button with Orpheus and Eurydices.

Astraea, the star goddess, in molded black glass and in brass with a cut-out top and 'screen' background.

The brass button at left with the Neo-Classic , leaf-designed border has a pressure-molded wood insert showing Europa on the bull. On the right is a molded black horn button showing the warrior Ajax.

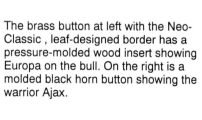

2 Mythologies

Some of the Shinto-based beliefs of Japan have been illustrated on buttons, as have Norse gods, but the vast majority of mythological scenes and characters on buttons have come from the ancient Greek and Roman tales. These were popular throughout the entire period of the western world's Neo-Classical movement, 1760 to 1870 or so. Button manufacturers, who were more than aware that the public was entranced by the tales of heroes and delightfully tragic stories of gods and goddesses, supplied a seemingly endless variety of buttons with mythological scenes. There are more versions of Minerva on buttons than any other character of the pantheon, except for Cupid. It is no exaggeration to say that hundreds of different Cupid-themed buttons were manufactured. To differentiate the Cupid buttons from those picturing assorted putti or even similarly-winged fairies, look for Cupid's accoutrements: the quiver, a bow, and arrows.

The public appetite for Greco/Roman culture certainly was not confined to mythological stories; the epic poems of ancient Greek heroes, and the historical tales of Roman warriors inspired countless buttons as well. (Even depictions of nothing more than their armour and weaponry were appreciated by the button-buying public.) Most of the stories, though based in history, were so fictionalized that they had become interconnected with the myths.

A mermaid on a one-piece brass button in high relief, with tail curled around the border.

The Roman goddess Minerva, after Cupid the most prevalent subject for mythological buttons. Minerva often looks like a man but can be identified by the dragon atop her helmet. This is an extra-large, early-nineteenth-century, heavy, one-piece brass button trimmed with riveted cut-steels around the border.

Mercury, from the sculpture by Praxiteles, in molded brass on a one-piece button at left, and in molded black horn at right.

Another lovely version of Minerva, as a brass escutcheon on a carved wooden button with riveted steel facets, early to mid-19th century.

The Greek god Hermes shown at left on a thin blued-steel disc with brass escutcheon, and at right on one-piece pierced brass.

At left is Ganymede and at center is Apollo, driving his chariot to the sun—a lovely, detailed, one-piece brass button. At right is Charon, with the Trojan warrior Aeneas.

Left: a concave brass disc, centered with a brass of Zeus drawn in a chariot; center: black horn with a brass escutcheon of Venus (the cresent moon she wears at the top of her head is a distinguishing feature) and right, a one-piece, dyed, pierced brass button showing Fortuna, Goddess of luck, with her cornucopia and wheel of fortune. Early to mid-nineteenth century.

Bellum in the center, pierced brass, and at left, Urania, the Muse of Astrology. At right, a copper button with a copper escutcheon of Jupiter and Minerva over a decorative wooden background, mid- to late-nineteenth century.

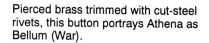

Pierced brass trimmed with cut-steel rivets, this button portrays Athena as Bellum (War).

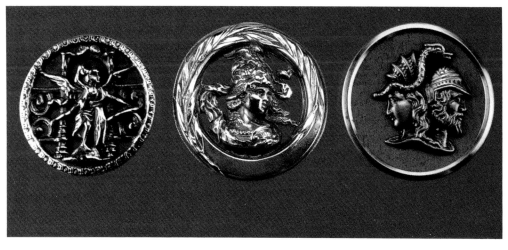

Brass buttons, from left: Dionysus, Bacchus, Aeolus the God of the Wind in pierced brass, Queen Hippolyte of the Amazons, and the lion. At center, a one-piece copper button of Pan playing his pipes.

Left: a pressed brass harpy; center, seahorse of inlaid silver in compostion; right: Cupid riding a seahorse, mid- to late nineteenth century.

At top, molded intaglio black glass, head of Minerva; at center, a centaur of brass, the Sibyl, and Ulysses returning from the seige of Troy; at bottom, a molded black glass head of Medusa with hair made of snakes.

At left, Mars, the God of War; at right, a portrait of the hero Hector, in brass buttons of the mid- to late nineteenth century.

Left: Ceres, goddess of the harvest, on a cut-out of brass, attached to a tin-rimmed button with a decorative wood background; center: another Ceres in a molded glass cameo; right: Minerva, in a brass rim with a pierced-brass layer over it. Mid- to late nineteenth century.

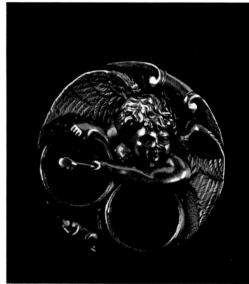

At left, Neptune and his horses on a dyed, pressed-brass button; at right, a lovely pierced-brass rendition of Neptune with a seahorse rising out the the wave at the right, ca. late nineteenth century.

A wonderful Cupid button showing him as a drummer, the brass button pierced for the drum-heads, ca. mid-19th century.

A sculptural brass Neptune, god of the sea, with his trident, over a decorative wooden background; at right, Cupid astride a dolphin and carrying Neptune's trident, in a dyed, pressed-brass 'picture button', ca. mid- and late nineteenth century.

Opposite page top:
An assortment of Cupid buttons, clockwise from top: pierced brass, white-metal 'Austrian tiny', pressed brass, acid-painted black glass, pierced hallmarked silver, painted enamel on brass with cut-steel border, mother-of-pearl with brass escutcheon, and pressed tin; in the center, molded black-horn.

Opposite page bottom:
An assortment of Victorian-era Cupid buttons in brass, tin, and, at bottom center, molded celluloid.

Cupid sailing a boat, a High-Victorian, overly-busy design. This is a deluxe button with an iridescent pearl base and a sterling and gilt escutcheon.

An assortment of mid-Victorian astronomical designs including, at upper left, Saturn in red dyed brass with cut steel trim; a small pressed brass with the symbols for the sun, Venus, Mars, and the moon; tôle with the moon and Mars symbol; in the center row, the moon, a comet and stars molded in black glass, a red dyed vegetable ivory 'whistle' button (one hole on top, two on bottom) engraved with the cresent moon and stars, and a cup-shaped tin with engraved brass background and a molded glass sun face; on the bottom, the North Star in the starry sky above the water embossed on a mottled, dyed vegetable ivory button, and a small molded metal button with thunderclouds and attached steel lightening bolts. *Saturn button Courtesy of M. W. Speights*

These are *putti*, not Cupids, flanking a large lyre, mid-nineteenth century. Cupids are always shown equipped with a quiver, bow, and arrows in addition to their wings.

A lovely Neo-Classic Cupid holding the horns of plenty.

3 The Heavens

Throughout the Victorian-era, people were intrigued by the heavens. Books, artwork, and products illustrating both astrology (the myths associated with the skies) and astronomy (the scientific study of the solar system) were enthusiastically received by the public. And once again, buttons reflected these dual interests.

Astrological designs were just as popular with the Victorians as they have been in the twentieth century. This assortment of nineteenth-century zodiac buttons includes the three one-piece molded-brass examples at left; three molded black glass buttons, one with a plain finish, one gold, and one silver-lustered. At far right, enamel on brass, a carp swallowing the moon, from Japanese astrology.

The moon in various aspects on nineteenth-century buttons including brass, blued steel, steel-cup, black glass, mother-of-pearl, and at the top, a vegetable ivory (tagua nut) crescent in an unusually large size, 3/4" to 1 1/2".

Comets. These do not depict 'Haley's Comet', which appeared in 1835 and 1910, for their age is wrong. They were manufactured in reaction to both the 'Comet Donati' in 1865, and the 'Great Comet' which appeared in 1882, both of which caused quite a sensation. From left, dyed embossed brass, molded black-horn, brass and black glass over a celluloid background set in brass, engraved brass disc with an added brass man in the moon, tin-backed button with cut-out brass border and wooden background, engraved grey pearl with inset rhinestone stars, one-piece brass with riveted steel facets, and, in the center, an engraved and pigmented black pearl disc mounted in a heavy silver frame with prong-set paste border—a deluxe button, mid-nineteenth century.

An assortment of nineteenth-century buttons with star designs, in mother-of-pearl, brass, black glass, enamel, glass, and black horn.

The Aurora Borealis (or Northern Lights) was of great interest to the people of the 1800s, and it is not, therefore, surprising to find that it was featured on buttons. The Aurora was so closely associated with North America that it was depicted in the background of many of the pro-immigration posters throught Europe, subliminally symbolizing America as a miraculous or magical destination. Not until the 1950s did scientists actually discover what causes the lights. These buttons demonstrate how artists of the nineteenth century portrayed the sight: top row, from left, molded white-metal, backmarked 'Paris'; cameo-carved shaded-pearl, and pressed brass marked 'Paris'; center: two molded black glass buttons with silver luster; left, iridescent luster; bottom, engraved shimmery mother-of-pearl mounted in brass.

4 The Grand Tour

Throughout the eighteenth and nineteenth centuries, inquisitive Europeans traveled abroad on the 'Grand Tour', with the Roman ruins, Venice, Naples and the Greek Isles as the favorite destinations. A popular rite-of-passage for young men of the upper classes, this travel was, in the eighteenth century, a difficult and often perilous journey suited only for the most adventurous.

The travelers often returned home from the 'Grand Tour' laden with buttons, including Venetian mosaics and cameos, jade from the Orient, and carved staghorn from Germany's Black Forest.

A three-dimensional, carved cameo stag-horn button from the Black Forest area of Germany, a favorite destination of Victorian travelers, ca. mid-1800s.

Two extraordinarily large and beautiful executed stag-horn silhouette-style dress trims from the Black Forest area.
Courtesy of Robert Selman

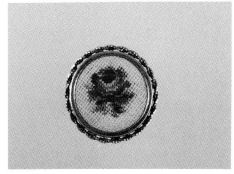

A petit-point embroidery from Austria mounted in hallmarked sterling, late nineteenth century. Another button— new when purchased in Vienna in the 1960s—is a copy of this one in the front, but it is mounted in a cheap brass setting and the fabric has not yellowed.

Two Black Forest-type stag horn carvings, neither as early nor as high in quality as the ones above. The left, a silhouette-style carving, has holes high at the sides to be sewn on as a trim rather than used as a button. The squirrel, in a realistic carving style, is a very effective example of the artistry possible by using both the inner white bone and outer rough area, late 1800s-1930.

Early examples of metalwork in buttons: at the left, a nineteenth century damascene from Toledo, Spain, where the technique has long been at its best. Damascene is accomplished by engraving grooves onto a copper or steel suface and then beating gold or silver into the recessed areas. At the right is a niello button with a cast shank, a very old example from Turkey.

Mosaics

Mosaics set as jewelry and buttons were one of the favorite items for eighteenth- and nineteenth century tourists to bring home from Italy. Antique mosaic buttons are often included in groups of semi-precious jewelry, not because of the intrinsic value of the material, but because of the delicate and intensive workmanship. Mosaic jewelry is sold there even today, though the new ones are of a far different level of workmanship

Mosaics consist of the mosaic itself—tesserae (little bits) of glass and stone assembled into a design—and the frame into which it is laid, usually onyx, glass, marble, or slate. There are two main types, known as Piètra Dura (or Florentine) and Venetian.

Piètra Dura buttons are the rarest and are always much-sought-after. Piètra Dura pieces were made by cutting a design out of the background piece, usually of onyx, and setting in a scene made up of vari-colored sections of semi-precious stones, rather like an assembled jigsaw puzzle. The stones were chosen for their color, and often included turquoise, coral, malachite, lapis, carnelian, onyx, and marble.

The Venetian mosaics, also known as micro-mosaics, had inlaid designs made from far more minute pieces of stone, or often of colored glass. The best description of them I know of was written by Mark Twain, in *Innocents Abroad*, in 1869:

> These artists will take particles no larger than a mustard seed, and piece them together on a sleeve button or a shirt stud, so smoothly and with such nice adjustment of the delicate shades of colour the pieces bear, as to form a pigmy rose with stem, thorn, leaves, petals, and all so softly and as truthfully tinted as though Nature had done it herself. They will counterfeit a fly, or a high-toned bug, or the ruined Coliseum, within the cramped circle of a breastpin, and do it so deftly and so neatly that many might think a master painted it.

Later examples of Venetian mosaic, also from Italy, are far less detailed; they are not done nearly as neatly, often roughly textured on the surface, for they were neither assembled nor finished with finesse.

The buttons are most often quite small-sized for a man's waistcoat (vest). The commonest designs are ancient buildings or ruins, and flowers, especially roses. The rarest are of people, followed by animals, and heads.

The smaller and more detailed the design of a Venetian micro-mosaic, the more value it has to a collector. On the other hand, Piètra-Dura are usually larger buttons and have less detailed designs, yet they are the most valued of all.

Piètra-dura, a hardstone inlay technique also known as 'Florentine' work, was rarely used for buttons. This extremely fine piètra-dura work of butterflies and ladybugs in black onyx is rimmed and shanked in 18k gold. 1 1/8" *Courtesy of Bruce and Jane Beck*

The reverse of the button above.

A very rare piètra-dura dog's head inlaid in black onyx and mounted in brass.

Micro-mosaics of fine quality in the upper row and of average quality in the lower row. The man is an unusual subject and (oval) shape. All are 1/2" buttons set in brass for use on men's waistcoats in the mid-nineteenth century.

Micro-mosaics of fine quality in medium-sized buttons and studs. The symbolic Lion of St. Mark is at left. The view of the Roman Coliseum, a favorite stop of those on the 'Grand Tour', is a particularly fine mosaic. The realistic flower, bird and strawberry are rare subjects for mosaics. 1".

A much later mosaic with a rough-textured top. The tesserae (little bits) of glass were not set evenly nor ground smooth. Nevertheless, the unusual cut-steel setting and oval shape make this a desirable example. 1", ca. 1890s to 1910.

Tortoiseshell buttons, inlaid and decorated. The sea tortoise behind them is a shirt-stud box—a tortoise made of tortoise! The button at left was inlaid with pearl. Behind it, a faceted tortoise button with a gold pin shank. The grape design is inlaid with brass and pearl tesserae. The bird button just left of center is a wonderful example of the finest gold and silver inlay work known as *piqué*. The two at the far right are mourning buttons with carved jet cameos attached to them, ca. early to late nineteenth century.

Coral, the mainstay of Naples' economy in the mid-1800s, was widely used for Victorian jewelry, but was seldom used for buttons. These are men's waistcoat buttons, and though very simple, were treated like jewels with gold shanks and a silver pinshank on the ball at right.

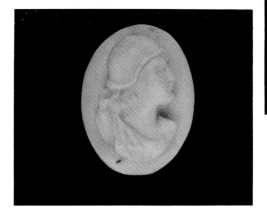

Helmet-shell carved cameo showing a bit of irony, for the figure is helmeted.

A lava cameo from Italy, mid-nineteenth century, mounted in silver. The lava stone used for such cameos following Napoleon's Pompeii excavations was from Mt. Vesuvius. Not expensive when originally sold, antique lava-cameo jewelry and buttons are now hard to find and valuable, although the color is far from attractive—in fact, it looks like carved, dried mud!

Assorted carved pearl cameos, late nineteenth century. Top, a fox-head, and under it a carved scene of a lady fishing, mounted in brass and ringed with cut-steels. The two buttons in the next row are of special quality: both are mounted in silver, have pearl back- grounds and a separate pierced and carved layer of pearl above. In the last row are a horse's head set in brass and rimmed with cut-steels, a dyed pear with steel leaves, and a carved, engraved and gilded fan.

Deluxe carved cameos from the mid-nineteenth century in Italy. The cameo was the most popular form of jewelry throughout the Victorian era. The quality varied widely. Cameo carving, which had for centuries been a gem and hard-stone technique, was first done with shell around 1820. Until the 1870s, carved shells were considered mere imitations of true cameos, until Queen Victoria popularized them, preferring them to stone ones. By the late 1890s, cameos were out of style. Top, a carved carnelian set in a solid gold waistcoat button. Left, a shell portrait of Bacchus with a grape leaf in his hair. The very deep lava-carving is mounted in brass. *Lava cameo Courtesy of M. W. Speights*

Painted ivory miniatures under glass, from India. The top two are set in 22 K gold and feature the Taj Mahal in Agra and the Qutab Minar, in Delhi. At the bottom is a charming little silver-mounted button with a miniature painting (on ivory) of a tiger riding on a bullock cart, early to mid-nineteenth century.

Fabulous set of ivory miniatures with paintings of Indian buildings under glass. Included are an extra large button and four smaller ones portraying the Taj Mahal in Agra, two views of the Red Fort in New Delhi, and one view of the summer Lake Palace of the Maharajah of Udaipur. Mounted in heavy silver, the largest is just over 2 1/4"; the rest are 1", ca. early to mid-nineteenth century.
Courtesy of Bruce and Jane Beck

This button from India was made from a tiger's claw inlaid with filigree silver. Tiger's claws have long been made into jewelry and amulets in India. Clearly this is a very old example: the claw has changed color and is petrifying.

Inlaid jade, a technique perfected only in India and Persia centuries ago. This is a very rare button with gold wire inlaid around the border and around each of the recessed, red-foil, rock crystal-topped rays. In the center is an oval carnelian with engraved Sanskrit writing, 2 1/2" across in pale green/white jade. It is at least 300 years old, and probably much older. Since there is no natural jade deposit in India, Chinese jade was brought to India for artisans to work, and then it was returned to China.
Courtesy of Bruce and Jane Beck

Opposite page top:

Chinese jade buttons and one red agate. The flower at the top is far more deeply 3-dimensional than is possible to photograph. The two outer buttons at the end of the next row are engraved seals. The beautifully-shaped button at the lower center is a Buddhist symbol called the 'endless knot' and the pierced button to its left has the figure of a man in the outline. The top button, the ball-shaped ones, and the seals on the outside of the second row are very old examples, probably dating well before the eighteenth century.

Opposite page bottom:

Jade buttons such as these are of great antiquity. The most recent one in this group is the second from the right in the upper row, a jade disc with an inlaid, engraved pearl scene inlaid, dating from the mid- to late 1800s. Some of the others date back to the Yuan (fourteenth to fifteenth centuries) and the Ming (fifteenth century) dynasties. The Chinese people sewed small pieces of jade on their clothing as early as 1122 to 770 B.C., and have maintained a steady history of jade fasteners ever since.

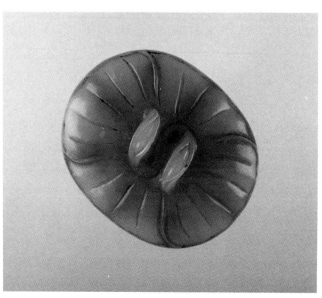

The back of the inlaid jade showing its two shanks carved in the shape of lotus-buds.

A very large carved ivory dragon, deeply undercut with a screw-in round turret-like ivory shank, and a carved signature and seal on reverse.

Carved and engraved jade with a dragon design. The jade is thick and oddly-shaped, with three different sets of curved needle shanks on the reverse. This rare button, which is nearly 3" across, was made many centuries ago, probably before the Yuan dynasty (1260-1370 A.D.).

Assorted buttons from China, including (from the top) three *cloisonné* enamels (the butterfly is very early), a painted enamel swan, a silver and enamel ball from a Chinese robe, engraved ivory mounted in silver, and a filigree silver button set with lapis lazuli and coral. 1/2"–1 1/8".

An oversized, convex tortoiseshell button with an engraved and gilded dragon design.

A sterling silver dragon with red enameled mouth and Chinese hallmarks on the reverse.

A Chinese enamel and silver cicada-shaped button, probably eighteenth century.

These small, one-piece, gilded brass buttons with oriental designs were not made *in* China, but *for* China. Known as 'trade gilts', they were made for the Oriental market by manufacturers in America, France and England. Ships sailed into Canton laden with buttons, furs, gold jewelry, and woolens, and sailed home with silks, porcelains, fans, tea, and spices. The first American voyage to Canton took place in 1785. During the American Civil War, ship traffic to China ceased and was never reinstituted. These buttons date from the mid-nineteenth century.

Men and women's Chinese robe buttons of ball shape with repoussé designs. The second from the top is made of gold.

5 Transportation

Until the middle of the nineteenth century, travel was conducted by foot, horse-back, coach, and ship. The advent of trains, however, brought at least the possiblity —if not always the reality—of travel to the masses. Each mode of transportation is featured on countless buttons, reflections of the realities of everyday life.

A rare, small, cast-brass button with a whale design from the early 1800s.

Two-piece, gilded brass button from the mid-1800s.

A lovely cast silver ship button, Dutch, early 1700s.

A small, engraved, one-piece gilded brass button with a ship pictured, ca. 1830 to 1850.

Steel button with etched and painted ship design, made in France.

Old, true scrimshawed ivory buttons such as these are hard to find. They are all from the early 1800s and were fashioned by sailors on long, often tedious whaling expeditions. The ship design is highly desirable, with a copper shank set into the back. The square button has an inlaid circle of black baleen (whale upper jaw-bone) in the center. The plain, domed button has a huge ivory loop shank that screws into the back, unlike the self-shank which is carved into the engraved, crudely shaped bottom buttons.

Black glass buttons with engraved and molded ship designs, ca. mid-1800s.

A small, two-piece, gilded brass button showing an early steam vessel.

A rare and perfectly lovely *emaux-peint* (painted enamel) in an oval iron setting, ca. late 1700s or early 1800s.

Another lovely painted enamel sailing scene set in a riveted, cut steel border. French, in the Romantic style, ca. early 1800s.

Sailboats on buttons of assorted materials, clockwise from top: pressed brass, dyed mother-of-pearl with pewter escutcheon, engraved black glass, acid-etched black glass, relief-pressed black glass, and etched mother-of-pearl.

Sail and row boats on brass buttons with various decorative techniques, ca. late nineteenth century.

A rare subject—a hot air balloon— and an unusual *emaux-peint* on a decorative brass base. This is from the late nineteenth century, a time of sentimental feelings during the centennial of the French Revolution; it recalls the first ballooning escapades of Montgolfier in eighteenth century Paris.

These buttons show a coach, a carriage, and a sleigh, far more common ways for the average man to travel about. At top and bottom are pressed brass 'picture buttons'; the center button is tortoiseshell with a sterling escutcheon.

Late-nineteenth-century buttons with hot air balloon designs. All are brass, except for the small steel-cup with a brass balloon set on a pearl background, at top.

It is surprising, in view of the extraordinary and far-reaching effect that train travel had on life in the last half of the nineteenth century, that there are not more buttons with train designs. The top one is gold lustered, molded black glass, ca. mid-1800s. The other two are brass and tin from the late nineteenth century.

6 Foreign Lands and People

Both the tales and souvenirs of travelers returning home from the 'Grand Tour' added new subjects to the decorative arts at home, as images based on exotic locales entered the repetoire. This, of course, had a tremendous impact on button manufacture. English, French, and German buttons of the last half of the nineteenth century are replete with scenes of far-away lands, buildings, and depictions of the seemingly exotic citizens of foreign lands.

From the earliest days of the nineteenth century, Napoleon's forces were exploring and conquering Egypt. For two decades, the French presence there kept the public's interest. Later in the century, after the French had long departed, the British took control of Egypt and once again manufacturers geared up to supply a curious public with Egyptian-like objects of all kinds, buttons included.

This button is rare, and the earliest of those seen here. It shows a pharoah's head painted directly on onyx and set in gold under glass, ca. 1800-1810.

Two early-nineteenth century Egyptian-styled French buttons. Napoleon's explorations in Egypt were simultaneous with these buttons. Left, a heavy steel disc with a cut-out brass musician riveted on with star-cut faceted steels; right, a one-piece impressed brass button with enamel trim, portraying Amon, the main god of Egypt, being fanned.

Champlevé enamel on brass showing a walking figure, ca. mid-1800s.

Assorted Egyptian-themed buttons made with various techniques. These are all from the last half of the nineteenth century. The bottom button shows the cat goddess. 1 1/2" average.

Egyptian scenes in a variety of materials. Top row: white enamel paint on black glass, a painted enamel sphinx with a man's face (probably a caricature), a small brass button with a cut-out top and velvet background, and a one-piece gilded brass button. Middle row: a convex one-piece pressed brass, punched and engraved steel disc, and one-piece molded glass with steel border. Bottom row: Two-piece brass with black painted background, horn inlaid with pearl, a pressed brass 'picture button', and a high relief pressed brass. The buttons at center and at upper right are from the Napoleonic times in Egypt, the rest from the later British influence.

Brass-rimmed button with a wooden background and a cut-out of a man riding a camel.

Black glass wafer button with gold luster, engraved with a sphinx, pre-1850.

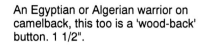

An Egyptian or Algerian warrior on camelback, this too is a 'wood-back' button. 1 1/2".

French legionnaire with his rifle in the air, on a one-piece molded brass button.

Called "Ghengis Khan" by collectors, this very large button with a complex battle scene is made of molded blue glass set in brass.

The Western mind was just as fascinated by the people of the Orient and manufacturers produced many buttons reflecting this. These are in many materials and techniques. All date ca. 1845-1890, and include brass buttons, a silver dragon, black glass, and lavender glass.

Chinese scenes including top: pressed brass and a pierced brass with steel fan riveted on; the rest include a *champlevé* enamel on brass, a wood-back, pressed and pierced brass. At center, a large molded milk-glass button. 3/4" to 2".

This image is taken from a print of the Zulu War of 1879, showing the death of the Prince Imperial of France, Louis Napoleon, the only son of Napoleon III and the Empress Eugenie. It may seem odd that the son of the French Emperor was ambushed and killed while on a patrol for British forces in Africa, but Napoleon III was an Anglophile and young Louis spent much time with the English.

A native African woman and son on a pressed brass button.

An African woman in a tree, shown on a wood background on this brass button. From her ornate outfit and detailed face, it is likely there is a historic purpose behind this button.

A native on a giraffe, in pressed brass. Such 'picture buttons' were mass-produced, some of them in great quantity, and can be easy to find through button dealers; others were not as popular or had limited runs and are now hard to find. This is a very uncommon one.

Princess of India, known as Lalla Rookh, in pressed brass.

An Indian mahout (elephant trainer) shown sleeping on his elephant, on a rare embossed iron sporting button. Iron was not common for such buttons.

A native South Seas islander, in pressed brass.

The tales of settlers heading 'west' in the United States were of great interest to Europeans, and buttons—such as this pressed brass of a Native American Indian in full feathered headdress—addressed that interest.

A molded black horn button with a rare subject—a Native American astride a horse being attacked by a mountain lion.

Small, molded brass button showing a Native American warrior on horseback.

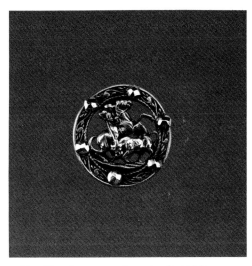

A Spanish toreador and his bull, in a brass 'steel-cup' with faceted edge, ca. mid-1800s.

The Picador, a member of a Spanish bull-fighting team on a pierced brass button with faceted-steel rivets.

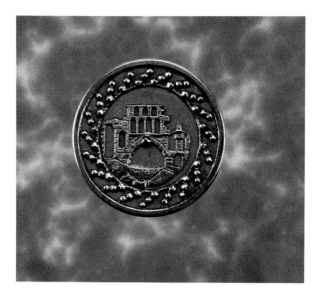

'Cleopatra's Needle' on a small brass picture button. There is a fantastic story behind this monument which now can be seen in Central Park in New York:

Thousands of different nineteenth century button designs show buildings from around the world, including this one with the aquaduct in Rome. Rome was the destination of many Western Europeans who embarked on the 'Grand Tour'. This brass-rimmed, tin-backed button has added white metal decor.

An etched pearl scene of the Mid-East.

Black glass with buildings and scenes from around the world.

Molded black glass, with iridescent luster.

Assortment of metal buttons from the
nineteenth century with buildings and
scenes from around the world.

Opposite page top:
Windmills in assorted materials, including pressed brass, pierced and etched shaded-pearl, and engraved tôle, ca. 1800s. 3/4"–1 1/2".

Castles on buttons of black glass and mother-of-pearl.

Every kind of building has shown up on a button: these black glass, mid-nineteenth century examples include the U. S. Capital, a country church, and an old school house.

Black glass buttons with assorted finishes and molded with water mill scenes.

Opposite page bottom:
More windmills. At left, iridescent black glass, pressed brass, a lithograph set in a pierced brass frame, and cranberry glass with an engraved mill. Bottom row, a steel-cup button decorated with a brass mill held in by a riveted steel sail, and two brass 'picture buttons', ca. mid-to late 1800s. 3/4"–1 3/4".

Pierced brass button with a goat confronting a statue on a pedastal in a Neo-Classic garden, complete with ruins in the background.

7 Home and Garden

Besides those showing foreign lands and exotic people, there are an equal number of buttons picturing the ordinary places and people of Europe and America. Their homes, schools, churches, farms, and mills were faithfully copied as were scenes of the life around those places, including farm workers, millers, shepherds, blacksmiths and others.

The proverbial English stone cottage and garden has become a trite image, but gardens were of extreme import to the people of the late eighteenth and nineteenth centuries and thus showed up on buttons as well.

Gardens were part of estate life during the eighteenth century. Man was an integral part of Neo-Classical gardens: wide walkways and serene retreats with formal benches were added for his comfort. Roman arches and sculptures of nude goddesses or sturdy heroes stood silently amid the vegetation. Fountains, pillars, and urns on pedestals were used as focal points. There were even reproductions of Roman ruins or Greek temples erected in the midst of large gardens.

By the late nineteenth century, gardens were a staple of the homes of all classes and the focus had changed from controlled and formal Neo-Classic gardens to Romantic gardens, viewed as a normal outgrowth of Nature.

The everyday life at home also was pictured on buttons. Children, along with their favorite games, pets, stories, and fables, are the theme of many Victorian-era buttons.

Buttons often showed sentimental and loving couples, but some pictured the raunchier sides of love and life, as well. (This sort of erotica is known in all of the decorative arts.)

A watercolor painting of a Neo-Classic garden.

Garden scenes with cupolas, ruins, and footbridges; molded black glass at left, a stencilled, dyed pearl at upper right, and three of brass.

Flower baskets filled with flowers and/or gardening tools. All of these buttons are made of black glass, with various luster finishes. The center one was set in a thick, drum-shaped brass mounting.

Brass buttons picturing women strolling in gardens. The upper left one—a wonderfully detailed and humorous scene of a mother protecting her child from geese.

Flowers in urns, all made of brass. The middle button, trimmed with steel, is the oldest, from the mid-1800s. The others date from the 1870s to 1880s.

Brass buttons (and one of steel, upper right) with garden scenes, ca. 1870-1890s.

The fruits of gardening, along with some of the tools needed, illustrated on buttons of brass, pewter, and black horn.

It was by no means only the 'exotic' that appealed to the button-wearing public in the nineteenth century. These buttons feature 'just plain home' scenes of houses in black glass, brass, and mother-of-pearl.

Each of these buttons showing ordinary homes is made of mother-of-pearl that has been etched, engraved, and/or cameo carved; they all are rather special with a high level of workmanship.

'Home Sweet Home'. Top, a beautifully engraved grey pearl with a woman and chickens in front of a farm house. Below is an engraved pearl and small gold-lustered black glass button with houses. The large button at bottom is known as an 'ivoroid', a molded celluloid picture set in brass, a type today's collectors covet.

These buttons have scenes of ordinary folk at home and at work.

Children playing together, on brass buttons, late 1800s.

Children on buttons of the nineteenth century: top left, a mother feeding a baby, and right, a happy baby. The left and right buttons below, called the 'Laughing Child' and the 'Crying Child', were orignally seen in a mid-nineteenth century German bisque sculpture which was reproduced in 1885 in England by the Torquay Terracota Company. The very popular image was also copied on other items, including these buttons. Bottom center, a button known as 'pulling hair', particularly desired by collectors.

Little Bo-Peep and Little Boy Blue. From left, steel with a brass overlay, incised and painted black glass, and pressed brass, late 1800s.

A hallmarked English sterling button of a child (or a putti) on a hobby horse.

More children, in brass and in black glass. The bottom button is rare.

Children at play. All of these are brass buttons except for the molded horn at the far left, and the molded black-glass second from right. Ca. 1800s.

Well-known children's stories illustrated on clothing buttons. Top row: *Rapunzel* and *The Goose that Laid the Golden Egg.* Middle row: *White Swan, Jack the Giant Killer,* and *Hansel and Gretal.* Bottom row: *Little Red Riding Hood* in two versions, and *Robinson Crusoe,* ca. nineteenth century.

Opposite page:

Kate Greenaway scenes on buttons. Kate Greenaway was an English illustrator, often of children's books, whose work was very well-known during the mid- to late nineteenth century. "With her drawing she created an entire new world of delicately-poised nursery figures inhabiting a never-never countryside of arcadian purity far from the big city smoke. These agreeable and edifying sentiments enjoyed wide spread appeal, and went far in defining taste. . . Today Kate Greenaway's style appears essentially escapist but in her own lifetime. . . enjoyed lasting popularity."[1] Many Greenaway designs were copied by button-makers and some collectors now specialize in them. These buttons include brass, steel, black glass, and vegetable ivory, ca. 1875 to 1890.

Fables are another collectors' specialty, and well over one hundred different button designs with fables have been identified. This lovely one-piece pierced-brass button shows the 'Kitty and the Lizard'. Such designs on buttons were often directly copied from the classic nineteenth-century books of La Fontaine's or Aesop's fables, with engravings by Doré or illustrations by J. J. Grandeville.

Fable buttons in brass and pressed wood. Included are *The Fox and the Grapes, The Fox and the Crow, The Fox and the Stork, The Raven and the Fox,* and *The Wolf and the Crane,* and (at lower right) *The Peasant of the Danube* by La Fontaine, taken from a Grandeville illustration from 1837.

The pet dog, dear to the hearts of Victorians, was so well represented on buttons that some collectors specialize in dog buttons alone. A tiny fraction of the dog-themed buttons that were made are illustrated here, beginning with this painted and etched steel button with a spaniel, ca. 1850.

A wonderfully detailed painting on porcelain set in brass.

These buttons feature dogs with dog houses, in black glass and brass, ca. mid- to late 1800s.

Pet birds were also pictured by button makers, including these brass and steel examples from the late nineteenth century. They are pictured here at half their actual size.

Cats were not illustrated on nearly as many buttons as were dogs and today bring a premium from collectors. These are all black glass examples from the mid-nineteenth century, except for the delicately etched ivory glove button in the center.

Cats on metal buttons from the 1800s.

An engraving from a book of the 1870s illustrates the more genteel aspect of relationships. Button makers reflected everything around them, and this included romance. It was most often sentimentalized and idealized, but in some cases buttons were satirical, off-beat, and just plain naughty.

A silver button with an illustration of an eighteenth-century dancing couple, ca. mid- to late nineteenth century.

Romantic couples on assorted brass and silver buttons of the nineteenth century.

Buttons (and at the top, a lapel-stud) in brass, molded black horn, aluminum, tortoiseshell inlaid with mother-of-pearl, and silver plate. The wording on the French stud is *La Pantoufle*, or, "The Slipper," referring to the weapon with which the lady is threatening to hit the man who is lifting her skirt.

Three white metal buttons from France, recastings from the 1920s of buttons from the 1890s; another set was re-issued in the 1950s. The top illustrates an amourous lady caressing a man. The wording on the center button, translated, refers to being stabbed in an important part of one's anatomy, and the bottom simply translates to 'lady wrestlers'. These buttons are hard to find.

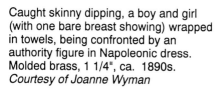

Caught skinny dipping, a boy and girl (with one bare breast showing) wrapped in towels, being confronted by an authority figure in Napoleonic dress. Molded brass, 1 1/4", ca. 1890s. *Courtesy of Joanne Wyman*

A very odd subject for a button: a lady in bed, patting the pillow. This two-piece, molded brass picture button is 1".

Although the young man on the ladder is intent on reaching his friend at the upper window, the dog seems equally intent that he not do so! Ca. 1880 to 1890.

From a set of three (see others under section on Impressionism) hand-painted ivory miniatures set under glass and rimmed with pastes, from the late 1800s. Nudes are far from common on buttons, and one done with such finesse in a deluxe button is particularly rare. *Courtesy of Lucille Weingarten*

What do you suppose he is peeking at so surreptiously? A small brass button, late-19th century.

Beautifully detailed répoussé brass button illustrating three vices: wine, women, and smoking. The background is filled with grape vines. Quite unusual, 1 1/2", ca. 1900 to 1920. *Courtesy of Joanne Wyman*

Molded brass in a basketweave pattern, with attached brass cutout. The naked Venus rising up from a clam shell is quite an unusual subject. 1 1/3".

A French beauty, nude and drinking wine, oblivious to the world! Silver plated brass, 1 1/4", ca. 1890s. *Courtesy of Bruce and Jane Beck*

Two-piece brass picture button of a naked lady toweling off after her bath.

A rather graphic depiction of the mythical Leda and the Swan, in a two-piece brass picture button, French, 1".

This astoundingly graphic French button shows part of a man leaning forward into the trees with his pants pulled down below his hips, and a woman's bare legs encircling his waist; a spike-collared mastiff is biting the man's naked bottom. Caught in the act by the master's watch dog? *Courtesy of Joanne Wyman*

A mustachioed soldier peeking through the bushes at legs in the foreground, suggestively positioned to show a couple *en flagrante*, lying on the ground. The lady's leg shows a garter and high-buttoned shoe, the man's, a boot and trousers. Cast pewter, probably a mid-twentieth-century copy of a late-nineteenth-century button.

This amazing little engraved black glass button pictures an outhouse, ca. 1860s-80s. Scatalogical buttons follow, so quit here if you are easily offended!

A very dimensional brass picture button with a rather humorous scene: a pretty woman is chatting with a man at the bottom window, while a man in a nightcap leaning out of the upper window has just emptied his chamber pot on the other's head. Is it the wife or the daughter who is the focus of so much attention? 1 1/3", ca. 1880-1900. *Courtesy of Joanne Wyman*

This very deeply répoussé brass button was most likely converted from a French lapel stud. It features a man with his trousers down, squatting against a tree stump, intently reading a newpaper named "The Patriot". 1 1/4", ca. 1870s to 1880s. *Courtesy of Joanne Wyman*

A French pewter reproduction of an earlier button, this very odd design shows a woman in peasant garb, holding her skirt away from her body and squatting. 1 1/4", ca. 1950s. *Courtesy of Joanne Wyman*

8 Romantic Medievalism

During the mid-nineteenth century, there was a revival of the attitudes and ideals of the previous century's Romantic Movement, combined with an intense admiration for the seemingly noble values of Medieval kingdoms. In part a counter-reaction to the restrictive formality of Neo-Classicism and its reliance on ancient Greco/Roman culture, this movement took inspiration from its own western-European past.

The restoration of the French monarchy and the popularity of the new, young English queen, Victoria, had brought about a sentimental interest in royal history, centering on Medieval French and English kingdoms.

The era's decorative-arts products reflected this; buttons in particular were often illustrated with medieval scenes, heroes, knights, and ladies. Buttons illustrating armour-clad warriors, helmets, and assorted weapons are related either to this trend or to the Neo-Classic mania already mentioned, depending on the types and styles of armour shown. It is important to recognize the differences in both the origination and intent of these designs and their actual appearance: for instance, Roman helmets are entirely unlike those worn by knights during the later period.

Known as 'Evangeline', from Longfellow's poem, this convex one-piece brass button pictures a lady in Medieval garb.

From left, King Arthur on an ornately designed, pierced brass button; a Medieval queen engraved on a thick white mother-of-pearl button, and another King Arthur of pierced brass centered within a large disc of smoked pearl.

The story of the troubador Blondel, personal minstrel to King Richard I, was illustrated on this little brass button.

From left, King Arthur, pierced brass with cut steel border, knights jousting (note the various shields around the border), a German knight with a horn, and a small metal button with a mounted knight and his jousting pike.

A warrior-knight, his flag held high, on horseback.

King Arthur on a lovely brass button with a pierced center and a cut steel decorated border.

At top, a brass button with a troubador kneeling with his lute; at bottom left, another troubador outside a castle (with cut out windows lined with tin to make them shine), and right, a pressed steel button with another troubador, called 'The Spanish Cavalier'.

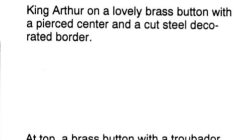

Pressure-molded horn with a Medieval knight in armor and helmet.

Brass buttons: from left, a knight, Sir Lancelot, and a knight with a shield and a mace, ca. 1880 to 1990s.

9 Fairies

The popularity of tales of the Medieval age of European history extended to local folk legends as well. In Northern Europe, and particularly in England, the wizardry and mysticism in Arthurian literature (such as that of Sir Gawaine and the Green Man) fueled appreciation for local lore about the spirit-creatures of fields and forests. Ancient Irish tales, old Welsh myths, and traditional Saxon peasant beliefs about the mischief and exploits of the 'little people'—fairies, pixies, leprechauns, red-caps, and their sinister counterparts: gnomes, hags, specters, and goblins—were suddenly all the rage.

During the same mid-nineteenth-century period, "...devotees of the newly fashionable Spiritualist movement were busily attempting to make contact with members of the spirit world."[2] Queen Victoria herself gave credibility to the movement in 1861 by using a medium in attempts to contact her late, much-lamented prince, Albert. "This general fascination with the supernatural manifested itself in art through fairy painting, a remarkable genre which flourished around the mid-nineteenth century."[3]

Fairy painters shared an idyllic view of nature with the artists of the concurrent Pre-Raphaelite movement. Both manifested fears about the increasing mechanization, urbanization, and industrialization of British society. Both also provided an alternative view—not a reflection of life around them, but of the opposite—of what they thought life ought to be, idealized and utopian, innocent and magical. Fairy painters presented an image to believe in, "...an ideal world which existed somewhere at the heart of the British countryside."[4]

Fairy themes enjoyed a considerable vogue in literature and on stage, as well as in these paintings, from about 1840 to 1900. Many Victorian 'picture buttons' feature fairy scenes: a number of these buttons are thought by today's collectors to picture putti, cupids and naked children, but actually depict fairies copied directly from the paintings. Most fairy paintings—and this is obvious in the button designs—pictured a microscopic world where insects were huge, birds were transportation for child-like fairy figures, mushrooms were shelters, acorns were vessels, and flowers were used as hats or skirts.

Other button designs were based on, or even closely copied from, the stage sets of contemporary fairy-themed theatrical productions—most notably Shakespeare's *A Midsummer-Night's Dream* and *The Tempest*, which enjoyed many revivals throughout the mid- to late nineteenth century.

Other staged productions also played to the same theme. From 1840 to 1861, J.R. Planché (a sort of Ziegfeld-like impresario) staged annual *Fairy Extravaganzas* in London; his lavish stage sets also served as inspiration to decorative arts designers.

Gnomes with lilies of the valley on a brass, two-piece picture button with a painted tin back.

Creatures from the more sinister side of the fairy world. At left, a gilded, painted shaded pearl button from France, and at right, a green snail, cameo-carved button, both ca. 1880s.

The Arthurian legend of Sir Gawaine and the Green Man, originally from a Celtic pagan cult, is the subject of these two buttons, pierced sterling-silver at left, and pressed brass. The story deals with a 'vegetation man', a piece of nature himself, who was a part of the bushes and vines.

This is an exact copy of *Listening to the Fairies*, a painting by Curo von Bodenhausen. It was reproduced in 1909 as a lithograph, and became quite popular. The button is rimmed in brass and features a pewter medallion centered on a painted base.

An idealized, sensual, butterfly-winged fairy carrying light to her tiny world. Brass picture button with heart and fleur-de-lis border.

Taken from a fairy painting, this creature wears a hollyhock cap and is riding a butterfly. (Note the tiny spurs!) The fairy is pewter, centered on a brass-rimmed, copper button.

Two fairies chasing butterflies in pierced brass and, at left, engraved vegetable ivory. The top button, a fairy 'lighting the way', is tin. The large one—a beautifully-made button marked "Paris" on the reverse—is made of tinted brass and features a fairy using a dragonfly to pull his wheeled board.

Two fairy buttons with birds, fairies in a garden, a fairy piping for a dancing pup, and at lower right, a mischievious fairy using a mask to scare a poor dog! All brass, two-piece picture buttons, from the late nineteenth century.

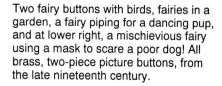

Fairies and birds were commonly depicted in paintings of this genre. The birds were usually being ridden, as they are in four of the buttons pictured. The button at the upper right is a 'wood-back'; the central brass medallion and thin wooden wafer are both mounted in a brass frame. At lower left, a later two-piece brass picture button from the end of the era. The others are medallions atop flat metal bases with separate metal rims.

Ariel, the spirit of the air and the lead fairy from Shakespeare's *The Tempest*, is shown on this brass-rimmed button with a pewter scene set atop a painted background, finished with a tin back. The 'water' at the edge of the shore is a highly polished steel liner, ca. 1880 to 1895.

Puck, the mischievous fairy from Shakespeare's *A Midsummer Night's Dream.* His true origins in myth were far more sinister: he derived from the diabolic forces of the devil , and was a hobgoblin with a roving eye and wicked humor, out to create domestic havoc. His bat-shaped, rather than butterfly-like wings identify him. The button is dyed brass with a tinted background; its design was copied from a Paul Konewka graphic, ca. 1880 to 1895.

Oberon and Titania from Shakespeare's *A Midsummer Night's Dream.* Oberon, the fairy king (from a Medieval myth) is seen hovering above the sleeping Titania. Titania was actually the goddess Diana in her third manifestation, as the Enchantress. Red tinted brass with a painted background.

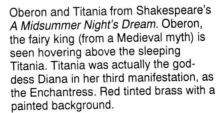

Aluminum painted and engraved to look like tortoiseshell. The iris has additional hand-punched detailing. Old aluminum buttons are of high quality and desired by collectors, though later ones are not. When this button was made, aluminum was a luxury item more expensive than gold. (Napoleon III actualy scrapped the official French silverware in favor of a new aluminum set in the 1870s.) First discovered in 1827 but not used in industry before 1854, the price plummeted towards the end of the century when a method of easily extracting it was found. *Courtesy of Bruce and Jane Beck*

Medium-sized black-glass button with an incised floral design.

A chrysanthemum of carved wood attached to a wooden base decorates this button from the 1825 to 1835 period when this flower was new to the West.

10 Romantic Realism: The Naturalist Movement

The sentiment for the land, the romanticized view of nature, and the environment of the fairies led artists to experiment with highly detailed views of this 'secret' world—the forests, fields, and meadows. Detailed depictions of leaves, flowers, and twigs were seen as intimate connections to this better world.

The overwhelming variety of plant and flower-related buttons of this period is a result of their designers, who were of course artists involved in the Romantic movement and dedicated to Naturalism. They had a great love for flowers along with an intense interest in their symbolism. This made flowers and all other plant forms the most common decorative motif for nineteenth-century decorative arts: ceramics, books, jewelry, and so on. But there is an additional reason for the amazing numbers of floral designs on buttons and other products.

The study of botany as a science had long led many intrepid (and wealthy) naturalists to go in search of unique specimens of plant life. For instance, in 1776, France's Chretien-Guillaume de Lamoignon De Malesherbes had left his position as the King's Master of the Royal Household to travel, in order to collect plants and trees for his chateau's garden, which was already very impressive. He brought back trees from all over the new world, including Dogwoods from Virginia, Junipers from Pennsylvania, Canadian spruce, and Brazilian nut woods. "He even had an entire stand of English elms shipped from Dover on a specially commisioned packet and transplanted.[5]

The Empress Josephine of France, first wife of Napoleon Bonaparte, was another devotee of botanical-specimen collecting. In the fantastic gardens of her home (where she lived after her divorce from the Emperor) "no fewer than 184 new species flowered for the first time"[6] in France. She spent an absolute fortune assembling and maintaining them, and was directly responsible for introducing "many plants, shrubs, and trees that are now commonplace: eucalyptus, hibiscus, phlox, cactuses, rhododendrons, dahlias, double jacinthas, and rare tulips."[7]

In England, the passion for botany was just as intense; by the early-nineteenth century, it had reached enormous proportions, with English enthusiasts searching faraway lands for new plant specimens, and the public awaiting each new discovery These imports always created a sensation, a point not missed by manufacturers who fully catered to the fashion: all manner of products were decorated with the latest botanicals. Jewelry, in particular, blossomed with such designs.

Floral buttons are often specifically related to the introduction of particular flowers into Western culture. For instance, the pansy was first developed around 1830, but in 1861, when the very brightly-colored, velvety-leaved blossoms that we now know were cultivated, they created a sensation and were used as the main theme of countless decorative-arts products.

The tiger lily was first brought to England from Canton, China, in 1804, and wisteria arrived in 1817. The potentilla arrived in 1822, and the much beloved petunia first came to England in 1831. Azaleas, magnolias, and gardenias were all new to Western society during this period, as were, from China, chrysanthemum and several new types of roses. They showed up quickly in lithographs, cards, and most certainly, on buttons.

The mania for naturalism and Romantic Realism led to another phenomenon in button manufacture—that of bugs on buttons. All of the creatures that lived in nature, especially in the romanticized, idealized, microscopic world of hidden fairy creatures—insects, snails, lizards, snakes, and the like—were included in the overall trend to floral and natural subjects.

Birds were another focus of the designers, still searching nature for inspiration, as were other little critters running about the meadows, streams, and forests (squirrels, etcetera).

Opposite page:
Roses on buttons: top row from left, molded brass, an ornate scallop-edged brass button with a separate brass rose atop a velvet background, a reverse-intaglio rose set under glass in a brass base, hand-painted china, inlaid black glass. Bottom, a brass wood-back button with the rose held by steel rivets, an elegant pierced mother-of-pearl, and wood with a molded compostion rose attached. The center button is a stunning iridescent pearl with silver and gilding applied.

Roses have long been the most popular
flower, in life and on buttons. These
include mother-of-pearl, black glass,
brass, and painted glass examples, ca.
1850 to 1920. The top button is the
oldest, the glass one at upper right by
far the newest.

This heavy, one-piece brass button shows a lily-of-the-valley with applied brass leaves and cut-steel flowers.

Lilies-of-the-valley in assorted materials including brass, glass, black glass, and four of inlaid horn, including the rare (dyed) blue horn button at center, ca. mid- to late nineteenth century.

An assortment of molded, etched, and incised black glass floral buttons. The center button is a very thick wafer of black glass with a silver flower attached, ca. mid-1800s.

Pansies in brass, black glass, tôle rimmed with steel, and painted enamel on brass, ca. 1861 to 1865.

The nineteenth century could be called the Century of the Flower; from beginning to end, the passionate interest in botanical subjects was a continual inspiration. Seen here are assorted flowers on brass buttons.

Water lilies and cattails on brass and pewter buttons of the nineteenth century. 3/4"–1 1/2".

A lovely black glass button with a fern. Ferns are not as common on buttons as flowers are, but can be found. "The popularity of ferns in the decorative arts of the late-nineteenth century was due to the development of the 'Wardian case', a glass box designed for the cultivation of ferns, by Dr. N. B. Ward, for which Victorian ladies developed an almost manic enthusiasm."[8]

Palms in urns, a common sight in Victorian homes, on a one-piece, pressed brass button and at right, incised and painted black glass.

A yucca plant on a gilded brass button, ca. 1870s to 1880s.

Another type of fern, made with inlaid silver in a tortoiseshell button.

Leaves of all kinds appear on many nineteenth and twentieth century buttons; these are all from the 1800s.

Acorns and grains in black glass and brass.

Bamboo trees on nineteenth century buttons. From left, brass with a cut out tree over a mother-of-pearl background, pressed brass one-piece gilt, engraved silver, and a pierced brass button with a wood background.

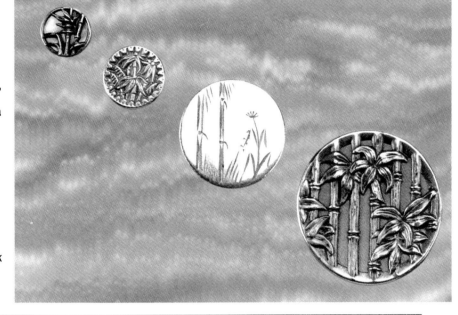

Buttons with wheat and, harder to find, with corn. Materials include brass, black glass, pewter (center bottom) and a brass and silver inlay in composition.

Strawberries. Top row from left, steel cup with pearl and a strawberry vine attached with steel rivets, pressed brass, and pierced brass. Bottom row, pierced pewter, brass with a steel strawberry riveted on, and pressed brass, ca. 1840 to 1900.

Pears with brass in the center and black glass with various lusters.

Cherries in brass and black glass, mid- to late nineteenth century.

An assortment of berries on buttons of brass, tin, black glass, and vegetable ivory, ca. 1860-1900.

Grapes. Top row, inlaid pearl chips and silver, molded black-glass, painted and faceted black glass, painted enamel set with enamel *perriéres* mounted in brass, and black glass. Middle row, steel cup with pearl background, brass rim and leaves, and steel grapes, a brass rimmed tin -back button, and a pressed brass picture button. Bottom row, transfer on camphor glass, gold-plated (gilded) brass, and green-dyed flat steel with brass decor, ca. 1850 to 1890.

Butterflies appear on buttons and are indeed decorative, but they are only one type of many buttons with bugs. Pictured are buttons of abalone, mother-of-pearl, brass, black glass, aluminum, pewter, inlaid composition, wood, and enamel. Except for the more modern top button, all are from the nineteenth century.

Pressed brass picture buttons flank a black glass one; all show bees caught in spider webs.

(Well, I don't care what you say, I'm not wearing these!) Spider buttons of brass, molded composition, and black glass, and one poor little enameled brass bee in the center. Ca. 1890–1920.

Various beetles and caterpillars on mother-of-pearl, brass, black glass, and bottom right, painted on horn.

Bees. The left button, brass set in steel, is from the very early nineteenth century and may relate to the 'B' symbol of the Napoleonic court. (See Chapter 3.)

Bees on brass and molded of black glass, early to mid-1800s.

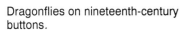

Dragonflies on nineteenth-century buttons.

Assorted insects, including a grasshopper at lower left on dyed brass. The two oval buttons are inlays in horn.

Flies on buttons of brass, black glass, and pewter, mid-nineteenth century. Even when one understands the reasons behind these buttons, it seems odd to *want* to have flies sitting on you!

Bees on buttons, including a very rare black glass overlaid with a sheet of white glass and a brass bee atop, ca. early to mid-1800s.

Assorted newts, salamanders and lizards on brass, pearl, painted glass, and black glass buttons. The button at far right has an interesting steel 'window' in the center.

Bats on black glass, gold lustered black glass, and brass buttons.

Frogs were surprisingly popular on buttons from this era, as seen by this small grouping of black horn, black glass, brass, pewter, and tôle examples.

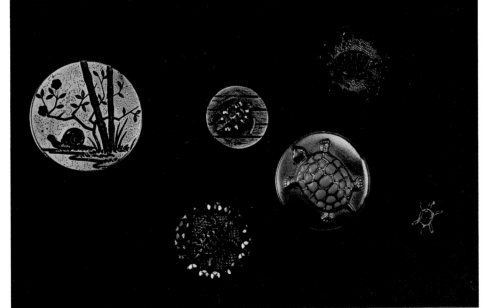

A snail impressed on a brass button, and turtles of black glass, brass, and enamel on brass.

Fish are not common on buttons, but here are a few from the Victorian era, along with a shrimp and a seahorse, in brass, molded horn, and grey pearl.

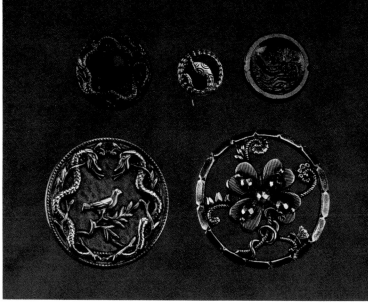

Snakes for milady's buttons include iridescent black glass examples at the top with a small brass button in between, and two sinuous snake designs in brass at the bottom, ca. mid- to late 1800s.

Birds in black glass.

Three very desirable bird buttons, early transfers on porcelain. The one set in brass at the right has 'Liverpool transfer' decoration, named after the town in England where the transfer technique was first perfected. Birds are rarer on such buttons than are people. Ca. early 1800s.

Peacocks in all sorts of materials. Top row, a molded glass disc set in a brass frame, pressed brass, pierced brass, and another pressed brass. Middle row, pressed brass, hand-painted Satsuma pottery, and brass with tin shining through the cutouts. Bottom row, gold-lustered black glass, tin with painted pierced areas, gold inlaid in tortoiseshell, painted blue glass, and painted camphor glass. The button off to the left, known as a 'peacock's eye', is a form of paperweight with gold foil and blue coloring under glass. 1/2"–2".

An assortment of birds on various metal buttons of the 1800s. Each of these is a different breed of bird. Each approximately 1 1/2".

Opposite page:
Some collectors specialize by type of bird, since bird buttons were made in such profusion. This is a grouping of owl buttons in brass, steel, cranberry glass, black glass, wood, silver, and mother-of-pearl. The large one second from the bottom has yellow glass eyes.

Roosters and chickens on brass and black glass buttons.

More black glass birds with assorted molding and finishing techniques. One has pearl 'eggs' attached.

Big-horned sheep. Left, silver-lustered black glass, and right, pressed brass picture button, ca. 1800s.

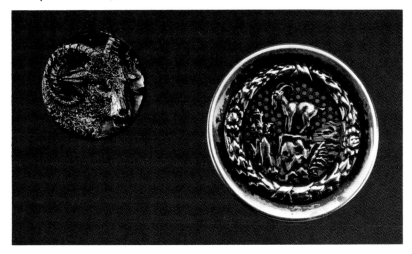

Squirrels in blonde horn, black glass, brass, pewter, and steel.

11 Animal Life

Animals of all sorts were pictured on buttons. They often had to do with sports and hunting, both popular general themes for buttons. You probably cannot name a sport or a hobby that has not been pictured on a button! Men had worn buttons with sporting and hunting themes since the eighteenth century, on their sporting clothing, but in the 1860s, horse-shoe shaped jewelry came into fashion for general wear, and many such buttons were produced at that time. Sports-themed buttons and jewelry had another vogue in the 1880s and 90s and were *de rigeur* for stylish women.

An extraordinary silver stag's head pinned on a thick wooden base. This was a very deluxe button in its day and is still a collector's joy.

Deer in the forest on variously finished black glass buttons. 5/8".

Two carved ivory deer, one mounted in silver and, at right, one mounted in brass and sheet iron. Although these superficially resemble the carved antler Black Forest buttons, they are not at all the same. This type of ivory work was a specialty of artists in Dieppe, France, where these buttons were made.

Deer in assorted poses, in metal buttons. The little one at the top is drinking from a stream.

Rabbits multiplying! Buttons from the nineteenth century including brass, black glass, molded blonde horn, silver plate, and steel. 1/2"–1 1/2'.

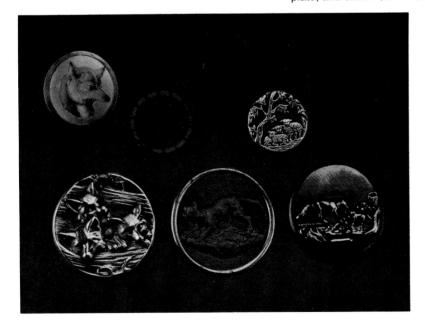

The fox was used more often used as a button subject than the wolf. Most fox buttons were worn on hunting coats. Pictured here are an early porcelain transfer mounted in brass, and others of pressed brass, wood, silver, and black glass. All date from between 1815 and 1880.

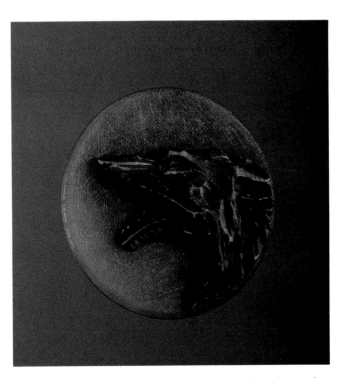

This large, cameo-carved horn button is rare. Horn is not a common material for this technique, and the wolf's head is an unusual subject, mid- to late 1800s.

Wild boars are uncommon on buttons. The left button, brass with a mother-of-pearl background, is a man's waistcoat button, and the right button is from a hunting coat, late 1800s.

Wild animals are less common than domestic animals on nineteenth century buttons. Left row from top, a zebra in relief on black glass (zebras are very rarely seen in buttons), a vegetable ivory camel, and a black glass dromedary. Second row, a monkey (also a rare subject) in black glass, and a large pressed brass 'picture button' of a giraffe. Third row, a pressed brass elephant, and a crocodile in gold-lustered black glass. Fourth row, a funny brass button with a circle of seventeen elephants, an elephant molded in black glass, and an alligator in brass.

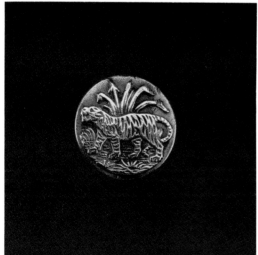
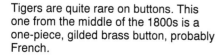

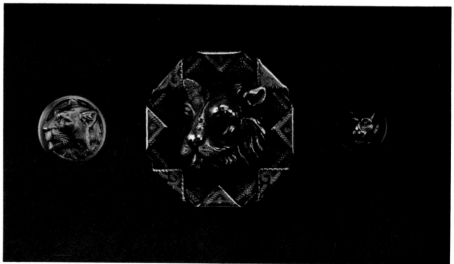

Tigers are quite rare on buttons. This one from the middle of the 1800s is a one-piece, gilded brass button, probably French.

Lionesses are less common on buttons than lions. At left, a deeply pressed brass rare design; at center, a very desirable 'handkerchief-corner' button of heavy, one-piece brass with a three-dimensional head in the center; at right, a cup-shaped vegetable ivory with a brass head escutcheon, ca. early to mid-1800s.

Lions' heads of brass, molded horn (an unusual example) and molded brass.

More lions, in molded black horn, pressed tin, and pressed wood mounted in metal. The latter is an unsual type of hunting coat button from the early 1800s.

Of all the wild animals, lions are the most often seen in button design. These are brass and black glass examples from the mid- to late 1800s. The one at right is seen with a deer it has killed.

Target buttons are unusual, and were made for hunting coats in the nineteenth century. These materials include brass, vegetable ivory, shaded pearl, grey pearl, and black glass.

Some hunting scene buttons were made for clothing men hunted in or wore to their hunt clubs. These buttons, however, which picture hunters in action, were for street-wear. The scenes include hunting dogs attacking a deer, a lady hunting with a falcon, a man stabbing a deer in the throat, and men with their hunting dogs.

Dogs also appear on hunt buttons. At top is a rare, intaglio, gilded brass button. On either end of the second row are black horn buttons with brass escutcheons. The others are gilded brass, ca. 1830 to 1880s.

These buttons were worn by men on their hunt clothes. The rarest are those that picture 'foreign' wild animals and people, or those made of unusual materials such as the scallop-edged red-dyed horn buttons at the top.

These fox buttons come from jackets worn to hunt clubs (where the fox was, after all, the favorite target). A silver button is at top center, above a molded horn example; the rest are brass.

Man's best friend in the nineteenth century may have been the horse, which is well represented on buttons. Brass buttons and a pressed black horn in the center, ca. mid-1880s.

Horses, in brass. The three in the center row are from hunt clothes.

Two rare, reverse-painted small glass buttons mounted in brass, made to be worn on men's waistcoats. The craftsmanship is wonderful on these two, made before 1850.

Horses in brass, steel, and black glass. The center button is a steel cup with a brass ringed border surrounding a lovely molded horse's head.

Horses with riders, including a lady riding sidesaddle on the lower right. The middle button is sterling silver, the one below it black horn. The two outer buttons of the second row are from hunting coats.

Steeplechase riders on buttons of tortoiseshell inlaid with pearl, brass, silvered brass, and black glass, ca. 1860 to 1890.

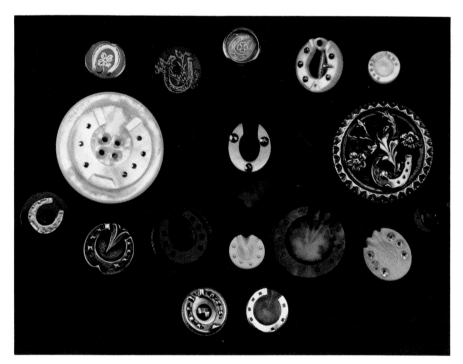

Gambler's buttons like these horse-shoes have far more to do with luck than with horses! The collection includes, top row across: enamel on silver, vegetable ivory, reverse-painted glass set in gold waistcoat (rare), a mother-of-pearl realistic, carved pearl. Second row: carved mother-of-pearl with steel 'nails', a very unusual natural horn square with a pearl horseshoe pinned on with silver 'nails', and pressed brass. Third row: inlaid horn, pressed brass, black glass, carved ivory realistic with silver 'nails', vegetable ivory realistic, carved ivory set with paste gems, and black glass. At the bottom are two with metal overlays, on pearl at left and blonde horn at right, ca. 1850 to 1890s.

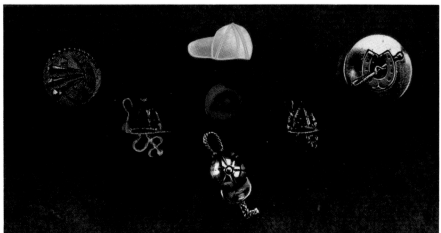

These buttons were worn by horsemen in the nineteenth century. Included are two realistics of mother-of-pearl and sterling silver.

These buttons with gambling themes include dice and cards in tin, black glass, porcelain, red horn, glass set in brass, steel, sterling, black horn and a lithograph set in brass.

Buttons with sporting equipment for hunting, fishing, tennis, shuttlecock, croquet, chess, and archery. The buttons are of dyed brass, pressed brass, silver plate, steel, black glass, and *cloisonné* enamel.

Fishing buttons are much harder to find than hunting buttons. At the center is a very large and lovely brass screen-backed button with a hook on it. Above it is a cameo-carved pearl mounted in steel, ca. mid- to late 1800s. 1/2"–2".

These nineteenth-century brass buttons show people at sport: two skating scenes and tennis scenes. (Note the cute little dog at the lady's feet on the lower right button.) 4/5"–1 1/2".

Two sets of lithographed waistcoat buttons from the 1890 to 1910 era, mounted in brass and portraying various sights related to sports.

Sculling and rowing scenes on buttons
of pewter and brass, nineteenth century.

A rare steel cup button with a gentleman
engaged in lawn bowling, with steel
rivets for bowling balls.

A rare little grouping of gilded brass
buttons showing the sport of curling, ca.
mid-1800s.

This brass picture button, quite a rarity,
has never before appeared in print. It
shows a baseball game with the umpire,
a mustachioed batter, and an incoming
ball, ca. 1880s or 1890s. *Courtesy of
Bruce and Jane Beck*

Brass buttons of the nineteenth century
showing mountain climbers at left, and a
sporting coat button with a man playing
cricket at right.

12 Music and Entertainment: Operas and Operettas

Successful plays, favorite performers, popular musicals, and operas inspired jewelry and buttons with familiar scenes or characters. Of these, opera is by far the best represented of the theatrical arts on buttons.

Just as young people now come home from rock concerts with pin-back buttons advertising their favorite groups, opera-goers in the nineteenth and early twentieth centuries purchased metal (usually brass) 'picture' buttons with scenes from the opera they had just seen. Usually manufactured in conjunction with the first production of a title (provided it proved to be a hit), these buttons can often be positively identified, not through manufacturer's records, but from old drawings and photos of the same productions. The scenes on these buttons are frequently copied from the stage sets, the costumes from the exact wardrobes, and even the actors' faces are at times so faithfully reproduced that they can be named.

The golden age of opera was 1880 to 1910, the period of manufacture of most of the buttons as well. There are two kinds of operas–Grand and Light. Grand opera began in 1580, in Italy. Most of the stories are based on tragedy, some fictional, some historical.

Light operas, or operettas, were generally amusing farces, first developed in Vienna in the mid-1800s. In France, Jacques Offenbach popularized them; in England, Gilbert and Sullivan. Gilbert and Sullivan's works now define the genre. Their fourteen operettas, written in London between 1871 and 1896, "still have a fervent following. When they first appeared they were sensationally popular. Their characters appeared on dishes, wallpaper, wapping paper, fans, postcards, games, buttons, and dozens of other items that are now collectible."[9]

Brass picture buttons featuring a lady playing the piano and a harpist with her dog.

Assorted musicians on metal buttons of the 1800s. The rarest button here is the largest one, far right, known as St. Cecelia at her organ. The top button pictures a famous man named Ole Bull, a Swede who started his own settlement in America and was said to descend from his mountain estate to assuage the complaints of the townspeople with his wonderful violin talents. 4/5"–1 1/2'.

Musical instruments of assorted materials. Clockwise from top: a harp (with a naked lady on its front) of black glass, etched and gilded bells on black glass, brass horn, steel and brass lyre, brass violin, celluloid and brass lyre, brass mandolin, brass drum, brass lute, brass banjo, and pressed horn lyre in the center, ca. mid- to late nineteenth century.

Assorted metal buttons with a circus theme. The Victorian era's citizens loved the circus and supported many different small traveling troupes as well as larger extravaganzas. A dog of sillver-plated brass with a non-plated center, a lion—an unusual solid cast-aluminum button, and a clown are all shown bursting through paper hoops. The rarest button here is the bareback rider at lower right. *First,* third, and *fourth buttons, lower row. Courtesy of M. W. Speights*

A 'gem' tintype waistcoat button with a picture of the singer Jenny Lind, taken from an engraved print. Jenny Lind was another of P. T. Barnum's imports to America. Known as the 'Swedish Nightingale', she was said to have the voice of an angel. Her first American appearance was in New York City in 1850; the tour lasted a year and a half and engendered many buttons, especially for men's waistcoats.

Jumbo, a huge (12 ft. tall) and famous elephant, inspired these buttons. Most of the elephant buttons from the 1880s were related to big game hunting, but these are attributable to the 'Jumbo mania' that swept England and America. Jumbo was originally brought from Egypt to the London Zoo. When the zoo accepted Barnum's offer of $10,000 for the elephant, English children were devastated. Parliament officially

objected to the sale, but the deed was done, and in 1882 P. T. Barnum brought the pachyderm to America. There would have undoubtedly been many more Jumbo buttons produced, but the unfortunate elephant was killed by a train in Canada not long after his arrival in North America. The top button is an early twentieth century work clothes button. Below it are three molded black glass examples from 1882 or 1883.

Jenny Lind buttons include three different molded glass cameos set in waistcoat buttons. The glass center of the left button—by far the commonest of those shown—came in a variety of colors and was made by the Waterbury Button Co in Connecticut, for her tour to the United States. The large molded black horn button is far harder to find than are the waistcoats, ca. 1850 to 1852.

A very rare image of Ira Aldridge, a renowned black actor of the mid- to late nineteenth century, appears on a one-piece pressed brass button. A tragedian, he achieved his greatest fame while touring as Andromachus and (in Shakespear's *Othello*) Iago

Julia Dean, an American actress, in *Round-Up*, a romantic comedy of 1907, New York.

Edwin Booth was one of the greatest stage actors in American nineteenth century theater history, although his fame has been overshadowed by that of his infamous younger brother, the lesser actor John Wilkes Booth, who assassinated President Lincoln. Rather surprisingly, the public's appreciation of Edwin Booth's acting career did not end after that event, and he continued to star in countless roles, as attested by this pressed brass picture button from the 1870 to 1880 period.

Tintype 'gem' photo set as a waistcoat button. Actresss Adah Isaacs Menken (1835-1868), whose main claim to fame was from her stage role in *Muzeppa* and her scandalous exit from stage–riding, in a nude-colored body stocking, strapped to the back of a galloping horse. It bought down the house at theatres worldwide.

Shakespeare's plays were produced over and over again throughout the nineteenth century. This pressed brass picture button shows a scene from a production of *Macbeth* that features Lady MacBeth descending the stairs, her torch held high above her, late 1800s.

The child star Minnie Maddern, who later found even more fame as the adult actress Mrs. Fisk. Black glass molded in intaglio in imitation of a framed portrait, mid-1800s.

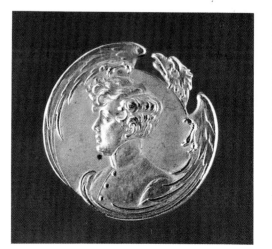

Sarah Berhardt as she appeared in the play *L'Aiglon* (The Eaglet, or baby eagle), the story about the tragic young Prince Imperial of France, Louis Napoleon, only son of Napoleon III. (See Zulu War button earlier in this chapter.) Bernhardt toured the world in this play and photographs from the time show that the button's design is a very accurate one. This silver button is but one of many that feature the same design, in different levels of quality and materials, and is a particularly deluxe example; the eagle border is die-cut and the center gilded. *Courtesy of Bruce and Jane Beck*

This button, based on the theatrical picture archives, is Minnie Maddern Fiske, starring as Mary Magdalene in 1902, New York. This one-piece pressed-brass button has cut-steel riveted trim.

Lillie Langtry as shown on buttons of pressed aluminum and pressed brass set in a Bakelite body. The image of Lillie with the mirror was then a popular one. She was the type of woman known as a 'professional beauty': famous for her looks, courted by kings and commoners alike, often used as a model for the era's artists, and an occassional actress. Early in the 1900s, she moved to America, bought land in northern California's Guenoc Valley, built a mansion and planted a vineyard. (The vineyard still exists, bottling wines under the names Langtry and Guenoc.)

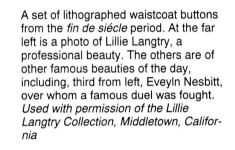

A set of lithographed waistcoat buttons from the *fin de siécle* period. At the far left is a photo of Lillie Langtry, a professional beauty. The others are of other famous beauties of the day, including, third from left, Eveyln Nesbitt, over whom a famous duel was fought. *Used with permission of the Lillie Langtry Collection, Middletown, California*

Although these have been said to portray Sarah Bernhardt, they really bear more resemblence to Lillie Langtry. Bernhardt had a narrow, gaunt face, while Lillie's was more rounded, with a large chin, as seen here. 3/4"–1 1/2".

By Sardou and Moreau, the French opera *Madame Sans Gene* from which this picture was copied, is the story of Napoleon Bonaparte and Josephine. This button of champlevé enamel is set in brass, 1915.

From the opera *Don Quichotte* by Jules Massenet, this button shows Don Quixote from the original Cervantes novel. One-piece pressed brass, 1910.

Derived from the story of *The Hunchback of Notre Dame*, Alexander Dargonizhsky's opera *Esmeralda* was featured on this two-piece, pressed brass picture button during the mid-nineteenth century.

A really lovely silver version of a famous scene in *The Three Musketeers*, which also was made into an opera, *Les Trois Mousquetaires* by Isidore De Laura, the inspiration for this button.

Flamenco dancers, from silver escutcheons on dyed mother-of-pearl buttons. These buttons were undoubtedly inspired by a certain popular dancing couple—they are too unusual and the details too distinct to have simply been stock designs, ca. 1880 to 1915.

Lucy and Edgar, from the opera *Lucia di Lammermoor* by Donzinetti, are shown in this button with a rough textured, pressed brass center, tin collet, and molded brass rim.

On this pressed-brass button appear Paul et Virginie, title characters from the 1876 opera by Victor Masse.

Inspired by Giacomo Puccini's opera *Madame Butterfly,* this simply beautiful button was made with an unusual technique, including an ornately molded wooden base framing a pierced brass insert. Note the butterfly on the upper edge of the bamboo-like border.

Pressed-brass and wood button in a design taken directly from the costume of the lead soprano for the opera *The Immortal Hour,* as seen in a contemporary photograph of the production. Although now almost unheard of, *The Immortal Hour,* by Rutland Boughton, was a phenomenal sucess. It premiered in 1922 at London's Regent Theatre and was revived three times in the next four years. A fairy story, it seemed to bring a necessary fantasy to war-weary, superficially cynical Britains.

The two clowns from *E. Pagliacci,* by Raggiero Leon Cavallo (1892). Right, Canio; left, Scaramouche.

In a design from Charles Gounod's opera *Faust,* these two brass buttons show Marguerite alone at left in a pierced brass style with cut steel rivets edging it, and with her spinning wheel at right.

One of my very favorite buttons, from the opera *Rigoletto* by Giuseppe Verdi. The ornate but wonderfully balanced design shows the jester (Rigoletto) popping through an open window. One-piece, pierced brass.

Two buttons from different productions of Georges Bizet's 1875 opera *Carmen.* At left with a molded copper inset and leather background, in a brass-rimmed tin button, and a facet-edged steel cup with a molded and detailed brass center, in very high relief.

This button shows Brunhilde, from Wagner's *The Valkyrie* (1870), astride her horse and being carried to the heavens . A powerful design in pressed brass set in a tin button.

Wagner's opera *Die Gotterdamerung* (1876) featured Brunhilde, seen here in front of a castle. The button's dyed, pressed brass and the shiny, tin liner behind cut-out windows give the button a great look.

All three of these buttons were manufactured because of the popularity of Richard Wagner's opera *Lohengrin*. Left, Lohengrin in his swanboat; right, 'Lohengrin's Arrival'; bottom, Lohengrin's departure and farewell to Elsa.

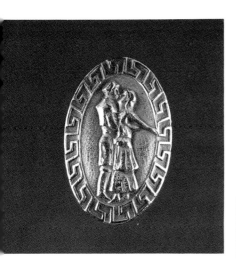

The Merry Widow was the most popular operetta of 1907 in New York, starring Donald Brian and Ethel Jackson. A photograph of the production shows that the button design copied this production in every tiny detail.

Gilbert and Sullivan's hit operetta *Pinafore* gave birth to the design of these buttons. From left, pressed brass with painted background, showing the young sailor; black glass incised and gilded with the letters HMSP (Her Majesty's Ship Pinafore); and a brass rim and brass cut out of the sailor above a decorative wooden background set in a tin back.

Also from the opera *The Mikado*, a very detailed, one-piece, pressed brass button.

The most popular operetta ever written, Gilbert and Sullivan's *The Mikado*, was first produced in London in 1885, immediately accompanied by several corresponding button designs. This two-piece, pressed brass picture button shows the Mikado (at left behind fan), his umbrella bearer, and two kneeling supplicants.

From the 1885 New York production of *The Mikado*, this is a perfect (if unfortunate) likeness of Elsie Cameron, who starred as Katisha.

Also from the 1885 New York *Mikado*, three little maids: Yum-Yum, Peep-Bo, and Pitti-Sing. The convex brass button was engraved in relief.

Another *Mikado* image, on a brass insert and collet in a tin button.

Another button from the 1885 New York version of *The Mikado*, featuring Geraldine Ulmar in the role of Yum-Yum, on a brass inset in a polished wooden button.

Chapter 7. Buttons of the Fin de Siècle and Edwardian Eras: 1885-1910

Queen Victoria's reign ended with her death in 1901, but the influence of the Victorian Age itself had really ended a decade earlier with the emergence of a new era, encompassing three related periods: the Gay Nineties, the *Fin de Siècle*, and the Edwardian Age. In literal terms, the Edwardian Age was quite short—King Edward ruled England from 1901 to 1910—but the cultural influences and attitudes we associate with it began early in the 1890s and ended with the advent of World War I in 1914. The Fin de Siècle is the French equivalent—a time of gaiety and pleasure, fashion, and progress; in America, the same trends defined the Gay Nineties. All are interrelated, and the terms are used here interchangeably.

By the time Edward the VII became the king of England, he was little more than a gambler, hunter, and aging playboy, yet in these last golden years of the British Empire he was beloved and respected by his subjects. His lifestyle was one of personal pleasure, comfort, and sport, setting a standard of self-indulgent excess. His Queen, Alexandra, was a role model for Edwardian women, famed for both her fashion sense and her conduct.

Edward loved women, literally and figuratively, and during this era that bears his name, the female face and form was celebrated. A woman's hair—usually worn swept up, but in a rather loose, seemingly informal way—was a very important part of her image, and make-up was absolutely frowned upon. The whiter the skin the better—even if it took frequent applications of borax, lemon juice, and sour milk to achieve it.

The lovely Art Nouveau-style designs featuring beautiful ladies date from this era. (See Part II, Art Styles.) So do the Gibson Girls.

The Gibson Girl was a feminine ideal created in the 1890s by artist Charles Dana Gibson. Although modelled originally on his wife, Irene Langhorne, Gibson Girls were actually composites of his stereotypical ideal. Tall, beautiful, and with regal bearing, the Gibson Girl in her various incarnations became omnipresent; her image decorated plates, spoons, wallpaper, tabletops, boxes, brooches, buttons, and so on.

For the parts of society that could enjoy it, this was an era of elegance, civility, conspicuous consumption, and shameless pursuit of the 'good life'. In England and Europe there was a tradition of royalty and court, of titled families and privelege, but in America it was the new industrialists who served that function. Vast fortunes supported the flamboyant lifestyles of the Vanderbilts, the Whitneys, the Rockefellers, the Astors, the Palmers, and many others.

The wives of these wealthy industrialists were "national figures, characters from a fairy story, for they lived on a scale that even Russian Grand Dukes found impressive. Their jewels, their yachts, their palaces (actually, mansions and summer homes of unbelievable size and luxury), servants, clothes, and carriages were of breathless interest to thousands of Americans who dreamed of success on the same terms."[1]

Art designers Carl Fabergé and René Lalique made wonderful buttons for their wealthy or royal customers. There were also precious-gem and vermeil buttons from lesser jewelers. For the rest of the populace, paste-set jewelry and buttons captured a similar look of grace and elegance.

Edward VII, King of England, and Queen Alexandra, who wore a multi-strand pearl choker to hide a tracheotomy scar. Other women copied her and began the fashion of "dog-collar" necklaces. Here the couple appears on a photo-centered glove button in a tin frame, 3/8", ca. 1901.

Queen Mary, wife of King George V, crowned in 1912, pictured on a men's waistcoat button.

Hand-painted china buttons ladies typical of the Edwardian ideal. Faces are more unusual on painted china buttons than are floral designs.

Opposite page:
These 'Gay Nineties' buttons—large, glass-centered metal made for ladies coats, were worn not by the wealthy but by those trying to emulate them. They are indicative of the ostentation of the era, 1 1/4" to 2".

Most of the painted and/or transfer-decorated china shirtwaist (lady's blouse) buttons like these were stud-backed, but these are all self-shanked examples. It is quite unusual to find one with a black background. Although buttons of this type were also commercially produced, the hand-painting of china was an art practiced at home by thousands of proper young ladies during the Edwardian era; far more plates and vases were painted than buttons.

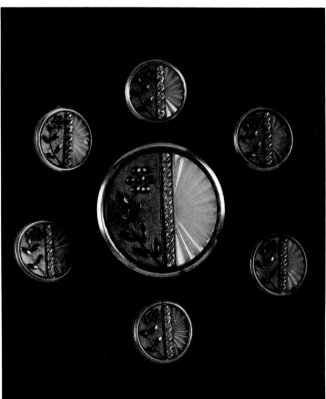

Signed on the metal shanks with both maker's marks and hallmarks, these are true jeweled buttons, made of vermeil (gold-coated sterling) set with emeralds, garnets, and pearls, ca. 1885 to 1895.

A lovely set for a lady's dress, brass-mounted with gold-lustered black glass flower design on one side and opalescent glass sunray on the other.

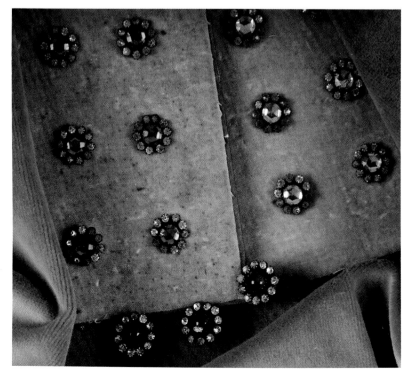

These glamorous paste-rimmed buttons with colored glass centers were sold on tan velvet cards marked 'Austria'. Even though these were made of rhinestone, they were still considered deluxe. 3/4".

The beauty of women was never more idealized than in the Edwardian era. One of the standards of beauty was the 'Gibson Girl', self-assured and elegant. This example is scorched onto wood, a technique known as pyrography. Pyrography was a craze from approximately 1895 through 1915. As was the case with china painting, ladies were encouraged to take up the art at home and they turned out large numbers of items; nevertheless, such woodburned buttons are quite hard to find.

Mother-of-pearl used as a background in brass and steel buttons, 1" to 1 1/2".

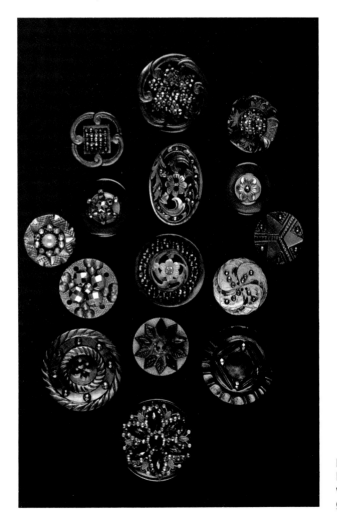

Two very stylish, fur-clad, turbanned and plumed ladies *á la Poiret*, ca. 1910 to 1920. The lady on the right is Gaby Deslys, a famous French musical-comedy actress of the era who made her American debut in 1911 at New York's Winter Garden Theatre. These rare, high-quality lithographs in double-shanked aluminum mountings were made in Czechoslovakia and measure just over 1 1/4".

Elegant mother-of-pearl buttons, French, from the *fin de siècle*, trimmed with cut steels, pearls, rhinestones, and gilt, 1" to 2".

The life of an Edwardian gentleman was one of private clubs, hunts, and for many, saloons and gambling halls.

During the Fin de Siècle, Paris became the world's fashion capital. The first true couturiér was Paul Poiret, whose influence between 1900 and 1920 permeated all facets of design, not simply clothing. He brought new colors to the forefront, using both the bright hues of the Impressionistic artists—red, yellow, green, and orange—and the darker reds and blues of the Orient. (See Part II, Art Styles.)

Poiret brought radical changes to womens' fashions. He glorified a new female body type: instead of the plump, rounded, bustled, and stuffed lady of previous years, Poiret championed the tall, angular, narrow-hipped look—the perfect figure for his long, slim tunics and straight, waistless sheaths. Turbans trimmed with beaded fringes and feathered plumes, and similarly-decorated hairbands, became the rage.

Dancing—in halls, hotel dining rooms, or private ballrooms—was a popular leisure activity. In 1912 a new dance sensation known as the tango literally swept the world. It was celebrated by participants, excoriated in print, and damned in the pulpits. In spite of the controversy—or perhaps because of it—the tango became an absolute mania. Poiret's turbans, tunics, and long slim lines lent themselves beautifully to the graceful steps of a well-danced tango.

In 1912, as Liberty & Company had done in London nearly half a century earlier, and with similar results (See Chapter 17, Arts and Crafts, in Part II, Art Styles), Poiret "opened a shop in Paris where the fashionable could buy embroideries, curtains, fabrics, wallpaper, painted screens, rugs, and all manner of other items in a distinctive Poiret image....". "Through his boutiques....Poiret really did change modern taste."[2]

Although he popularized many Chinese everyday items (for more than a decade mah-jong was the favorite parlor game in the western world), Poiret's oriental-style designs for wallpaper, fabrics, graphics, etc., were actually based on patterns and colors more common to India and the Middle East.

These were not respectable! As lithographed mens' waistcoat buttons of the 1890s, they were among those in the 'Downfall of Man' sets. It is said that decent women would not allow them to be worn in their presence, so men wore such buttons at their clubs, on gambling boats, etc. Shown are a jigging dancer, a couple doing the 'scandalous' tango, a champagne bottle and glass, a French can-can dancer, a gambling scene with eight men and four less-than-reputable women playing baccarat, and a billiard game between a lady in a Gibson-girl hairdo and shirtwaist. The gentleman, having shed his jacket, is clad in only his shirtsleeves, waistcoat, and high, starched collar—intimating that he is no gentleman, and his companion, by association, is no lady!

Sheet music from the height of the tango craze, ca. 1913. The multitude of happy devils cavorting around the borders tell the story of this scandalous dance craze! Wicked or not, perfectly respectable couples on three continents were simply wild about it. The lady is wearing a plumed cloche hat, a style popularized by fashion designer Paul Poiret.

Paul Poiret brought the Buddha into fashion for commercial graphics, jewelry, and buttons throughout Europe and America from approximately 1910 to 1925.

Pictured with an eighteenth-century Tibetan bronze Buddha are some other, non-religious, strictly decorative Buddha buttons from 1910 on: jade, Bakelite, celluloid, wood, glass, brass, white metal, black glass, and electroplated plastic, up to 2" in diameter.

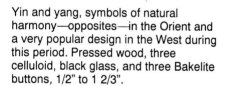

Poiret influenced public taste enough to support the manufacture of buttons with such odd themes as the carved and dyed vegetable ivory mah-jong tile at left and the celluloid Chinaman and rice bowl with chopsticks, ca. 1912 to 1915.

Yin and yang, symbols of natural harmony—opposites—in the Orient and a very popular design in the West during this period. Pressed wood, three celluloid, black glass, and three Bakelite buttons, 1/2" to 1 2/3".

A hand-painted, wooden button featuring Japanese lanterns, ca. 1912 to 1915.

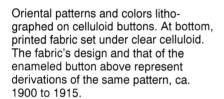

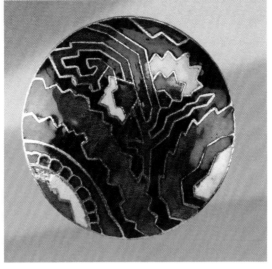

Oriental patterns and colors lithographed on celluloid buttons. At bottom, printed fabric set under clear celluloid. The fabric's design and that of the enameled button above represent derivations of the same pattern, ca. 1900 to 1915.

The colors and patterns of the Orient, translated *á la Poiret* into a jazzy enamel button: the less frazzled-looking original of this design was the *gul*, a motif common to Persian carpets.

A charming set of buttons, small red enamelled brass scarabs, ca. 1895.

Another 'foreign' look became quite popular during this same period; Egyptian themes and design motifs appeared everywhere, as they had earlier in the nineteenth century. Buttons featured scarabs, lilies, heiroglyphics, etc. While the previous vogues for pseudo-Egyptian styled goods were related to military campaigns, this fad stemmed from actress Sarah Bernhardt's very successful stage revival of Cleopatra. Bernhardt's performance was so well-received that her friendly rival, Lillie Langtry, went on tour with a version of her own.

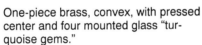

One-piece brass, convex, with pressed center and four mounted glass "turquoise gems."

An unusual enameled and pierced brass button showing the influence of both pseudo-oriental and Egyptian styles. The lady is wearing a fringed, mideastern type of turban, French, ca. 1912.

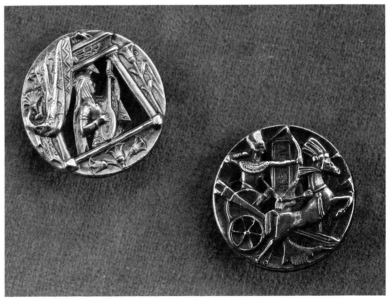

Two pierced-brass buttons from the late nineteenth century, an Art Nouveau-influenced lady with a lute and an archer in a chariot.

Amusement parks were very well-attended; park-goers were enchanted with a brand new and thrilling ride, the Ferris Wheel, first invented for the Columbian Exposition in Chicago in 1893.

International expositions and world's fairs were huge successes wherever held. The Paris International Exposition in 1900, the 1901 Pan-American Exposition in Buffalo, N.Y., and St. Louis World's Fair in 1904 were enormous hits with the public. (Three of America's favorite treats were first introduced at the St. Louis fair: iced tea, ice-cream cones, and hotdogs.)

The bicycle was the biggest fad in Europe and America from 1895-1899. It is nearly impossible to overstate the size and enthusiam of the bicycling fever, or to imagine how universal it was, and how large an industry it became. Literally thousands of bicycle companies sprang up to meet the demand, from one-man operations to large factories.

Automobiles weren't the invention of one man or country, but of several simultaneous efforts, including Germany's Karl Benz and America's Henry Ford, in1893. They got off to a particularly strong start in France under Louis Renault: bicycle racing was practically the national sport and legions of French cyclists had already developed a large network of good, smooth roads. In America, the cyclists were responsible for the decent roads that did exist, for the early roadmaps, and for the rules of driving etiquette.

As the automobile caught on, the bicycle declined. Automobiling became, by 1910, a perfect Sunday diversion for those who could afford it. This new pastime popularized ladies' hats with wide sashes to keep them on in the wind, and 'dusters'—long linen coats for both men and women that buttoned from neck to ankle to keep the road dust from ruining their clothing. The buttons on these coats "...came in brass, silver, cloissoné, enamel, jet—even a brass car on abalone shell. All vaunted automobiles or automotive designs."[3]

The first flight of a heavier-than-air craft took place when Orville Wright lifted off in 1903; his bi-plane's first flight—220 feet—lasted only 12 seconds, but a later attempt the same day lasted for more than 60 seconds. Other flight pioneers worldwide almost immediately succeeded in duplicating and improving on Wright's technology.

Molded black glass, made during the time of the 400th anniversary of Columbus's voyage to America in 1892. The button, appearing here at twice its size, shows Columbus standing next to a pedastal, his right hand resting on a globe, copied directly from a statue in Philadelphia, ca. 1892 to 1893.

A stamped, tin souvenir stud button from Chicago's Columbian Exposition,1893.

Meet Me in St. Louis! A rare and lovely button of painted enamel on brass; a commemorative button from the St. Louis World's Fair,1904.

The bicycle was important transportation to the citizens of the last half of the nineteenth century, but it not until the 1890s did the 'safety' cycle with twin wheels replace the high-wheeler (known as the 'ordinary' or 'bone-breaker'). Between 1895 and 1900, bicycling became a worldwide sensation. Top row: a velvet background showcases an aluminum bicycling lady rimmed in brass, cheap tin button with brass escutcheon, and embossed vegetable ivory. Bottom row: two-piece pressed white metal, silver plate, and molded brass picture button, ca. 1880 to 1900. *Button at lower right Courtesy of M. W. Speights*

The Hawaiian Islands' last royal ruler, Queen Lydia Kamekeha Liliuokalani, gave up her throne in 1893, and Hawaii became a republic. Button makers did not let this event pass unnoticed! Her romanticized likeness was forever captured on this small tin button.

Thematic buttons from the dusters worn by early drivers and passengers, male and female. From the top: brass escutcheon on enamel, set in brass; brass with engraved iridescent pearl background and plated brass auto atop (a deluxe example symbolizing a star-lit evening drive); a cameo carved pearl; pierced mother-of-pearl with brass auto held on with cut steel rivets; an embossed leather sheet set in a silver-plated button frame, silver plated pressed copper; pressed white metal; pressure-molded natural horn; pressed brass picture button. *The six top buttons Courtesy of M. W. Speights*

Waistcoat buttons with lithographs of Edwardian era automobile passengers in duster coats; the center lady is also wearing the *de rigeur* broad-sashed hat, ca. 1910. *Top and bottom examples Courtesy of M. W. Speights*

Manufactured shortly after Orville Wright's first flight in 1903, these buttons with the bi-plane and fenced farmfield designs commemorate the event. Two-piece stamped brass with tin backs.

A deluxe, French, painted enamel copper button with a rare subject: an early 'fantasy' flight scene. Long before man succeeded in flying, he dreamed of ways like this to attempt it, ca. late nineteenth century.

The Klondike Gold Rush in Bonanza Creek, Canada began in 1896. This waistcoat button made from a gold nugget was linked to that event. A rarity, it measures just over 1/2" long. *Courtesy of Bruce and Jane Beck*

The Edwardian period was also a time of discovery and exploration. The Klondike Gold Rush began at Bonanza Creek, Alaska, in 1896 and although thousands upon thousands tried to strike it rich, less than a few hundred really found enough gold to fund their desires. By 1900, the rush had ended, but the arctic had caught the imagination of the public. One of the smitten would-be goldminers who went to Alaska was the author Jack London: he found gold not in the Klondike, but in writing about it. *Son of the Wolf*, in 1900, was followed in 1903 by the very successful *Call of the Wild*. London did much to flame interest in the frozen north.

The North Pole was first discovered in 1892, but it took seventeen years and eight attempts for Admiral Robert Peary—accompanied by four Eskimos and one shipmate—to become the first white man to reach it, in 1909. Manufacturers quickly produced buttons with designs based on actual photos brought back from the expedition.[4]

Not all of the public imagination was caught up in events to the north: in 1913, the Panama Canal, a huge engineering project that linked the shipping route between the Pacific and Atlantic oceans, was completed (after twenty-two years of attempts by France, and nine more by the U.S.). The ten hour passage through the canal was a mere forty-one miles, shaving 10,698 miles off the former route around the dangerous base of South America.

For all its glamour and invention, the Fin de Siècle period also saw the rise of violence worldwide. Workers began to form unions to fight bad working conditions, and strikes became violent seiges as labor unrest grew and politicized. Socialism became more focused and communism began to develop. The Social Revolutionary Party was founded in Russia in 1901, and the Bolsheviks, under Trotsky and Lenin, in 1903.

International conflicts and localized wars marred the years after 1895. The British were embroiled in the Boer Wars in Africa (1899-1902) and the Americans fought the Spanish-American War in Cuba (1898).

U.S. gunboats also steamed into China in 1900 during the Boxer Rebellion to protect western diplomats and missionaries. By 1910, the young emperor of China was forced to abdicate, ending centuries of imperial rule. The fabled 'Summer Palace' was sacked, its treasures carted off: many carved-jade buttons of great antiquity found their way to western markets after this event.

Assassination of world leaders was rampant. Twelve major royal or political leaders were killed by anarchists between 1896 and 1915: the Empress of Austria, the King of Italy, the King and Queen of Serbia, the King and Crown Prince of Portugal, the Egyptian Premier, the Russian Premier, the King of Greece, the Archduke of Austria and his wife (the act which led directly into World War I), and America's President William McKinley.

Cheaply stamped brass coat buttons were made to take advantage of the excitement following Admiral Peary's expedition to the North Pole, 1909. The one featuring Peary's parka-enclosed face is easier to find than the polar bear and U. S. flag or the Eskimo in front of the aurora borealis; there are three more designs known, including a much finer quality button featuring Peary's ship, the *Roosevelt*.

The printed fabric dress button shows a gunboat steaming into action. In 1900, the U.S. Navy steamed into China.

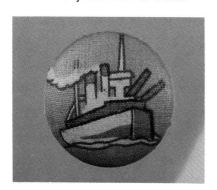

This two-piece stamped brass coat button commemorates the opening of the Panama Canal in 1913.

You can't believe everything you read! The public was fascinated with the Arctic and product after product used that fact: these ca. 1900-1915 bone underwear buttons—as plain a type of button as has ever been made—were marketed with the magical "Sitka" name and the not-quite-true claim of "ivory!"

The Socialist Party emblem in enamel on brass. 'Workers of the World Unite' was a rallying cry for The International Workers of the World, or 'Wobblies', founded in 1905.

Patriotic coat buttons, designed as carved mother-of-pearl flag mounted on smoky pearl at left, and engraving of the *Maine* on mother-of-pearl at right, shown actual size, ca. 1898. *Engraved button Courtesy of M. W. Speights*

English military officers' glove buttons, worn during the Boer Wars (1900) in Africa. Natural horn, 3/8" to 1/2". *Courtesy of Duttons for Buttons, England.*

A brass civilian button commemorating the 1898 sinking of the American battleship *Maine* while anchored in Havana Harbor, an act which led to the Spanish-American War. *Courtesy of Bruce and Jane Beck*

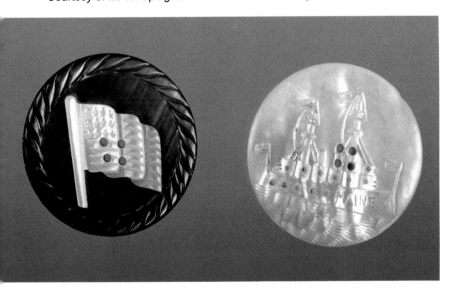

A stud-backed, pewter lapel button, featuring a grim Uncle Sam carrying a rifle, worn to show support for U. S. troops during the Spanish-American War in 1898.

On a hunting trip in Mississippi in 1902, American President Teddy Roosevelt refused to shoot a bear cub; the moment was immortalized by political cartoonist Cliff Berryman and caught the public's fancy resulting in the manufacture of the perennially popular stuffed teddy bear. Before long, Steiff (of Germany) and Horsman were marketing Teddy's Bears and Selchow & Righter was selling Roosevelt Bears. The teddy bear soon became a decorative motif, adorning boxes, postcards, tea sets, lamps, puzzles, and of course, buttons.

Pictured are true Teddy Bear buttons dating from the beginning of the legend. Of those shown here, the top brass button is the rarest: it shows a bear holding a Rough Rider type of hat over his heart and a rifle over his shoulder. Below it and at bottom are pressed brass buttons with bears in relief. The three celluloid centered tin buttons in the middle were made for childrens' pajamas ca. 1907 to 1909 and were offered in a variety of colors, 3/4" to 1".

Billy Possum was a negative nickname for President William Howard Taft, Roosevelt's hand-picked successor. The nickname referred to his Taft's obesity and his reputation for plodding. This is not a button of quality manufacture, but is nevertheless a desirable political item, made of pressed brass with a tin back.

Another Taft possum-themed political campaign clothing button—the possum golfing—a very rare button, far more so than the previous one. It is pressed of two-piece brass.

A stud-backed lapel button with a woven silk picture of a French soldier in battle. It says *Le Poilu*, literally "the hairy one," a slang term for French soldiers dating from the time of the Franco-Prussian war through World War One.

German national emblem, the crowned eagle, in gilded black glass at left, and painted on a two-piece tin button at right, ca. 1910 to 1915.

The latest weapons of war—tanks and airplanes—on post-war buttons for the homefront. The tank was a very exciting and mysterious new invention during World War I. The tank corps replaced the cavalry: rather than the centuries-old tradition of horses leading the way into battle, now the tanks lumbered into battle. First used in France at the battle at Cambrai in 1917, the earliest tanks were lozenge-shaped, as seen in the button at right (an airplane is above it). Tanks evolved quickly through many variations in size and style: the center button shows a tank with a slightly later but very different shape. At left, artillery with a shell exploding in the air above it. The center button is celluloid; the others, are Burwood or Syrocco—trade names for various pressed wood compositions, ca. 1920s.

Kaiser Wilhelm of Germany's intense rivalry with his uncle, England's King Edward VII, evolved into World War I when the Kaiser attempted to become the only world-wide sovereign. Seeking to conquer and annex territories, Wilhelm attacked Belgium, France, England, and Poland, declaring war on Russia and, finally, the United States. The Great War, or the War To End All Wars as it was concurrently known, lasted from 1914 -1919.

New technologies made armies no longer dependant on feet and horses for mobility: cars, motorcycles, trucks, and armoured tanks, along with airplanes and Zeppelins, were used as weapons of war for the first time during this war, taking both men and their arsenals further and faster than ever before. These new weapons seemed frightenly impersonal in their indiscriminate abitilities to destroy and made this war particularly horrifying to the citizenry.

The war caused massive sociological and economic upheavals worldwide. For the leisure class, elegance was an early casualty. For the general population, basic cultural standards crumbled as the war dragged on, devastating families everywhere. The aftereffects of W.W.I permanently altered fashion, industry, the workplace, gender roles, politics, and transportation. Society based on privileged birth was destroyed.

Celluloid buttons from the United States of the World War One era: a patriotic, tri-colored representation of the American flag, and an ivoroid (celluloid made to imitate ivory) with a lithographed American soldier or 'doughboy'. Although not deluxe, the soldier button is quite unusual and desirable.

Marked 'France' on the reverse, these embroidered fabric, metal-backed buttons featuring regimental insignia were not for uniforms, but for men's formal dress wear.

Chapter 9.
Mourning: The Face of Pain

A very rare, early-eighteenth-century mourning button with a drilled shank on the reverse, relief-cast in heavy pewter and signed. The angel is writing the deceased's name on a placque above a broken pillar, 1 3/4".

Mourning the death of a loved one is a rather private affair today, but it was once a very public art governed by a rigid etiquette. During the seventeenth, eighteenth, and nineteenth centuries, mourning in western cultures was refined and regulated until it became so encompassing that dress, activities, home decor, and even the depth and expression of one's grief was subjected to rules.

There developed a distinct difference in the symbolic trappings of mourning during these centuries. Skeletons, skulls, and the macabre were standard fare throughout the 1600's while eighteenth-century propriety called for Neo-Classic urns, eternal flames, broken pillars, weeping willows, and weeping women. The citizens of the nineteenth century took pleasure in the maudlin: be-ribboned bouquets of dying flowers adorned doorways, prints featured such images as stoic but grim fathers and sobbing youngsters, and paintings of cloying sentiment combined with spiritual overtones—perhaps deathbed scenes of angels with long golden hair and flowing gowns sadly caressing ethereally perfect, though very dead, children. These pictures decorated many homes' parlors.

Pearls became the symbol of tears (so chosen because they came from water) and were therefore considered appropriate for mourning jewelry. Seed pearls—tiny natural pearls—were used extensively in jewelry of all types throughout the eighteenth century and the first half of the nineteenth, but were rarely used after that.

Locks of human hair from the dearly departed were made into mementos: woven and set into jewelry, intricately braided into chains for watches, or even used strand by strand to form elaborate and sorrowful scenes or floral still-lifes, which were then framed and hung on the parlor wall. In 1861, *Godey's Ladies Book* reminded readers that "hair is at once the most delicate and lasting of our materials and survives like love...with a lock of hair we may...look up to heaven...and say: 'I have a piece of thee here.'"[1]

The late Victorian era was the 'golden age of mourning,' in which social mourning procedures were prescribed in stages, with different rules applying to each. Full mourning—the first and deepest stage—lasted a year and a day, and was observed by immediate relatives, servants, and staff. "Second wives were expected to go into mourning for a recently-deceased previous Mrs., when she acquired the poor woman's husband."[2] Half-mourning then lasted for another six months, followed by three months of quarter-mourning. (For more distant relatives and in-laws, half-mourning, rather than full-mourning, was acceptable.) Half and quarter-mourning periods had broader choices of clothing and jewelry.

Very rare, mid-eighteenth century black lacquered *papier-mâché* mourning button painted *en grisaille*; it shows a Neo-Classic urn with ram's head handles. *Courtesy of Bruce and Jane Beck*

In full mourning, women wore black, completely covered in crepe fabric; half-mourning included grey, purple, and dark reds. Quarter-mourning was a transition back to a normal way of dress; outfits were simply trimmed or edged with black ribbons, black-glass fringes, etc.

Accessories, jewelry, and buttons also reflected the different stages of mourning. Full mourning required matte or dull finishes. Half-mourning jewelry, though still black, was often finished with a partially gleaming and partially matte surface.

When a country's president or sovereign died, the entire population observed the event according to the social rules of mourning. In addition, the nobility had its own etiquette about mourning within court life. "It is hardly likely that the members of the English Court, plunged into deepest black by the death of some distant member of the Royal Family quite unknown to them, were always displaying their true feelings." Official "court mournings were so frequent and...rigorously observed...that it was considered unwise to go on any journey with the Royal Family without...complete mourning...dress and ornaments." "These periods of mourning were absolutely dreaded by the ladies of the court."[3]

A rare button of woven human hair set under glass and rimmed in copper. Saving a loved one's hair in this way was the epitome of loving sentimentality, 1760 to 1790, 1 1/2". *Courtesy of Bruce and Jane Beck*

An extraordinary mid-eighteenth-century, French, brass-rimmed, under-glass mourning button with seed pearls (tiny natural pearls) and gold wire placed on a black painted ivory disc. It features a Neo-Classic weeping willow tree and a bunting-draped bier topped with an eternal flame, 1 1/2". *Courtesy of Bruce and Jane Beck*

But being "sad need not be synonymous with being unfashionable."[4] Indeed, fashion magazines themselves promoted the mourning industry, dictating elaborate rules for physical appearance; being unable to do anything about the proscribed colors and fabrics, women attempted to outdo one another in the design or richness of their outfits. Men were expected to show their bereavement only through a change in jewelry, ties, and gloves, but women's' mourning fashions included the outer- and under-wear from head to toe. Mourning hats and bonnets, ribbons, and veils, jewelry, buttons, gloves, handbags, shoes, and fans joined black dresses, skirts, chemises, and cloaks.

Charles Dickens criticized the excesses of the mourning industry in his satirical writings by complaining that the entire structure was no more than social competitiveness—a desire to outshine one's neighbors even in sorrow, with the length and depth of one's grief, the expense of the funeral, and especially, through the purchase of any number of mourning accessories. The grief-stricken could order mourning stationary, handkerchiefs, and visiting cards edged in black, bed and table linens embroidered with black ribbons, bunting for the doors, and, for the well-dressed horse, tastefully somber bridle-rosettes and large purple plumes.

Queen Victoria was the single most instrumental influence on the ethic of mourning in England, and therefore in the Western world. When her beloved Prince Albert died in 1861, she plunged into deep despair and never really recovered, although she lived another 40 years! At first, she was copied and admired for her dedication to his memory and for her fashionably black appearance, but eventually her grief was simply too much for even her most loyal supporters: she actually stayed in full mourning for twenty years, quite excessive even in those times of extreme excess.

Victoria set the standard for black accessories. Jet was the only material that the Queen's jewelers used for her buttons and jewelry, and the fashionable women and men on five continents followed suit. Almost immediately, the once small English jet-mining industry centered in the little town of Whitby became an international business. "Visitors to Whitby complained that the town had an excessively mournful aspect, as every window was filled with a sombre display of jet jewelery [sic]."[5] The sources for this coal-like mineral were finite and within decades, jet mining died out entirely.

The soft black gleam of polished jet ornaments had already been copied by enterprising manufacturers in other industries; far more buttons and jewelry items were

A basket of gold wire with seed pearl flowers was placed inside this unusual mourning button from mid-eighteenth century France. The very odd construction features two convex glass discs bound by a tight copper band, 1 1/2". *Courtesy of Bruce and Jane Beck*

True jet, hand-carved into an unusual and very desirable button. Jet was used extensively in jewelry, but buttons—made for a select few—are very difficult to find, ca. 1850 to 1865, 4/5".

Very rare mid-eighteenth century mourning button in the Neo-Classic style, showing a lady languishing on an ovoid urn. This fabulous *en grisaille* enamel button has a blue background set on a thin, hand-hammered *répousé* brass disc backed with iron. Unusually large, 2 1/4". *Courtesy of Bruce and Jane Beck*

made to look like jet than ever were made from true jet. The Bohemian manufacture of black glass ('French-Jet') ornaments and accessories in particular became a huge industry. Onyx, black rubber, molded and dyed horn, and crape-stone were also used for jet look-alike jewelry. True jet jewelry is not common; it is quite lightweight, not cold to the touch, and can be easily etched with a sharp knife. These tests distinguish it from the competitive products; in addition, while black glass was always molded, jet couldn't be—it was carved, either by hand or machine.

Crepe-stone jewelry was made to match the black crepe fabric mandated for mourning costumes. There are two kinds: the first was truly stone, made from onyx that had been treated with acid to give it the appearance of crepe, a process patented in the United States in 1874. Before long, this was copied by the black glass industry in Bohemia; glass buttons or beads were covered with wax, then put into acid to give them the desired ridged and wrinkled appearance.

Not until the turn of the twentieth century were women's clothes sold 'off the rack'; the first of these were mourning outfits. By 1915, there were retail stores dedicated solely to mourning fashions.

The death-knell for the institution of mourning itself began to sound with the huge numbers of deaths in World War I. Beginning in 1918, just as the war ended, another horror swept the entire world: 22 million people died in the next two years during the Great Flu Epidemic, three times as many as had been killed in the war. Almost no families were untouched by untimely death.

In combination, the Great War and the flu deaths brought the mourning industry to an end. The number of deaths was so overwhelming that there was no time to stop and mourn: both the war-work and life had to continue despite the losses. Mourning had become a dispensable luxury.

Besides the ending of the mourning industry, two other changes in society were apparent. One was a change in behavior. People longed to put sorrow behind them. Women in particular had no intention of returning to the restricted lives they had lived, with its complicated social regimens.

There was also a change in the moral values of society. The reasons were deeply emotional: young adults reacted to having seen so much sorrow and death by adopting a 'live for today' attitude of personal and sexual freedom. The overall effect was a forced merriment, which led directly to the period known as the 'Roaring Twenties'. A new attitude of unfettered freedom and possible happiness was sought publicly.

By 1920, the entire structure of a long and elegant era had collapsed.

These black glass buttons were used on women's mourning clothes. At right center, a half-mourning button with a highly polished edge and dull-finished center. The bottom row contains dull-finished molded and/or passementerie buttons. (Passementerie consist of tiny beads of black glass that were individually riveted to a metal framework). Both the largest button and the smaller one at upper right are imitation crepestone, glass made to match the crepe fabric that was ubiquitous during mourning periods. The three between them were sandblasted to match oufits of moiré silk, ca. 1850 to 1900, 1/2" to 1 1/4".

Dull-finished, flat, oval black glass shirt buttons and two different cufflinks of dull-finished black glass. These accessories, plus a black arm-band, comprised a man's 'full-mourning' costume, ca. 1850 to 1900.

A man's lapel stud button advertising the Widow Jones, a turn-of-the century men's clothing shop in New York. It is a brass-rimmed, lithographed celluloid, featuring a widow in 'full-mourning' dress, ca. 1895 to 1905, 1 1/2".

Made of molded, black dyed horn, these two British family crest buttons were worn by the liveried household staff during times of 'house' mourning. Mourning crest buttons are scarce, ca. 1860 to 1910.

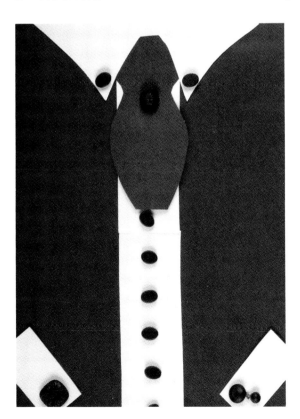

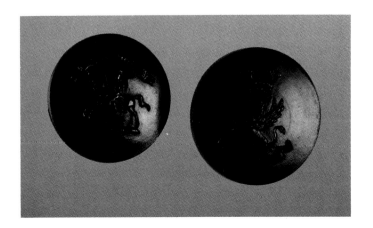

Chapter 10.
Roaring, Depressed, and Recovered:
1920-1942

The new woman! In the 1920s, suffragettes and flappers alike asserted their independance in every way possible. The face on this 1920s postcard is a bone underwear button: such cards are hard to find and avidly sought by postcard collectors.

In the years immediately following the Great War, western society changed completely. Instead of glory, the war's end brought confusion: the years of sorrow and devastation had shaken people's faith in their most precious beliefs—manners and mores were questioned, attacked, and revised. The age of elegance had given way to an age of self-expression, to a giddy sense of relief "expressed in hectic celebration and a general frivolity in design."[1] This became known as the 'Roaring Twenties'.

Overnight, or so it seemed to the more conservative members of society who were trying to no avail to hang on to pre-war standards, 'normal' women (as opposed to simply 'bad' women) wore make-up. Painted fingernails debuted in 1925. For the first time, skirts were raised above the ankle; some women even exposed the knee—very daring, and still rather scandalous. "In 1913 the average woman's costume used some 19 yards of cloth. By 1928 only 7 yards were needed."[2] Women by the thousands 'bobbed' (cut short) their hair, their crowning glory in the eyes of most men, causing much dismay.

This 'new' woman—the bachelorette, the flapper, the suffragette—was suddenly (horrors!) smoking, eating alone in restaurants, driving, voting, working though she didn't need to, and engaging in physical sports.

"During the twenties...an entirely new factor influenced fashion...women's growing participation in sports...It all started with Suzanne Lenglen, the great tennis player. Emerging in 1921, she replaced [the Poiret lady] as the typical twentieth-century woman, adding an athletic note to the slim, elegant, androgynous figure. Before Suzanne, women who played tennis wore [floor] length dresses over corsets and starched petticoats, and their hair was firmly covered with a hat."[3]

Actress Clara Bow, the 'IT' girl, and many of the other vamps of stage and screen with their bobbed jet-black hair and bright red 'bee-sting' lips, strove, through nature or cosmetics, to have whiter-than-white skin. Betty Boop, a cartoon character, was another version of this look.

A painted bone underwear button with a bob-haired flapper. This is similar to the image of Clara Bow with her signature 'bee-sting' lips and wide eyes.

Garter buttons showing 'flappers': short-haired, heavily made-up, and sequined, these modern, independant, and rather scandalous women epitomize today's image of the 1920s. These buttons were not used to fasten garters—elasticized bands worn just above the knee— but were simply decorative. The silk and lace garter and matching night-time headband shown here were part of a set that also included a teddy top and robe. The buttons seen on the lingerie have plume feathers, and the one at far right has a black satin bow hanging from it; such additions are unusual. Although flappers or even 'vamps' are by far the most common images, there are, as in the fourth button, rare examples with other themes—the tongue-in-cheek button picturing a policeman with his hand up in the 'stop' position is full of innuendo! Actual size, 1".

The 1920s woman was not afraid to show her ankles or her athletic skill to a man! The tennis scene on this scarce and unusually large celluloid wafer button was engraved and pigmented, and the steel tennis balls riveted on.

The flamingo as a decoration has become a maligned sterotype, but it really was once the most fashionable of items. The flamingo button here is painted wood. Florida itself was thought a nirvana: exotic, far-off, idyllic. There was a huge effort in 1924 to sell land in Florida to outsiders; the market grew

immensely, led by speculative financiers, and then collapsed in the Great Florida land bust of 1926! The red celluloid button with the lady bicycling amidst the palm trees features a typically indoctrinaire scene of the 'good life' in Florida. Both buttons ca. 1924 to 1930.

The discovery and opening of the sealed tomb of Tutankhamen, by England's 5th Earl of (Lord) Carnarvon in 1922, brought the image of the 'boy-king' and his kingdom to fame—oddly enough, for the first time: he was so insignificant in Egyptian history that over the centuries grave robbers had not even bothered to search for the tomb. Still, to the western world, 'King Tut' was an overnight sensation! His death mask became one of the most familiar images of the twentieth century, and 'Egyptianism' took hold.

Its influence was rampant, provoking "a flood of imitative, Egyptian-style jewelry, such as scarab and 'Ba' bird pendants, necklaces, and earrings. "The extraordinary beauty of the head-dresses and collars, combining dully shining metals with brilliantly deep colored ...lapis lazuli, turquoise, and carnelian, opened up new possibilities to modern designers."[4]

A flapper in a short, spaghetti-strapped, sequinned sheath, relaxing with her pet parrot. (The parrot was another pervasive 1920s image.) An unusual button for its time, this young lady has far more than her ankles showing! Made to be worn on a man's vest, this under-glass painted intaglio was made in Czechoslovakia in the 1920s, 1/2".

The world's attention was riveted on Egypt when King Tutankhamen's tomb was discovered in 1922, and its treasures were brought out. Manufacturers produced all manner of 'King Tut' and other Egyptological items. These molded Syrocco buttons reflect the craze: a plane flying over pyramids and a lady wearing the headdress of a goddess.

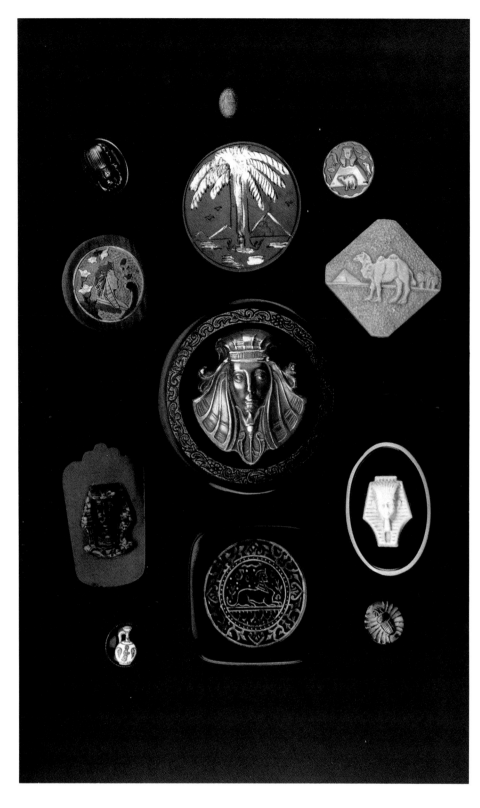

Starting at the top, clockwise, these 1920s buttons include a glass imitation faience scarab mounted in brass, a pressed brass picture button, a pressed celluloid wafer a laminated and layered celluloid featuring Tut's mask, a molded and painted black glass scarab, an engraved and pigmented celluloid sphinx, a cloisonné enamelled brass ewer, a celluloid wafer with attached hollow molded celluloid head; composition with painted brass, and a pierced and molded brass scarab. In the upper center, an engraved and painted pyramid scene, and finally, a huge, celluloid disc topped with a brass head in very high relief.

One of the two important new color combinations in use throughout the twenties was red with black: the fashion industry promoted it for women's clothing and accessories. The vogue stemmed in part from the ongoing passion for all things oriental. Black and red lacquered items—oriental standards—were considered particularly stylish choices for the home. Red lacquer, or cinnabar, also was very popular for jewelry; most of the cinnabar buttons, brooches, etc., imported from China during the 1920s were brand new, but some were antique examples.

The new black and white color combination was even more pervasive. It has been suggested that "...the ubiquitous presence from 1914 onward of black and white in clothing and accessories reflected and served the dramatic contrast of black and white photography which had entered the cultural life of the epoch. Designers played with transparent and opaque materials which reflected light, juxtaposing, for example, onyx and crystal glass beads."[5]

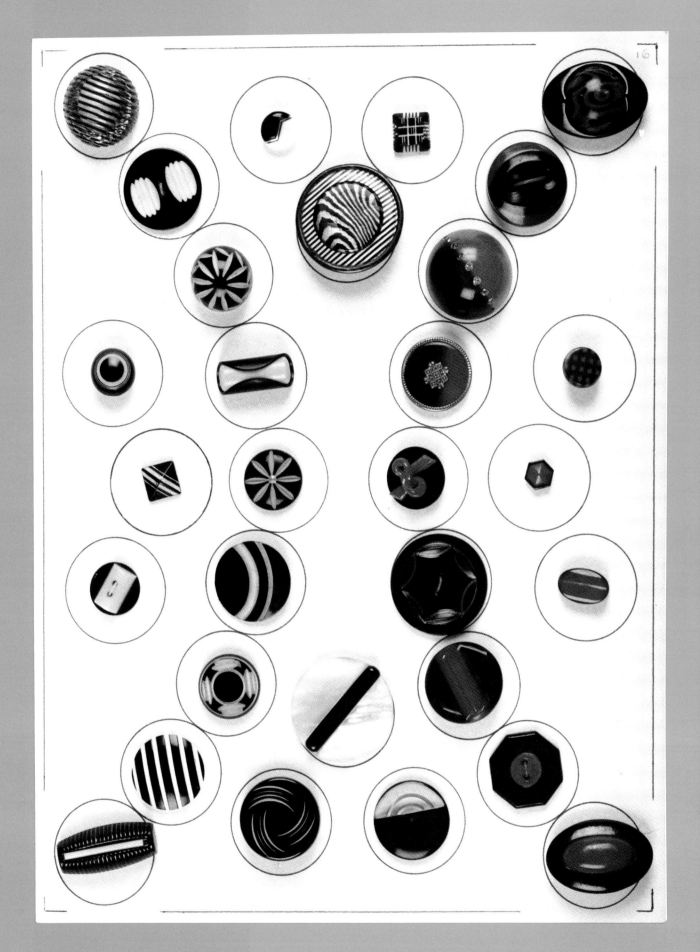

Red & black and black & white, the two
color combinations of the 1920s, seen in
buttons of the period made of glass,
celluloid, Bakelite, vegetable ivory
(tagua nut), and mother-of-pearl.

A collection of 1920s and 1930s 'Scotty' buttons in celluloid, plastics, wood, Syrocco, glass, fabric, brass, and Bakelite.

Art Deco was in vogue and these stark color contrasts stemmed from that influence as well. Black and white enamel work joined such material combinations as ebony with ivory, onyx with marcasites, black glass with white glass, and black and white celluloids. Black Bakelite was often combined with bone, or was laminated to itself in various opaque/transparent patterns.

Scotch terriers, preferably a pair in perfect black and white balance, became a rage throughout the United States. For two decades the Scotty was one of the most prevalent subjects on inexpensive costume jewelry, in advertisements, on linens, kitchenware, clothing, and on buttons.

The fashionable dog of the 1920s and 1930s, the Scotch Terrier in molded white celluloid attached to a black celluloid base.

During the 1920s, the sharp contrasts of colors and the strong patterns of primitive art began to be appreciated, and for the first time, tribal items were looked at as more than anthropological artifacts. The dramatic effect of African sculpture and masks, the linear patterns of North-American Indian pottery and weavings, and the geometric planes of Pre-Columbian figurines from the Americas caught the eye of artists and designers who turned these motifs into important elements of the Cubistic Art movement. (See Part II, Art Styles.)

The public awareness of African, Oceanic, and Carribean arts really began in France, where, "in the twenties, everything black came into vogue, thanks to the French Colonial Art Exhibition of 1922 which introduced the eroticism of African sculpture to a wider French, if not international public. In 1925, the Art Deco exhibition reflected the influence of black African art on weavings, carpets, drapes, and many other furnishings."[6] Designers everywhere soon incorporated masks, shields, idols, and so on, in their works.

French café society was enchanted with black culture: "It is often noticed that the international society of the.....1920's was much less racially prejudiced than later generations: African Art, African Painting, the....gorgeous figure of Josephine Baker dancing in Parisian night-clubs, the elegance of jazz band leaders newly arrived from America....all added to a fascination with black culture."[7]

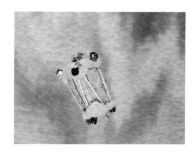

African drum, a complex, handmade beaded wood and deerskin button.

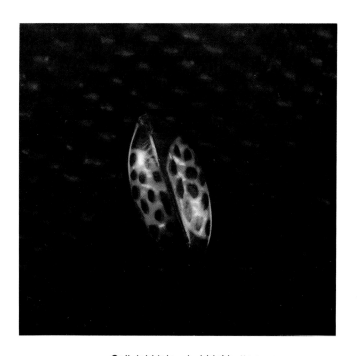

Celluloid 'glow-bubble' button, ca. 1920s, imitating African leopard fur. Exotic animal furs were the rage during this time. The button has a tin base with a translucent hollow celluloid dome over it. The glow comes from the shine of the polished tin showing through the thin celluloid bubble. The spots are litho-printed on the celluloid.

Shield-shaped celluloid buttons in the colors of the twenties.

This carved and painted Bakelite button with metal rings attached has Art Deco lines and the stereotypical 'African savage' look, ca. 1925 to 1930.

A sterling silver realistic button that appears to depict Josephine Baker, the American black singer who became a sensation on the Paris nightclub scene in the 1920s.

Perceptions of Black People in Buttons

From the end of slavery in the United States in the1860s, the popular view of racially black people has been determined by various societal factors, including literature, stage, music, movies, sports, politics, and television. Blacks have very often been the subject of decorative-arts products. Sometimes the images used were realistic; sometimes they were ignorant interpretations, more the effect of benign thoughtlessness than cruel intent. But throughout the years, the intent behind the designs has also quite often been hostile, sexually stereotypical, paternalistic, superior, or insulting. Black people have been viewed as 'noble savages' and simply savage, as 'Uncle Toms', Mammys, servants, buffoons, and so on. In France, the image of blacks–though generally more positive than that in America–has usually been unrealistically exotic.

Although buttons featuring black people are by no means common, the changes in American and French perceptions, and the ups and downs of race relations through the last 150 years, can be traced through the few that have been manufactured.

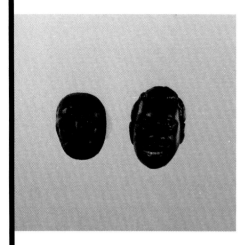

These rare buttons of black men were made before the Civil War in the mid-nineteenth century. At right, carved ebony with tiny ivory teeth and inlaid-glass eyes. At left, a molded black glass button that collectors refer to as 'Uncle Tom', from the book of that title. *Glass button Courtesy of M. W. Speights*

The stud-backed, pewter lapel button shown here—a caricature of a black man eating watermelon—illustrates a derogatory opinion of blacks in 1901.

The influence of Cubism on Art Deco can be seen in the facial lines of the African woman on this 1930s button. The imitation tortoiseshell base (made of Bakelite) has a brass head attached.

This glazed ceramic button features a rather realistic African woman in the 'noble-savage' tradition, ca. 1935 to 1940.

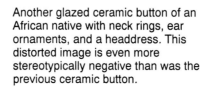

Another glazed ceramic button of an African native with neck rings, ear ornaments, and a headdress. This distorted image is even more stereotypically negative than was the previous ceramic button.

Enameled copper , modern.

An unusual hand-carved wooden black-faced button with a molded brass head-dress attached. This is a semi-realistic image of an Algerian or North African and was probably made in France, ca. 1930 to 1940s. *Courtesy of Judy Wehner*

By the 1950s, beginning in French society, but spreading quickly to the U.S. as well, the ethnographic-exotic look of African masks became part of the 'beatnik' decor and new Abstract Art-look. These buttons, painted wood at the left, and black-finished brass exemplify the look.

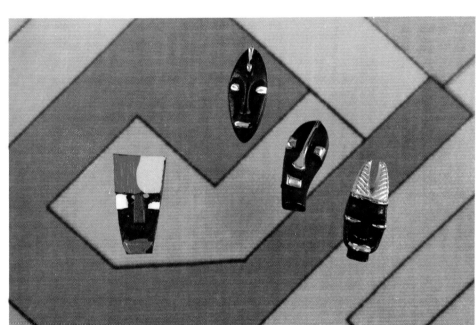

French painted-plastic 'natives' set. The French sterotypes are pretty apparent in these images. Very rare and sought after, these buttons are presently being duplicated in the Philipines and sold to collectors—the copies are larger and crudely painted. 1 1/8" & 1 1/4", ca. 1950.

In America in the 1930s, the most pervasive and popular black image was the mammy, a caricaturized maternal/servant figure. The stereotype was ostensibly one of fondness, but it was fraught with condecension. These two very rare buttons are hand-carved and painted wood, ca. 1930s.

This glazed and painted brass 'blackamoor' with jeweled turban and brass-ringed neckpiece was a stereotypical image often encountered in the early decades of the twentieth century, 3/4", ca. 1940s.

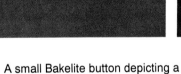

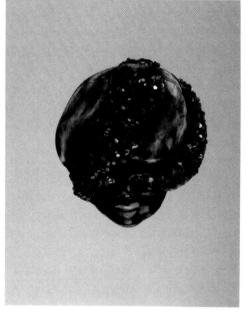

A small Bakelite button depicting a cartoon-like representation of a half-idiotic black man. Ca. 1930s.

These incredibly negative black's faces are molded of a plaster-like substance and have metal shanks inserted. 1 1/8", ca. 1950s.

Glazed ceramic with sparkly hair made from powdered glass.

Another popular image during the 1930s in the United States was Topsy, a so-called 'pickaninny' from the revival of the book Uncle Tom's Cabin. Although the two ceramic buttons at lower left date about 1990, the others are from the 1930s. Topsy's blonde companion was Little Eva, shown printed on a fabric-covered button (a Topsy button matches this one, but is elusive!) At the top are two hand-painted wooden buttons from Czechoslovakia, ca. 1935, trimmed with a fabric scarf at left, and fuzzy black pipe-cleaners at right.

Charles Augustus Lindbergh took off from the U.S. in his airplane *The Spirit of St. Louis* on May 20, 1927, and landed in Paris 33 1/2 hours later. He was suddenly the most popular hero American had known. Within two years, the airline industry that had developed in America for air-mail, was now equally important for passenger travel. Boeing Air Transport began the first cross-country service: the leg from Chicago to San Francisco took 22 1/2 hours.

By the end of the 1920s, a worldwide economic depression had set in. There had never before been such a vast and total collapse of currencies. Not only were private fortunes lost, but entire countries went broke. The Great Depression began in the United States with the stock market crash in 1929.

THE 1930s

The lifestyles, fashions, and behavioral patterns of Americans in the 1930s were as much a reaction to the Roaring Twenties as those of the 1920s had been to the Great War. The Great Depression saw families stripped of their incomes; life became a struggle for survival for many.

Monolopy replaced mah-jong as America's favorite parlor game; instead of being pre-occupied with the mysterious east, the public at large was thinking more about finances, fantasizing about being filthy rich, and worrying about ending up in the 'poorhouse' and 'going to jail.'

Although liquor sales were prohibited in the United States from 1919, 'bootlegging'—illegally selling alchohol—flourished; the 'cocktail' came into fashion in speakeasies (illegal bars), with over 120 different mixed drinks becoming popular. When President Roosevelt signed an ammendment repealing Prohibition in 1933, the speakeasies of the 1920s became the nightclubs of the 1930s. In nightclubs, the sounds of jazz were joined by swing tunes that people danced to—and thus were born the 'big bands'.

Brass realistically-shaped Liberty Bell, a commemorative button from the U.S. Sesquicentennial celebration in 1926.

Cheap two-piece brass commemorative button from 1927 showing *The Spirit of St Louis*, the monoplane Charles Lindbergh flew non-stop across the Atlantic Ocean from New York to Paris.

Buttons showing matches: from left, two Bakelite sew-throughs, painted celluloid, and a molded metal shanked-button with three matches stacked akimbo, ca. 1930s.

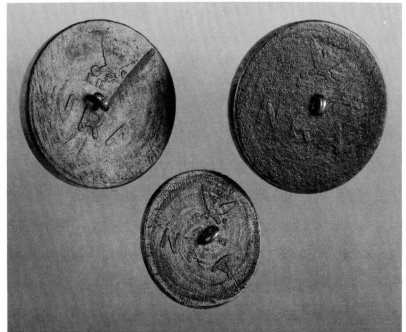

In 1933, President Roosevelt set up the National Recovery Administration (NRA) in an attempt to encourage industry and put the unemployed back to work. NRA markings appear on a wide array of items made under the provisions of this act, including buttons. All reported NRA buttons have been plain, utilitarian, and wooden—but they are by no means easy to find! The backmarks, impressed in the wood as shown, consist of the letters NRA and an eagle.

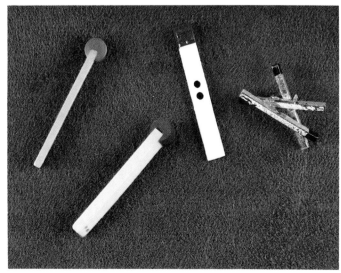

Opposite page:
By 1935, because cigarettes had acquired a cachet of glamour and sophistication, eight out of ten American men and five of every ten women smoked. These buttons, from three different sets, are hard to find. The largest are made of wood with faithfully-copied paper labels wrapped around them. The buttons on the card are molded plastic 'goofies' with printed labels. The two smaller ones at lower right appear to be made of brass, but are actually gilded celluloid with transfer decals attached. *Courtesy of Florence Dieckmann*

When Prohibition was repealed in 1933, Americans went wild for depictions of liquor: these buttons from the 1930s include, at left, two painted plaster bottles; at the top, a complete set of the 'big-three' cocktail buttons; at right, three from a set of five metal realistically-shaped buttons with applied decal labels of actual brands, all of which are forms of whiskey. The rare molded plastic button at the center is the 'drunk on a lamp-post', a common image of the time.

The 'big band' sound became more popular than jazz by the mid-1930s, and lasted well into the 1950s. The buttons in the top row include three members of a 'big-band' from a very rare set of molded metal 'goofies', and a flat Bakelite note. At the bottom are Bakelite guitar, saxaphone, and banjo.

An original salescard of 'goofies' showing not only the musically-related buttons, but delightful artwork on the card of an Art Deco-styled 'swing' band of the 1930s.

The hottest sound of the twenties was jazz, and the hottest new instrument was the saxophone. This hand-sewn leather designer's button, in stylish red & black, features both a brass guitar and a saxaphone, ca. 1920s.

An early football player, engraved on an unusual and partially enameled sterling silver button, ca. 1920s to 1930s.

Going to the horse-races and betting on the ponies became more and more popular as desperate people risked some or all of their money on chances to get rich quick. Individual sports did not hold nearly the appeal of spectator sports, especially football. Baseball also continued to capture the American public's imagination, and the great stars of that game were known in every household. There was an ongoing appreciation for golf, and women's participation in sports increased dramatically during the decade.

Winter sports did not have a strong following in the United States, when a darling, graceful young ice skater from Norway named Sonja Henie emerged from the Olympic games. Only sixteen when she won her first Olympic gold medal for figure skating in 1928 at St. Moritz, she followed with two more gold medals, in Lake Placid, New York, in 1932, and at Garmisch-Partenkirchen, Germany in 1936.

It was at the 1932 Lake Placid Olympic Winter Games that Henie first caught the eye of the American public; the reaction was not only adulation directed at Sonja herself, but also a tremendous interest in winter sports in general. Skiing became a popular mania; in their sporting goods department, Macy's Department Store in New York City built a twenty-foot hill covered with borax to imitate snow and offered skiing lessons on it! Sonja Henie remained an international celebrity after she retired from competition in 1936. She originated the touring ice shows, became a movie star in Hollywood, and was featured on buttons.

Before long, all winter sports were featured as decorative motifs on costume jewelry and buttons.

Plastic buttons with women bowling and playing tennis.

Celluloid button 'The Ponies', with painted metal insert and, at right, Bakelite with a very detailed racing scene on copper set into it, ca. 1930s.

Four molded celluloid buttons with football or baseball themes, ca. 1930s.

The 1930s and 1940s sportswoman of molded plastic in relief.

One of a rare set of small brass and painted decal, magazine cover buttons from the 1930s. The skiing lady is quite a romanticized image!

Skiing buttons of painted and embossed wood, from Czechoslovakia, 1930s.

Sonja Henie. The left button, of molded and painted wood, and the center one, a plaster intaglio in the back of a glass disc mounted in brass, were both made in Czechoslovakia; the red Bakelite button at the right from the United States. Each of the designs is taken directly from a photograph of her, right down to the exact outfits. The design of the Bakelite button was copied from a cover photo on a late-1930s ice show program.

The Olympics

The first Olympic Games were held in Olympia in the Elis region of Greece in 776 B.C. As a movement for international brotherhood, they were reinstituted in 1896 as the modern Olympics. The Eternal Flame carried from game to game was added in 1936 as the symbol of continuity.

The emblems of the modern games are changed every four years with each new venue, but the Olympic logo itself never changes; the five interlocking rings represent the continents of Africa, Australia, Eurasia, North America, and South America.

Clothing buttons have been made both as souvenirs (sold on location to visitors) and commemoratives (commercially distributed for public sale anywhere) for each of the Olympic Games throughout the twentieth century. Olympic buttons have usually featured the emblem of the particular host city. Button collectors seek Olympic-related buttons, but not nearly with such dilligence as do specialized collectors of Olympic memorabilia.

The pressed brass button at left is from the tragic 1972 Munich games, at which terrorists murdered members of the Israeli team. At right, a brass button from the games in Montreal, 1976.

Pressed brass Olympic souvenir button from Tokyo, 1964

The non-political image of the Games was shaken badly in 1980 when American President Jimmy Carter banned the U. S. team from competing in the Olympics in Moscow. The Soviets retaliated by refusing to send a team to the Los Angeles Games four years later. The left button is molded plastic from the 1980 Moscow games; the right button is nylon plastic.

A brass penguin on a celluloid button, inspired by the 1930s exploits of Admiral Bryd in Antarctica.

From 1933 to 1935, American aviator Richard Byrd was on expedition to the South Pole, having first flown a discovery mission there in 1929. His exploits were photographed for the public at home, and his every move reported on. When Byrd arranged to export a shipment of penguins to a few American zoos, the American public suddenly went wild for penguins. Manufacturers reacted by including penguin designs on all manner of objects, and the image of the 'tux-clad' birds appeared over and over in print as well, throughout the 1930s.

(Tragically, all of the penguins from Byrd's shipments became victims of viruses and impurities their lungs had never before been exposed to. Once veterinarians studied the problem, they discovered that the birds needed to be kept in protective sealed airspaces; the next round of penguins that were imported did survive and millions of Americans flocked to zoos to see them.)

In general, traveling was still the option of the wealthy. Great ocean liners, the new passenger airplanes, and the vaunted express trains all represented the 'good life' to the general public, who devoured stories and items featuring travels to far-off locales.

Pressure-embossed, hand-painted wooden penguin button from Czechoslovakia, ca. 1930s.

Penguin buttons are almost always from the 1930s when 'penguin fever' first hit. These include, at left, a silver Arctic explorer on Bakelite, a celluloid realistic, deluxe three-dimensional celluloid on celluloid, plastic, incised yellow glass, and a small celluloid realistic; bottom, white metal escutcheon on brass. Shown at 1/2 normal size.

A gentleman's lithographed waistcoat buttons from England picturing the great ocean liners of the 1920s and 1930s.
Courtesy of M. W. Speights

Realistically shaped luggage; the left two buttons are part of a set of four in painted wood; at right, molded celluloid, ca. 1930s.

A diesel passenger train in molded celluloid, a molded Burwood *Queen Mary*, a white metal car—part of a 'goofie' set of transportation modes of the 30s–and two planes, in plastic and in Burwood. (Molded wood pulp).

Home life in America in the 1930s was still family-oriented with traditional roles and rules. The radio had become omnipresent in homes all over the land; broadcast news, entertainment shows, comedies, and dramas all had huge audiences.

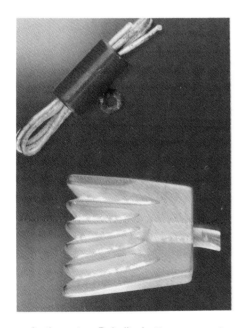

As these two Bakelite buttons suggest, women's work is never done! One shows a carved dust-pan, the other a laundry line made of rubber wire slipped through a red tube.

More women's work! Celluloid buttons joined by metal thimble and scissors, carved wood coffee cup and rolling pin, yarn-filled plastic basket, and two Bakelite clothes pins. The celluloid coffee service set at right is hard to find, ca. 1930s.

Bakelite hammer button.

Men's work was represented by far fewer buttons! (Does that mean that they had far less work to do?) Bakelite realistics, from the 1930s.

Photo-lithograph of an airship set in brass as a man's waistcoat button. *Courtesy of M. W. Speights*

An airship featured on a two-piece, pressed brass button, ca. 1930s.

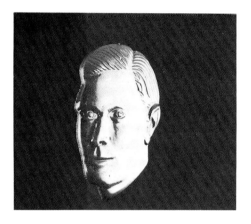

A very scarce, molded, celluloid realistic head of the Duke of Windsor. *Courtesy of Bruce and Jane Beck*

Following the abdication of England's Edward the VIII in 1937, his brother Bertie became King George VI. The white metal portrait button and the crowns were designed to satisfy public demand for souvenirs of his coronation. In May of 1939, King George and his Queen, Elizabeth, toured Canada for six weeks, becoming the first British sovereigns to ever visit the 'New World'; the button with the photograph was sold in Canada during this visit.

Radio

Serialized radio dramas were followed by millions who tuned in week after week for further developments. Tom Mix, the Cisco Kid, Hopalong Cassidy, Roy Rodgers, and other cowboy tales began as radio serializations. The producers of *The Shadow*, *The Green Hornet*, and many similar programs did their best to scare half to death the families seated together after dinner in front of their radio sets. Orson Welles succeeded best in a now infamous broadcast called *The War of the Worlds*.

Surprising numbers of listeners believed *The War of the Worlds'* hair-raising tale of Martians attacking the U.S. to be a live news broadcast, and panicked. The government actually issued rules afterwards to ensure that a dramatization never again would be mistaken for a true news event. Other space-related programs, such as *Buck Rogers* and *Flash Gordon*, were wildly successful, but certainly not taken seriously!

In 1937, the German air-ship *Hindenburg* crashed and burned at its landing dock in New Jersey, killing many passengers. The event stands out as more than just a death-knell for passenger air-ships: it also was being broadcast live on the very first transcontinental radio news program. Those who heard it never forgot the horror and emotion in the voice of the reporter who was describing a routine landing when the disaster occured.

German Count Ferdinand von Zeppelin's invention, the air-ship (blimp), had first flown in 1900. By 1916, German Zeppelins were used as weapons of war in attacks on Paris, and afterwards, as transatlantic passenger carriers, competing with the ocean-liners. The *Hindenburg* was not the first crash: the British commercial airship, the R101, had crashed in 1930 on its way to India, killing all aboard and there were other others as well. By the end of the 1930s, Zeppelins were history.

Another famous radio broadcast took place in England in May of 1937, announcing that David, the Prince of Wales, who had just become King Edward the VIII in 1936, would abdicate his throne to marry the woman he loved, American divorceé Wallis Simpson. The match was unacceptable to the British parliament. He was given the title of Duke of Windsor and left England forever. He and Mrs. Simpson did marry, and spent their lives traveling and living as fixtures in the world of high society. Although the new Duchess of Windsor was the woman half the world loved to hate, she was a fashion leader. Her taste in accessories and jewelry was both whimsical and ostentatious, and was widely emulated.

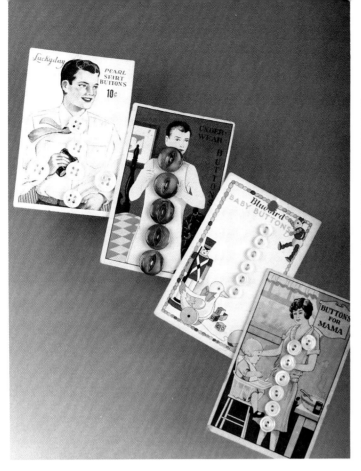

Original sales cards with mother-of-pearl shirt buttons from the 1930s. These are collectible for their great images of everyday life, such as the stages portrayed here—a carefree bachelor, the young married man, a new baby, and mother with child.

Martians were an intriguing subject in popular literature of the 1930s. Few products reflect this, though, for it was such an unknown image and people felt a bit sheepish about believing in it. These carved celluloid Martian buttons are exceedingly unusual, ca. 1930s.

Tom Mix and Hopalong Cassidy were two of the most popular radio cowboy heros, and all of these buttons may have been inspired by such shows. The two center buttons in the bottom row certainly were: the engraved and painted Bakelite boot was a radio premium offered to listeners as a keychain or a button, and the carved, painted, wooden head is a likeness of Tom Mix.

Two celluloid buttons reflecting the interest in space exploration in the 1930s. At left, a comet representation by a steel escutcheon, and at right, a glass-covered celluloid button base protects the interior design of a comet with star.

The Depression in the 1930s had the effects of adding sobering reality on some levels and fostering fantasy on others. Fashions were very quiet for daywear, and slinky, dramatic, long, and sensual for evenings. The gaudy and glittery was in style for both jewelry and clothing. The fashions looked rich, but in most cases the appearance was not reality. What had begun as acceptance of costume jewelry in the 1920s had become an enthusiastic vogue in the 1930s.

Clothing designer Coco Chanel herself had actually legitimized costume jewelry, gleefully christening it 'frankly fake', but it took more than a designer's say-so to make the costume-jewelry industry grow. Because of the financial depression and the need to rise out of it, at least emotionally, the "fashion for frankly artificial jewelry...became a necessity rather than a diverting whim."[8]

In Paris, the witty and even surrealistic fashions from designer Elsa Schiaparelli, decorated with amusing and often bizarre buttons, popularized the use of similarly odd or humourous costume accessories worldwide. The fantasy of elegance and glamour was further fueled in the 1930s by the great escapist therapy, the 'Silver Screen'.

Opposite page:
The glamour of the Duchess of Windsor's jewels and fashion designer Coco Chanel's embrace of costume jewelry led to widespread public use of rhinestones, as seen in these buttons of the 1930s and 1940s. Every one of these rhinestone buttons has prong-set, hand-mounted stones.

Thought to be a design by Elsa Schiaparelli, this button's rather dreadful mask-like face is hand-modeled clay with tiny glass teeth strung on a wire, ca. 1930s to 1942.

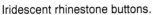

Iridescent rhinestone buttons.

Another possible Schiaparelli design is this large knight in armor on horseback with a jousting pike, made of white metal and pavé-set rhinestones, 2 1/4" across.
Courtesy of Bruce and Jane Beck

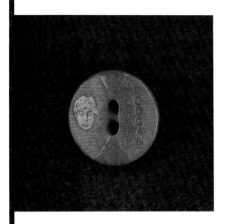

Jackie Coogan's embossed face and name appear on this vegetable ivory button commemorating his first hit movie, *The Kid*, ca. 1921, 2/3". *Courtesy of M. W. Speights*

Shirley Temple's face appears on a rare Czechoslovakian self-shanked glass button which was manufactured in many colors, ca. 1935, 3/4". *Courtesy of Mary Johnson.*

A very rare Bakelite button with a répoussé brass head of Shirley Temple, mounted under glass, self shanked and backmarked 'England, Copyright'; only one set of six of these buttons has ever been reported, ca. 1935, 1 1/2".

Hollywood

The first Hollywood motion picture was the 1903 silent classic, *The Great Train Robbery*. Mary Pickford, widely known as 'America's sweetheart', was the original child star, beginning her career at age sixteen in 1909. Only 5' tall, she continued in children's roles until she was thirty-four, but it was Jackie Coogan who became the first child super-star.

In 1921 when Coogan was five years old, Charlie Chaplin chose him to co-star in *The Kid*. Within two years, Coogan was the biggest box-office draw in America, above Rudolph Valentino and Douglas Fairbanks. Manufacturers tied into the popularity by marketing Jackie Coogan toy wagons, caps, clothing, and candy.

An even bigger success story with no parallel in the history of Hollywood was that of Shirley Temple. Born in 1929, by the age of three she appeared in small films. When she was five, she starred in *Stand Up and Cheer*, and the 'Shirley Temple smile', her singing and dancing, absolutely enchanted the country. She was a sensation. By the end of 1934, she starred in eight more movies, and was awarded a special Oscar by the film community.

Shirley Temple was the top box-office star in America from 1935-1938. By 1939, she was being paid $300,000.00 per movie, when the typical American worker with a wife and two kids made about $2200.00 a year. Every mother in America wanted her little darling to be just like Shirley, and manufacturers produced an unbelieveable variety of Shirley-related items, including dolls, clothing, tea sets, jewelry, and buttons.

Some of America's adult screen stars were also pictured on buttons during the 1930s. Manufacturers had discovered that not only could an image of a movie-star on a button sell that button, but that popular actors could be used as marketing tools to sell even plain buttons to the public. They began to offer carded sets of quite unremarkable buttons with the stars pictured on the cards; in return, the studios insisted that the button cards be actual advertisements for their latest movies.

Throughout the late 1930s and 1940s, Hollywood was a major fashion influence. Elsa Schiaparelli, recognizing that the stars on screen were far more influential with the public than fashion designers were, once said "What Hollywood designs today, you will all be wearing tomorrow."[9] These Bakelite buttons commemorate the movie version of *Steppin' Out*, and are trimmed with rhinestones and mother-of-pearl. They are reminiscent of Hollywood's big-budget musicals, with a top-hatted Fred Astaire and glamourous Ginger Rodgers gliding across a Bakelite dance floor.

Original sales cards of buttons from the late 1940s and early 1950s, each advertising a movie. The buttons on cards such as these are never very exciting and collectors should keep the cards intact as movie memorabilia; their value is not in the buttons!

A set of rare tin-framed clothing buttons with photographs of the six biggest contract players for M. G. M (Loretta Young, Robert Taylor, Errol Flynn, Clark Gable, Tyrone Power, and Myrna Loy) set under celluloid covers. They came in both rectangular and oval shapes, ca. 1938, just under 3/4".

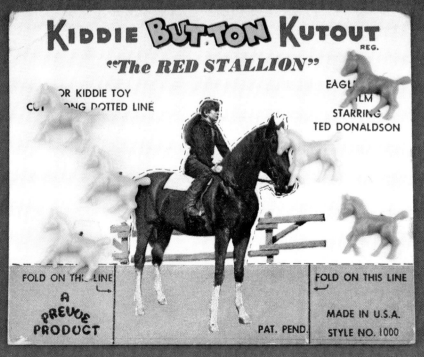

'Kiddie' button card advertises the sad Disney movie *The Yearling*.

A 'Kiddie Button Kutout' card of buttons advertising the movie *The Red Stallion*. *Courtesy of Judy Wehner*

Carmen Miranda shown with fruit on her head on this three-dimensional button made of copper electroplated over plaster.

The Carmen Miranda Influence

Oddly enough, although the absurdly flamboyant singer and dancer Carmen Miranda made no classic movies and was not considered a glamour queen, a superstar, or a great actress, she was nevertheless one of the most influential women in fashion from the late 1930s to the mid 1940s.

"Carmen Miranda in motion—accompanied by...torrid sambas...and supported by her legendary nine-inch platform-soled shoes—undulated and slithered her bare-midriffed personality across acres of glassy Bakelite floors in a sucession of luridly Technicolored musicals in the early 1940s."[10] She wore bananas, cherries, oranges, even whole pineapples, on her headresses and hanging around her neck on celluloid chains. With the "gaudiness (of) the tutti-frutti salad of junk jewelry that adorned every available square inch of her diminutive anatomy....she surpassed Hollywood's wildest dreams of itself...."[11]

In addition to Carmen Miranda's "enormous influence on the artificial-fruit industry (which) made the kitchens and dining rooms of America resemble orchards"[12], she was the impetus behind the costume-jewelry industry's trend to large and colorful fruit brooches, bracelets, earrings, and buttons. Astounding numbers of fruit-themed buttons—almost always large, gaudily colorful, and realistically-shaped—were produced during this period.

A deluxe realistic, silver with pavé rhinestone turban and hand-painted details. The paint is peeling, but the button is still very desirable. Carmen Miranda, wearing her signature fruit salad headdress, 1", 1940s. *Courtesy of Judy Wehner*

Fruit salad! Carmen Miranda inspired a generation of American women to deck themselves with fruit. These assorted buttons of plastic, wood, celluloid, and glass were typical of the thousands of fruit-themed buttons manufactured in the 1930s and 1940s.

Even fruitier! Buttons from three different deluxe sets: upper left, solid, molded celluloid with multi-colored rhinestones and hand-set leaves; right, celluloid with a very unusual satin finish and inlaid rhinestones; and heavy white metal buttons enameled and coated with glitter, the leaves trimmed with rhinestones.

More Fruit! These enameled metal buttons with dyed brass leaves are of a higher quality than most of the 1930s and 1940s fruit-themed button sets.

Left, molded and paint-trimmed hard plastic realistics; center, molded celluloid fruits attached to celluloid plates; right, molded celluloid, set with rhinestone trim.

Woody Woodpecker, transfer on plastic.
2/3", ca. 1990.

Cartoons

Animated cartoons were an important part of the movie-going experience. Whether as the feature, or as short fillers between motion picture, newsreels and popcorn advertisements, they were wildly popular. The brand-new film animation companies quickly learned—as was the case with radio serials—that characters with ongoing storylines kept the public returning to the theatres for more.

The cartoon industry was the provence of a limited number of companies. Warner Brothers did the Looney Tunes, starring a number of favorite characters, although Bugs Bunny could be called the leader of the pack. Woody Woodpecker had his own following as well. But no other cartoon character has ever had the success of Mickey Mouse, from the Walt Disney Corporation.

What is Inspector Clouseau looking for? Probably the missing button from the upper right corner! A set of Pink Panther plastic buttons on the original gift card, inspired by the series of 1960s-era movies starring Peter Sellers, 2/3", ca. 1984. *Courtesy of Kate McDermid.*

The Teen-age Mutant Ninja Turtles, very heavy, solid molded-plastic buttons from the hit cartoon series of the late 1980s.

The Looney Tunes characters were memorialized on darling white-plastic buttons from the fall of 1990. The transfer designs included Porky Pig, Bugs Bunny, Elmer Fudd, Yosemite Sam, Daffy Duck, Sylvester the Cat, Tweety Bird, Road Runner, and Wile E. Coyote.

Mickey

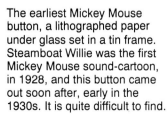

The earliest Mickey Mouse button, a lithographed paper under glass set in a tin frame. Steamboat Willie was the first Mickey Mouse sound-cartoon, in 1928, and this button came out soon after, early in the 1930s. It is quite difficult to find.

This glass dress trim from Czechoslovakia can be distinguished from buttons by the sewing holes, which are on the edges. This dates to the early 1930s, when Mickey Mouse had already reached international 'cult' status. Very rare.

This is the rarest Mickey Mouse button. It was sold, not as a button, but sewed onto children's sock garters and undershirts that were advertised by A. Stein & Company of New York in 1934. The image on the button, Mickey playing ice hockey, was taken from a movie 'still' advertising "Walt Disney's Mickey Mouse on Ice," from United Artists. The button is a two-piece brass with tin back, self shank with partly-silvered finish.

The buttons best known to Disney collectors are these, which were first issued in 1935, under liscence from the DuPont Viscoloid Company and were reissued with variations at least four times. They were sold on cards marked "Hollywood Button Company", with three, four, or six buttons to a card. The set of six sold for $.10! The version seen in the center, with the Mouse pointing to the right, was not reissued and is therefore much rarer than the rest

At first, the buttons were hand-painted in great detail. When reissued soon thereafter, they were unpainted, but had a rhinestone eye. The next reissue was totally undecorated, probably due to the constraints of hand labor and the deadlines of great consumer demand.

Later, in 1937 and 38, the Leo Phillips Company of New York produced a licensed spin-off of these buttons, an example of which is seen at the lower right: the same button-mold was used to produce these sew-through buttons; holes were drilled in the realistic bodies and they were attached to sew-through Bakelite-type (Catalin) bases.

The Disney Connection

The most successful merchandising ever done by a company must surely be that of the Walt Disney Corporation. In 1932, Joyce Hall, the founder of Hallmark Cards, became the first licensee for Disney-related items. Others quickly followed suit; in the years since, thousands of manufacturers worldwide have been licensed to produce innumerable decorative-arts products with Disney characters on them. (Many have produced merchandise without permission, however, a problem which to this day keeps several full-time Disney employees occupied.)

Clothing buttons have been produced under license since 1934. They are among the rarer Disney items—even some of the most devoted Disneyana collectors are quite unaware of their existence. The majority of these buttons were products of the 1930s, but Disney-themed fasteners have sporadically appeared since that time from manufacturers in the U.S. and several other countries. There have also been non-licensed buttons, very limited in production, most of which were sold directly to button collectors. Only the commercial, 'real' examples are discussed here, and to Disney collectors, these are the only ones of value or interest.

In the published literature on Disney collectibles, buttons are sadly lacking. These writers have not intentionally disregarded buttons—indeed they are usually thrilled to have an example if they find one—but they simply have not been aware of them! Most of the research on Disney memorabilia has been accomplished with the help of the early merchandising catalogues issued for retailers, and by Disney's own archives department. Unfortunately, the licensing agreements on file in the archives didn't mention buttons by name but instead called them notions or jewelry. Therefore, other Disney researchers have concluded that only one type of clothing button —the one most commonly found and that is listed in an early catalogue—was ever officially manufactured.

In my research, I have found many examples of Disney buttons from manufacturers around the world. Mickey Mouse appears on the majority, but Donald Duck, Pluto, Bambi, and Minnie Mouse have each been pictured on several buttons. Snow White and the Seven Dwarves have inspired several button sets. I know of only one licensed button each for the characters Bongo, Chip, or Pinnochio, and most recently, The Little Mermaid was the subject of a very colorful realistically-shaped plastic button.

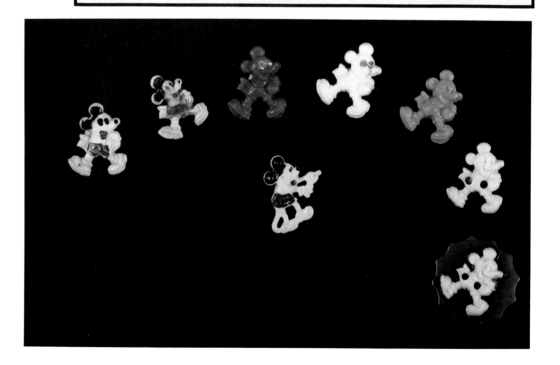

Mickey Mouse, on a brass two-piece button with a red painted background. Ca. 1950s. Courtesy of M.W.Speights

The glass buttons at the top with incised and painted Mickey Mouse heads came from Europe in the 1950s and 1960s. The printed fabric button may have been unlicensed. It dates from the same period.

The two buttons at the left are from Italy, late 1930s, and are molded wood-composition sew-throughs, painted by hand. The ones to the right, with both Mickey and Minnie Mouse, were from Australia late in the 1940s, and are of a molded plaster-like material, hand-painted.

Donald Duck buttons were issued in the same manner as were the Mickey Mouse ones, by the Hollywood Button Company, beginning in 1937. By the end of the 1930s, Donald was actually more popular than Mickey!

Pluto was the next character to be made into this type of button, as this original sales card from the Hollywood Button Company attests. Next to the card are plastic buttons from a set consisting of Pluto, Bambi, Chip, and Donald Duck. These were from Australia, in the early 1940s.

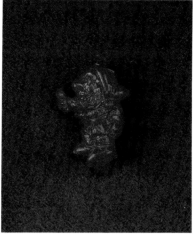

Following the phenomenol success of the animated film "Snow White" in the 1930s, several sets of 'Snow White and the 7 Dwarves' buttons were issued. They are all incredibly elusive, but the molded-plastic realistic set (one of which, Grumpy, is shown here) is the one most often seen. It is a challenge to find even one button, though, much less to assemble the whole set!

This is a very hard to assemble grouping of Snow White buttons, representing 5 different sets. Two sets seen here are complete: the Bakelite set of 8, with colored-paper decals reverse- pasted on the plastic dome-like covers (the 9th button shown here in this set is to illustrate the two colors it came in, very dark green, and mustard-yellow), and the 4 hand-painted white-plastic buttons across the 2nd row at the top. This set only came with the 4 characters shown, from the Brier Manufacturing Company of Providence, Rhode Island. In the center is a molded and painted wood button from Czechoslovakia. Under it are two of the dwarves from the easiest set to find, sew-through molded-plastic realistics. The printed-fabric button at the bottom is part of a very rare set with only six buttons to it.

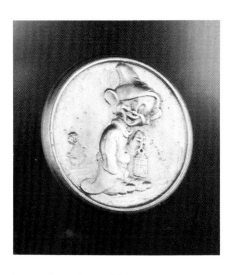

This is Bashful, from a rare molded-brass set of Snow White buttons, probably French. I have never seen a whole set and do not know how many it might consist of. *Courtesy of M.W. Speights*

Dopey from *Snow White:* this and the button to the left are the only ones of the seven dwarves that I have yet seen. It is not known how many more of the seven were made. Very rare. 1 1/8", molded two-piece brass button with self-shank, 1940s. *Courtesy of Judy Wehner*

Bambi, the animated feature cartoon success from Disney in 1942, seen on two-piece cheap metal buttons of the same type as in the Mickey playing ice-hockey seen earlier. They were most likely all made in Czecho-slovakia, but sold in the United States.

Bambi, of molded and painted plaster. Ca. 1944.

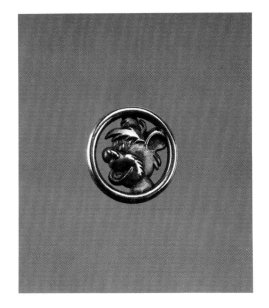

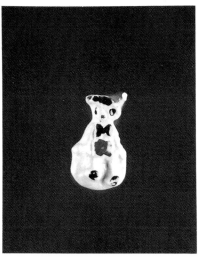

Bongo the bear, seen in an open-work copper-colored electro-plated plastic button, issued for the film "Fun and Fancy Free" in 1948.

Pinocchio, ca, late 1930s, molded plaster-like composi-tion, enamel-painted.

A set of gold-plated brass blazer buttons, made by the Theme Merchandise Company of Attleboro, Massachusetts, in 1986. They were sold in boxed sets of 8 buttons at the Pleasure Island shops in Disneyworld and Disneyland, from 1986 to 1988. There were less than 500 sets made in total.

Mickey Mouse, a transfer-print on white plastic buttons, from the early1980s in celebration of Mickey Mouse's 50th anniversary. Minnie Mouse and Donald Duck were also issued by the same firm, located in France, at the same time.

Donald Duck buttons, as previously described.

From France, in the 1990s, these are colorful plastic. *Courtesy of Diana Epstein and Millicent Safro, Tender Buttons, N.Y. and Chicago*

The Little Mermaid, ca. 1990, painted, molded plastic button backmarked 'Disney', and 'Applause™, CHINA'.

The 1930s ended with the very successful 1939 New York World's Fair, which followed the theme 'The World of Tomorrow'. Its symbols were the Trylon and the Perisphere, which appeared on almost every one of the thousands of products sold there, including a number of buttons.

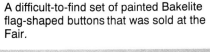

A difficult-to-find set of painted Bakelite flag-shaped buttons that was sold at the Fair.

These plastic buttons, molded with the shapes of North America and the United States, were quite popular when sold at the Fair. The left example is electro-plated, 1939.

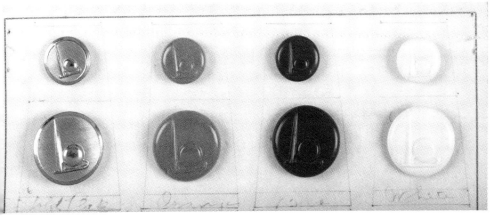

Left: painted, pressure-embossed wooden button with the flags of the Fair, the Trylon and Perisphere. Right: the same design on a large Bakelite coat button.

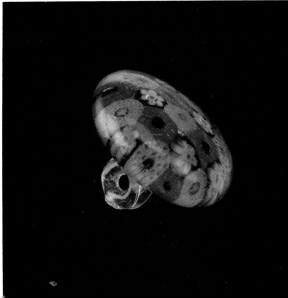

A huge and very heavy glass paper-weight button with a glass shank, from China. These millefiori paperweights were imported to be sold at the Fair in 1939, but the vast majority were desk weights, not buttons. Shown actual size.

Assorted clothing buttons commemorating the 1939 New York World's Fair. These buttons have all become quite scarce and are as sought by World's Fair collectors as they are by button lovers. An original sales card is upper left. The various buildings depicted on the sets, shown in all of the available colors, are the Aquacade, the Communications Building, the Trylon & Perisphere, the Chrysler Building, the Administration Building, and the Aviation Building.

The black Bakelite buttons inlaid with mother-of-pearl, still on their original sales cards, are very rare. The other buttons include, upper row, from right: molded plastic (this came in orange, blue, and yellow, and was the official button for the employees at the Fair), a lithographed print under celluloid mounted in metal as a vest button, and two molded plastic rectangles.

A set of 6 realistic heads of stereotypical couples of the type glorified in any number of Hollywood "B" movies of the 1930s: bon vivant, man about town and his stylish and snooty lady friend; the street 'tough' (complete with cigarette hanging from his lips), his red-headed moll, the hispanic macho-male and his fiery cutie.

Chapter 11. Realistics and Goofies

When a button is made in the actual shape of what it depicts, it is known as a realistic. Although realistics have been a relatively small part of total button manufacture, they account for a very large percentage, overall, of collectible buttons. Some experienced button collectors concentrate entirely on realistics, but it's also a wonderful category for a novice: no special study or knowledge is necessary to enjoy them and they are endlessly diverse in design. Boldface type has been used to identify buttons illustrated in this chapter.

ANTIQUE REALISTICS

Realistics were not particularly popular during the eighteenth and nineteenth centuries. Button makers and manufacturers offered them intermittently, in an assortment of materials, but antique realistics were simply curios. The subject matter of nineteenth century realistics was limited, and the designs were quite subtle. Moreover, since mixing different realistically-shaped buttons on one garment was not popular in Victorian fashion, they had no influence on the dress of the period.

Silver buttons have been made throughout several centuries, but were very seldom realistically shaped before the mid-twentieth century. One notable exception is a very old type of two-piece silver button from China known as a toggle, Usuallly

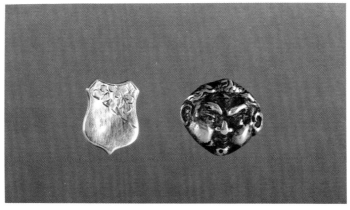

realistic in appearance, toggles depicted foo dogs, bats, the Buddha, frogs on lily pads, cicadas, butterflies, and so on; a very few were enamelled. The larger, realistically-shaped piece had from one to three loop shanks soldered to the back. The toggle itself was usually ball-shaped, but there are rare examples with realistic shapes: the **lotus-pod shaped toggle** attached to the **charming little blue bat** represented fertility.[1]

Also from China came **realistic jade buttons,** dating back several centuries. Almost always **of white jade,** they are far from common. Whether ornately sculpted or carved in a more simple fashion, nearly all were **flowers, cicadas,** or **bats**.

Mother-of-pearl realistics from the Victorian age were not common, but were always of fine quality; this lovely **dog's head carved from iridescent pearl** has faceted, cut-steel eyes and a tiny steel ball riveted firmly in his mouth.

Black glass buttons, particularly favored by the Victorians, were not often manufactured in realistic shapes. The most popular of these must have been **a shoe,** the one we most often find; more unusual was a **horseshoe.** The insect, a very rare example of a **realistic passementerie button,** was made from eleven faceted-glass pieces, each riveted on a metal base.

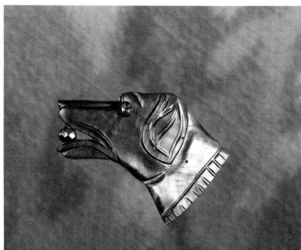

MODERN REALISTICS

In terms of their influence on fashion, realistic buttons are truly a twentieth century phenomenon. Twice during this century, realistic buttons have exerted a strong influence on dress and on culture, altering the public's perception of fashion along with their sense of propriety: from the mid-1930s to the mid-1950s, and from 1985 into the 1990s.

This unprecedented mania for novel-looking buttons had its catalyst in Elsa Schiaparelli. The Italian-born designer, the most creative couturier in Paris, delighted in the unexpected or even the shocking. Among the accessories she was known for were buttons: it has been said that she used buttons of every type except plain round ones! Schiaparelli's reputation and influence was such that famed artists—Jean Cocteau, Jean Schlumberger, Salvador Dali and others—designed buttons especially for her fashions.

The originality of Schiaparelli's buttons kicked off the tremendous rage for 'realistics' that was to last until the early 1950s. Button manufacture in general was stimulated by this fad, and buttons of all sorts took on added importance on clothing.

Sciaparelli's buttons were made of any number of materials in an enormous variety of themes to match her thematic clothing collections. "Schiaparelli rendered the mundane delightful with buttons in the form of shoelaces...spinning tops, spoons, padlocks, lollipops, Christmas-tree bells, coffee beans, fish hooks, the bobbins and weights of a fisherman's net, safety pins, paperclips" and so on. "She was never more waggish...than when she launched the dollar-sign button in 1933" right at the time of the U.S. economic collapse.[2] She had buttons made to look like butterflies and bees, drums and bagpipes, candies and cakes, ostriches, mermaids, eggplants, and acrobats.

Schiaparelli buttons themselves are, of course, few and far between and quite valuable. They were not mass-marketed or available on ready-to-wear clothing, so it is not *her* buttons that represent the collector's realistic-button choices, but those she inspired, from hundreds of manufacturers, cottage industries, and artisans worldwide.

These realistics included hundreds of subjects: "Bunches of fruits, little baskets of flowers, bowls of cherries, pieces of furniture, faces, plates of food, breads, musical instruments—almost anything that could be depicted was turned into a buttons for novelty's sake in the 1930s."[3]

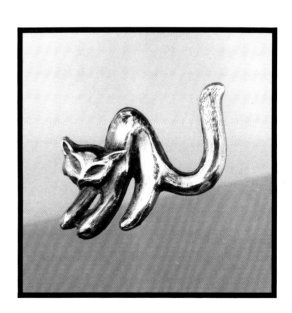

This cat button with its great Art Deco face and stance is a signed designer's button, French, in silver-plated copper. It has two shanks on the reverse.

Goofies

Some realistics were mass-produced in enormous numbers during the 1930s to 1950s period as variously-shaped sets of small buttons. These small buttons, sold in sets with a common, often lighthearted, theme, are known as 'goofies'.

The name goofie, often quite descriptive, has been widely used for many years, and though now in disfavor—some collectors consider it demeaning—the term lingers on. I think it is a fun and friendly name for a humorous and distinctive group of buttons and helps differentiate them from other modern types of realistically-shaped buttons.

Made between 1935 and 1955, of hard plastics, celluloid, Bakelite, metal, or glass, and normally less than 3/4" in length, goofies were mass-produced in vast numbers.

Collecting these buttons can be addictive. Some people specialize in favorite categories such as **birds, dogs**, **vegetable gardening,** fruit, flowers, **the circus, folk dancing,** and patriotism. It's really quite hard to think of a subject that wasn't used as a theme for goofie sets.

There are advantages to buying sets on the original sales cards: the number of buttons in sets varied, so having the card is the best way to determine what a set consisted of. Obviously, many more loose buttons survived than did carded sets, and they are not easy to find. Collectors usually buy goofies one by one and assemble the sets themselves; it can be quite a challenge!

Some particularly popular sets are sought by non-collectors as well: the **baseball set** of the 1930s is beloved by sports nuts, for example. Some of the most coveted goofie sets, made during the late thirties, featured assorted **brand-name pantry products,** including cans of food, boxes of cereal, and cleaning powders; these small white plastic buttons were wrapped in colorful paper labels, duplicates of the originals. Similar sets featured the leading cigarette brands, whiskeys, etcetera.

The last word in patriotic wear during the early forties was a set of six **All-American symbols:** the Statue of Liberty, the flag, the Capitol, Uncle Sam, an American Eagle, and the Liberty Bell.

Many of the more interesting and collectible goofie sets relate to certain specialty fields, such as sets of Walt Disney characters, World's Fair sets, and sets featuring movie stars. The collectors in these fields value the tiny treasures even more than do button collectors and avidly buy any they can find.

Other now hard-to-find sets were either poor sellers when first offered or were very deluxe and made in limited numbers.

Most of the plastic and celluloid goofies were made in the United States; the glass ones were almost all from Eastern Europe. Plastic, glass, and metal goofies were molded in one piece with self-shanks. Celluloid shanks were usually added separately, though a few were manufactured with inserted metal shanks. A number of early celluloid goofies had extra pieces that were added by hand to pre-molded bodies. The only other hand-work found on goofies is painted trim, or rarely, rhinestone trim.

The glass goofies were usually more conservative in design and theme than were the plastics. Celluloids were often the oddest of all, and some were even...well, goofy!

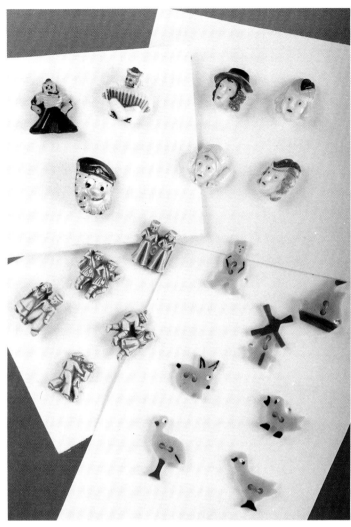

Not all of the modern realistics were goofies, or even mass-produced. Many were man-made or were machine-tooled on a smaller scale. In addition, a considerable number of realistically-shaped buttons were supplied by importers who employed native craftsmen and villagers in cottage industries worldwide. Realistics from these sources, though sometimes far from practical, were usually intended for use as buttons, though not always. A few, made from materials such as **coconut-shell** and sold in various exotic locales,were intended just as quaint souvenirs for tourists.

Commercial manufacture of realistics ended in the early 1950s and they faded totally from view; buttons in general were no longer in vogue and grew increasingly non-descript. A few button collectors—not the majority, who were in those days interested only in antique buttons—were the only real market for realistics throughout the next quarter-century .

It was not until the mid 1980s, when a newly-enthusiastic public and a newly-energized button industry came together with a resounding bang, that realistics again became an important part of button design. They are once again being manufactured in a vast array of themes.

Modern realistics (any button made since 1918 is considered modern by collectors) have been made of pearl, celluloid, wood, pewter, brass, silver, copper, Bakelite, ceramics, plaster, glass, plastics, bone, horn, leather, ivory, etc.

If I had to guess what was the most common realistic button of all, I would pick the ubiquitous leather knot, used on countless men's sports and overcoats over the years That (k)not withstanding, (sorry!) leather realistics are actually rather uncommon, but include **flat, embossed-leather footballs** with heavy brass shanks, sized for both men's and boy's fall coats.

Expensive realistic leather designer-buttons were made in France in the thirties. Marked Paris on the back, these were hand-tooled, beautifully-painted renditions of popular motifs, such as the fabulous **leather dog's head** seen here.

Sterling realistics were almost all made since 1920. New buttons are presently being made especially for today's collectors.

Numbers of realistic sterling buttons were made in Mexico, from the 1920s through the 1950s. Usually fashioned by silversmiths from Taxco, they featured **animals, people,** and **objects** in two basic types: one-piece silhouettes, or three-dimensional hollow realistics. Collectors of Taxco silver compete with button collectors for these little goodies. None of these buttons were actually imported in appreciable numbers, but were bought here by tourists or jewelry collectors.

Guatemalan silversmiths produced realistic, **mask-shaped** buttons during the 1930s and 40s, as did similar artisans in **Peru;** very heavy, **solid cast-silver heads** came from Ecuador and Guatemala a few years later. The country of origin is usually engraved on the back, but the word 'sterling', or numerical equivalents such as 900 or 975, always appears. Like the Mexican silver buttons, these were exported in limited quantities.

Native-American silver buttons were seldom made in realistic shapes, although **symbolic thunderbird** designs were fashioned.

Modern buttons made with ancient metal-working techniques, such as **niello** from Siam and **damascene** from Japan, came in many shapes, realistic **fans** and **butterflies** among them.

Damascene, an inlay in steel, originated with swordsmiths in the Damascus, the world's oldest city. A burr was used to deeply engrave a design in a steel base; silver and gold wires were pounded into these lines until the surface was level. The piece was then roughened with acid so that the final layer of black lacquer would adhere to the steel. The final step, a brisk buffing, revealed the gold and silver wire designs gleaming through the black. Japanese Damascene buttons were set in gilt mountings; a very few were set in sterling.

Niello work—a decorative treatment, not an inlay—was an early Russian craft in the 1400s, but has since been used throughout the Arabian and Southeast Asian areas. Always done on silver, the design was cut so that the area to remain silver-colored was in relief. Then the entire piece was blackened with a chemical finish of copper-sulphate, acid and lead. When the silver was polished, the black remained in the sunken areas.

These particular niello buttons, marked "Sterling-Made in Siam", date between 1945 and 1949. (In 1949, Siam changed its name to Thailand.) Although these are attractive buttons, the coating and engraving were lighter than was usual in quality niello work.

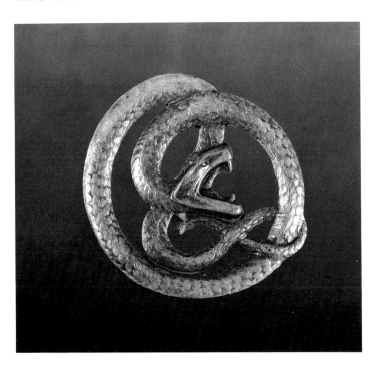

Other than the relatively few goofy sets that were manufactured in cast white metal, modern realistics of assorted white metals, brass, and aluminum were invariably light weight and were of cheaper construction than were those of the 1800s. Twentieth century manufacturers were more concerned with conserving material and keeping down costs: the curved, slightly convex, and coiled body of the **aluminum snake** is hollow on the underside, as is the **brass bowtie,** of nearly the exact same construction, though they seem quite different from the front.

Early-twentieth-century realistics of shell were often from the Mississippi River-based button companies in the United States. Small and uncomplicated designs such as **simple animals** were most frequently intended for children's wear.

Later and often larger mother-of-pearl realistics came from many lands. The workmanship varied. A number of beautiful realistics, about 1 1/4" long, made in Japan of very thin shell have a quality of workmanship not often seen on modern pearls; these intricately cut-out silhouettes of **tropical fish and birds** were also finely engraved on the surfaces and each has a tiny red-painted eye. (Unfortunately, they also have glued-on metal shanks which can easily come off.)

Many of the very large **Bethlehem pearls**—a souvenir and export item of long standing in the Holy Land—were made as both buttons and brooches. Traditionally round, some were realistically shaped. Most of these buttons were imported by American dealers from the 1940s through the 1960s, but they have again been available in recent years.

The earlier examples were usually well-designed and carved; the quality seemed to deteriorate over the years, as seen in the realistic **lady's head, crown,** and **crowns.**

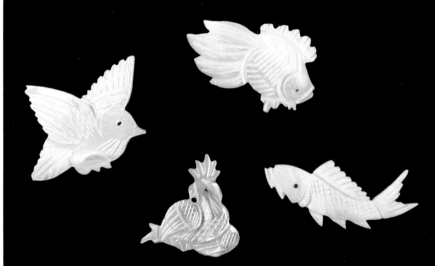

Both bone and ivory were used for realistic buttons since the early 1800s, but the majority were made after 1920. **Large, carved ivory flowers**—often orchids or hibiscus—were brought from Hawaii during the 1940s and 50s.

Other ivory realistics were made by Eskimo carvers. The earliest examples date back hundreds of years, and were toggles for fastening, or amulets in the likeness of seals, whales, or other figures; they were "sewn on clothing to ensure success in an undertaking".[4]

Such early examples are museum-pieces; nearly all of the Eskimo ivory realistics found now are modern. Already very scarce, the choicest ones were actually small sculptures. Carved throughout the first half of this century under the encouragement and guidance of dealers in North American native art, they featured such subjects as **polar bears, birds, fish,** and even the compelling **white baby seals.**

Africa was another source of both carved bone and ivory realistics. Interpretive of African folk-art, they have a great deal of primitive charm. Many were **fat, flat frogs**— say that quickly!—with sewing holes pierced through the center.

Similar **frogs, fish, turtles,** and **African huts** were carved from transluscent dark horn and imported as recently as the 1990s.

Any collector would be delighted to find a Japanese ivory realistic decorated in the desirable Shibayama style of inlay. This carved and nicely detailed **ivory comb and hairbrush set,** sold in Tokyo in the1930s, was deluxe even then.

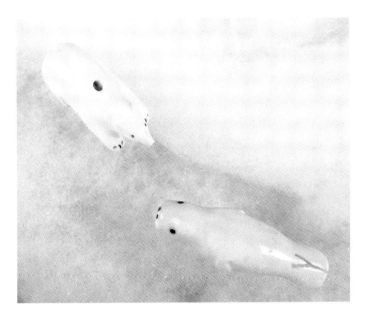

Wooden realistics were usually imaginative, but often erratic in quality: whether huge or small, some were finely carved, others were crude. Most commonly hand-made, they have been produced in astounding variety worldwide.

Some of the more singular examples, such as **foreign folk-art carvings**, have become rare. Particularly interesting and desirable is a set of six sculpted, painted, and gilded, royal **Moor's heads** from Spain. Other folk-carved **masks and heads** came from Ecuador, Mexico, and Italy. **Tribal heads** and **animal heads** from Africa, very crudely carved from a wood known as African teak, softer than regular teakwood and very black in color, were imported for clothing boutiques in the 1960s, but others had been purchased by collectors at least ten years earlier. Rosewood from the island of Madagascar was used by Kenyan woodcarvers to fashion buttons in less primitive style, including some shaped like **elephant heads mounted as trophies**, with tiny ivory tusks.

Collectors often find small, painted **wooden doll-like buttons,** but few realize what they are—tiny Kokeshi. Very popular in Japan as household ornaments, Kokeshi there are avidly collected. Always of wood in a stylized, cylindrical body form, Kokeshi have a distinct head, but no limbs (the arms, hands, and legs are not carved, but inferred) and the hair and features are painted without detail to "preserve and further exaggerate the basic simplicity of the piece".[5] Non-button Kokeshi range in size from 1" to 24".

If you are lucky enough to find a Kokeshi button, look at it very carefully—a very few lucky collectors have discovered that the head of their little button-doll unscrewed, and within the hollow body were tiny ivory dice.

The first mass-produced modern realistics were made of celluloid, early in the 1930s. At its production peak during that era, button designers took full advantage of its versatility: the best realistics ever attempted, as well as the worst ones ever achieved, were made of celluloid. An example of celluloid at its best is the button shaped like **fruit with a branch;** it features fine hand-worked details.

The large **celluloid pelican** exemplifies the elaborate modeling techniques manufacturers sometimes used. More than 170 individual, petal-like feathers appear to be layered and attached to the body, but it's actually a molded piece.

My favorite celluloid buttons were created in 1939: irresistibly odd, these realistics feature **breakfast and dinner** selections on plate-shaped buttons. The breakfast plate holds several strips of bacon, and two eggs, sunny-side-up. The main course on the dinner plate varied: chicken, steak, pork-chops, or fish were combined with different vegetables and potatoes. The foods were separately formed and colored, then arranged and attached by hand on the plates. Though these buttons were produced by the B. Blumenthal Company as commercial products, they were part of the deluxe line made under their most creative designer, Marion Weeber; they hardly deserve the label 'mass-produced'.

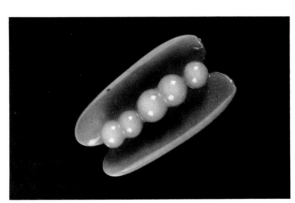

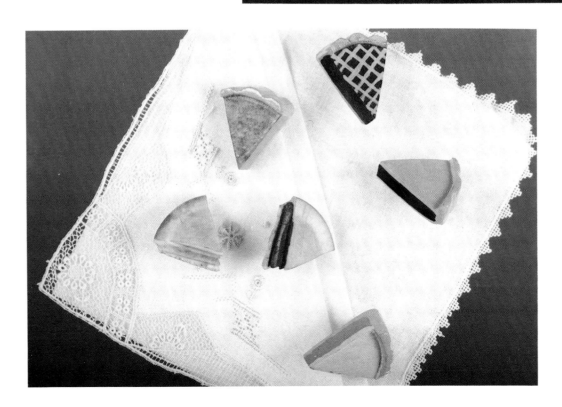

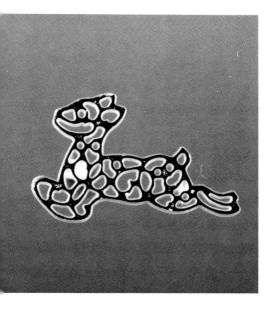

Bakelite was a very popular material for buttons and jewelry from the late 1920s through the 40s. The realistics were mainly a product of the 30s: most depicted animals or starkly designed industrial objects.

Bakelite was sometimes actually sculpted as were the very desirable **animal heads with embedded glass eyes**, wonderful examples of the Art Deco look.

The vast majority of glass buttons in realistic shapes were goofies, but a few molded glass realistics of the same era were bigger, and not from sets. The **bamboo-knot of pearlized glass,** hand-trimmed with just the right amount of color, is quite lovely and undoubtedly European.

A unique type of glass realistic came from Czechoslovakia: **small two-piece buttons, often animals or birds** with a coating of mirror-silver between the halves. When found in good condition, they are quite sparkly. Some are clear, others are bright blue, or red.

Glass blowers and artisans have made a few realistics, including Jacques Israel in the1940s, and Jackie Gooderham of St. Ste. Marie, Canada, and Julie Clinton of Washington in the 1990s. Other very fragile **blown-glass lamp-worked** buttons, and—I know from experience—are only for less rambunctious collectors.

Goofies were not the only type of plastic realistics. The button industry had a great deal of fun with the then-new material. Piercing it was a popular effect for a while; the **large leaping deer** is a rare and wonderful example.

One popular look for plastic was to imitate tortoise shell. In the 1930s, button-makers used it in big, solid, women's coat buttons, sometimes in realistic shapes: the smooth lines of the **huge sailing swan** show some late, residual influence from the Art Nouveau style; **the eagle,** from the patriotic, war-time 1940s, was found on a woolen jacket.

Life-sized and deliciously calorie-free, these **realistic candy** buttons from the 1940s were made of plastic, but be forewarned—these are already quite rare. If you get cravings for chocolate, it will take quite a search to find even one of these cuties. They were designed as peanut clusters, chocolate-covered cherries, fondants in pink, green, or white coatings, chocolate and vanilla buttercreams, and triple-layered nougats. Imagine the fun of walking around with these buttons on your best suit!

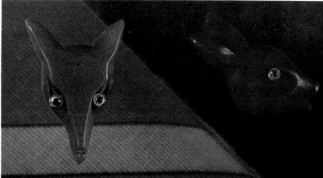

Courtesy of Laurel Brown

A number of other clay realistics came from craftsmen both here and abroad. An interesting group of glazed, self-shanked ceramic buttons came from Denmark in the late 1930s. A **cream-colored horse** with an almost Surreal look to it, various **flying birds,** and **plump fish** in earthy, mottled colors were among them.

The mid-century ceramic buttons usually had metal shanks put into the backs; some had clay self-shanks. The **sombrero,** large and plaster-like with a metal shank, still has quite a modern look. The little **doll in her colorful folk costume** was carefully hand-colored, then fired and glazed; it has a self-shank.

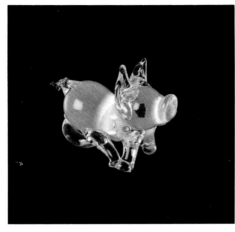

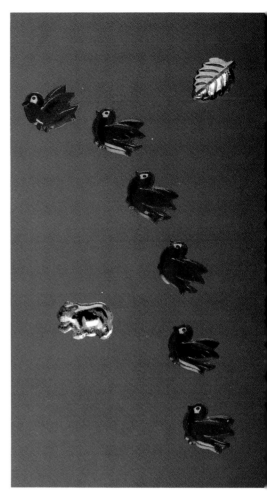

Numerous buttons made of **glazed ceramics** being designed today by artists. The buttons are usually intended for collectors, but are sometimes sold through shops or catalogues.

These new **ceramic realistics** are **sew-through buttons,** often quite large to be truly utilitarian, but very attractive and colorful: non-collectors like to sew them on hats, bags, or clothes, just as decorations. Collectors usually buy them by subject matter, for use in competition. And no doubt someone, somewhere, actually uses them as buttons!

Some of the finest porcelain buttons of any era were from the Japanese town of Arita. Made from a special, silky smooth clay, they were usually square, rectangular or in realistic shapes , but very seldom round. Molded in relief, with sometimes astonishing detail, then colored and glazed, many were then further finished with touches of gilding. The decorating on these buttons was done with perfect accuracy and delicate detail.

The realistics range in size from 3/4" to over 2 1/4", and include a **seahorse, fish, penguin, swan, squirrel, elephant, multi-colored fall leaf, daisy, foo dog, ship, Buddha,** and the most often seen, **various immortals or gods.** The largest Arita, a **dragon**, as well as the oversized **girl, cat, peacock,** and **butterfly,** each had two metal shanks on the back to help stabilize them on clothing; the rest had molded self-shanks. Both potters marks and the word 'Japan' are impressed into the backs. Arita buttons were made as early as the 1930s though most were imported in the 1960s.[6] Aritas have recently become very sought after and prices have risen tremendously.

The Maiden Vermont Button Company, a division of Danforth Pewterers, was founded in the mid-1980s, at the beginning of the button mania. They have been very successful at marketing pewter realistics—not until 1991 did they make their first round buttons. Sold to the general public in stores and through catalogues, Danforth's wonderfully creative and beautifully modelled buttons are often in sets. **Baskets, cats, barns, cabins, angels, plants, tractors, Christmas themes,** and **toys** are among the many shapes and subjects; all of them have been original designs, created by the co-founder of the company, Judi Danforth, a talented sculptress.

Maiden Vermont (Danforth) buttons are all marked on the back (although it is etched, and hard to see on some of them) and often dated. The marks are not standardized: initials or the full name Danforth or Maiden Vermont have been used. Although novel, these buttons are sturdy and practical fasteners as well.

J.H.B. International, one of the most innovative button companies of all time, markets huge numbers of buttons worldwide and is known for its novelty and realistic buttons—some are in sets but most are not.

It is not generally known that J.H.B. brought out the first mass-produced realistic since the days of the 1930s to 1950s button craze, and that this button pre-dated the new mania by ten years. It was only one button, a red glass lady-bug manufactured for J.H.B. in Germany, and the wave of interest was still a long way off, but it was a start. Most of J.H.B.'s realistics have, however, been small enamelled-metal buttons: a very **large variety** has been made. J.H.B. has the license to produce buttons based on the Peanuts cartoon strip. **Snoopy** has had many incarnations on these buttons! **Santa Claus, Snoopy, The Flying Ace, the Football Snoopy**, and **Joe Cool** are among them.

Button collectors buy many of the new, mass-produced commercial realistics. Very often, the buttons manufactured during the 1930s and 1940s were ignored by 'serious' collectors who wanted only antique examples. Today's collectors aren't going to make that mistake!

Card #74

ROVER
A JHB ORIGINAL

92951

KOALA BEAR
A JHB ORIGINAL

92825

TOBY
A JHB ORIGINAL
92956

MARTY
A JHB ORIGINAL
92952

LAMB
A JHB ORIGINAL
92973

CHICKEN LITTLE
A JHB ORIGINAL

92747

KITTY-HAWK
A JHB ORIGINAL

92953

PALACE GUARD
A JHB ORIGINAL

92971

SNOWMAN
A JHB ORIGINAL

92976

ST. NICK
A JHB ORIGINAL
92977

INNOCENCE
A JHB ORIGINAL

92972

SPRING CHICKEN
A JHB ORIGINAL

92954

FRUITS 'N VEGETABLES

CHILI PEPPER
A JHB ORIGINAL

92970

TOMATO
A JHB ORIGINAL

92701

EAR OF CORN
A JHB ORIGINAL

92705

MCINTOSH APPLE
A JHB ORIGINAL
93004

ORANGE BLOSSOM
A JHB ORIGINAL

93022

VINEYARD
A JHB ORIGINAL

92975

BANANAS
A JHB ORIGINAL

92704

LEMON
A JHB ORIGINAL

92702

PEAR
A JHB ORIGINAL

92955

STRAWBERRY PATCH
A JHB ORIGINAL
92703

WATERMELON
A JHB ORIGINAL

92582

PINEAPPLE
A JHB ORIGINAL

92583

CHERRY JUBILEE

92562

APLETS

92563

STRAWBERRY JAM

92560

Chapter 12. World War Two Home Front Buttons: 1940-1944

A Nazi uniform button. These have been reproduced, but the originals have a textured background not seen in the new versions.

A patriotic sales card with plastic 'goofies', buttons intended for children's wear. 'Homefront' jewelry was militaristic in design, but not military (i.e.official) —it was manufactured for the sweethearts and children back home. Each button is 3/4", ca. 1944.

During World War II, the governments of England and the United States instituted rules for the austere use and conservation of raw materials and resources. The news media aided in the effort to reduce consumer demand and increase co-operation with rules about rationed goods through editorials, cartoons, and posters. Food, gasoline, metals, and fabrics were among the most restricted items.

No-frills women's fashions, without lace, velvet, embroideries, fur trim, padded shoulders, flared skirts or turned-back cuffs, were called 'utility clothing' in England. For both men's and women's wear, there were restrictions in the numbers of pleats, pockets, and buttons manufacturers could use on one outfit.

"You can't ration fashion" was the industry's way of suggesting that although one had to conform to rigid rules about conserving materials, there still was room for style. Hats, not restricted, were very much in demand. Because there "were severe restrictions on tin, copper, rhodium, and silver, the jewelry trade was both taxed and vexed by the challenge of producing alluring ornamental jewelry..."[1] Clothing was adorned with patriotic, pro-military brooches and buttons—often of plastic—with the colors of the flags, wings, anchors, planes, and so on.

Kilroy was a particulary W.W.II fad: "The GI came and went, in Europe and the Pacific...and left behind some of his own ideas and a great many dead comrades. He also left behind a curious marking that was chalked on rocks, on city walls, on lavatories: 'Kilroy was here.' No one ever found out for sure who Kilroy was, where he came from, or why (soldiers) would care enough about him to scrawl his name across half the globe."[2]

Assorted W.W. II homefront buttons: the flag buttons are made of a cheap white metal; one is plated in brass, the other is hand-painted. The U.S. designs are plastic 'goofies'. The plane and hand (with thumbs-up symbol) are part of a scarce set of molded glass 'goofies'.

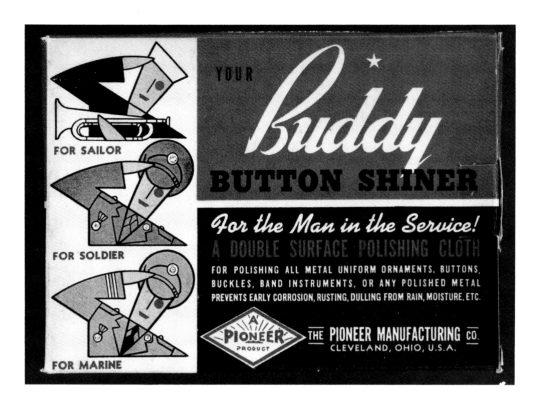

A cheery war-time kit to send to one's loved ones overseas, this box contained no more than a simple polishing cloth! The back of the box is an address label, ca.1945.

Victory buttons made of plastic, celluloid, pressed brass, aluminum, and one brass with pavé-set rhinestones, American, ca. 1945,.

Beethoven's 5th symphony, first performed in Vienna in 1808, has perhaps the most famous opening notes of any piece of music ever written: the rhythm of these four notes—dot dot dot dash—represents the letter 'V' in Morse code. Synonymous with 'Victory' throughout the years of World War II, the 'V' was a common motif on jewelry and buttons, sometimes in combination with the dots and dashes. *Courtesy of the 'V for VandeBerg' collection*

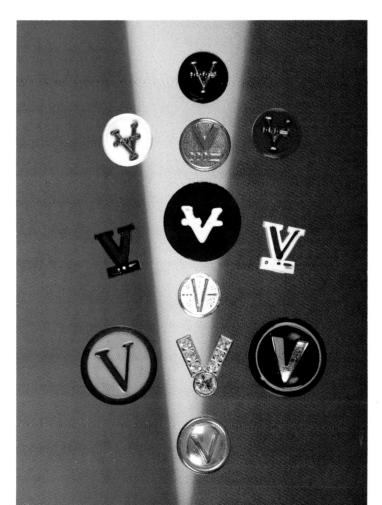

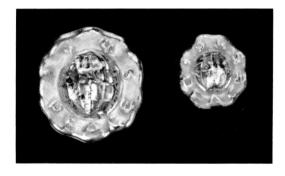

Hand-painted, molded ceramic/plaster buttons, the globe in the center and 'PEACE 1945' around the borders, 3/4" to 1 1/4".

A number of 'Kilroy Was Here' souvenirs appeared at war's end, this Japanese-made vegetable ivory button among them. (The Japanese were the only button producers who continued to use tagua nuts for commercial button production decades after the industry died out elsewhere.)

Chapter 13. Post War: 1945-1965

The Christian Dior 'New Look' silhouette on a molded plastic button, ca. 1948.

After the war, couturiérs in Paris, no longer limited to austerity fashions, brought back femininity with a vengeance. Designer Christian Dior opened his own salon in 1947, introducing his 'New Look' fashions: fitted top, full swirling skirt, and wasp-waist. The collection caused a sensation, and remained in vogue for over ten years.

Paris itself became a style—Paris-Style—a stereotype of everything chic. Returning servicemen brought home stories and images of a different world. They had traveled and seen much of Europe and the Far East; foreign cultures, especially that of France, began to find their way into middle America. *How are You Going to Keep Them Down on the Farm Now That They've Seen Paree?* was more than a catchy song, it was truthful.

Berets, can-can girls, the Eiffel Tower, champagne, café tables with umbrellas and wine bottles, and painters' palettes became the most popular images on wallpaper, kitchen canister sets, stationary, and so on.

Movies and songs extolled the life of 'Gay-Paree': *An American in Paris*, the most sucessful Hollywood musical of all time, and the song *I Love Paris in the Springtime*, were typical of the romantic, idealized view Americans had of France in the early 1950s.

The poodle dog was particulary omnipresent: poodles of every imaginable look, size, and material were churned out by giftware manufacturers. The poodle also became a mainstay of jewelry design, and for over a decade was the most popular pet in America.

The mania for all things French following the war included buttons. The plastic button has French postage stamps enclosed—one with the image of Marianne, the symbol of France. Also, a Japanese Satsuma pottery poodle and a cast metal poodle.

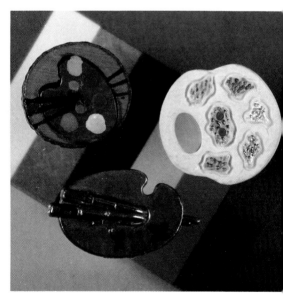

An artist's palette, also French-inspired, was one of the distinctive design motifs of the 1950s. These buttons are painted wood, painted brass, and embossed porcelain.

A set of commercially sold Schiaparelli buttons from the post WW II years. These are metal buttons with photos of scenes of Paris set under glass. *Courtesy of Lucille Weingarten.*

A lovely post-war designer button of silver plate, with a hand-hammered flower set with rhinestones.

Snakeskin or alligator purses and shoes were the height of sophistication; similar buttons were manufactured for the sake of co-ordination. Pictured are a French designer's set of snakeskin with brass letters, ca. 1955.

Pegasus, the winged horse, was another design mania, on jewelry, fabrics and wallpaper, ads, bookcovers, mirrors, and buttons. Although this mythological creature had been appearing off and on in cultures around the world for two thousand years, there is a theory that its prevalence during the post-war forties and fifties was a "need to de-fang...the threatening symbols of war" and "symbolized the new freedom of the air from menace."[1] (This seems odd, but the pegasus had also been a very popular motif in the 1920s, following the first use of airplanes in war.)

A highly specialized collection of Pegasus buttons of assorted materials. The large Art Deco, gold painted, wooden button is from a French courtier's collection. Other materials here include glass, black glass, ivory, enamel, brass, silver, copper, leather, pearl, Satsuma pottery, and Arita porcelain.

Opposite page:
Lucite, an acrylic plastic made by the DuPont Chemical Company, was a 'wonder' material used during W.W. II for airplane windshields. In the early 1950s, it became wildly popular for fashion accessories including purses, outrageous sunglasses, shoes, jewelry, and buttons. A hard, clear material that could be etched, cut, and embedded with other materials, Lucite did not yellow with age, as the transparent thermo-set plastics like Bakelite had.

Following the war, GIs stationed in Germany began to send and bring home Hummel figurines. The darling designs thrilled their mothers and sweethearts back home in America, and kicked off a huge collecting boom. This plastic button is one of many items other than figurines decorated in the same style.

Japan was occupied by Allied forces from 1945 to 1957. There was a concerted American effort to re-open the many Japanese manufacturing industries closed by the war. All Japanese goods made for export to the U.S. during these years were marked (made in) 'Occupied Japan'.

Button collecting was in full swing in America, and thousands of the lovely Japanese porcelain, pottery, and ivory buttons made before the war were imported for American collectors. Great numbers of Satsuma pottery buttons in particular were imported in the 1950s. All Satsuma buttons were made for export; therefore, they never pre-date the 1860s when Japan's trading ports were re-opened to the west after 150 years of isolation. There is often a significant difference in the quality of late-nineteenth-century Satsuma-ware and the pieces made in the 1950s.

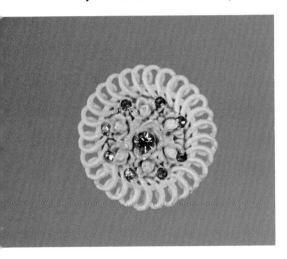

An extruded celluloid button set with rhinestones. The backmark, 'Occupied Japan,' makes it a rare cultural item, ca. 1945 to 1957.

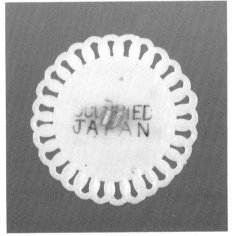

The stamped 'Occupied Japan' mark on the reverse of the button above. This is one of only a few marked 'O.J.' buttons.

These buttons are not marked 'Occupied Japan', but the sales card is. Finding one of these cards is difficult, ca. 1945 to 1957. *Courtesy Lynette Parmer.*

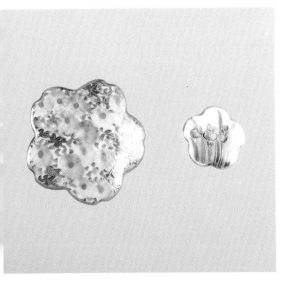

Kutani porcelain buttons from Japan, few and far between compared with Satsuma, though not nearly as valued by collectors. These can be differentiated from Satsumas by their blemish-free glaze; Satsuma pottery pieces all have a crackled glaze.

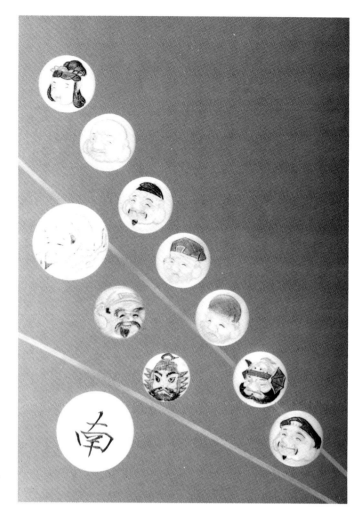

Japanese ivory buttons made before
World War II and exported to America in
the 1950s. The engraved faces are
those of the seven gods of good fortune.

Satsuma buttons with cobalt blue
backgrounds. Buttons with this coloring
were not at all common. The upper right
button is from the nineteenth century;
the rest ca. 1920 to 1950. 1"–2".

Antique Satsuma buttons of various
subjects. All of the buttons on the far
right, as well as the top center button,
are mounted in silver. Antique Satsumas
have far better detailing, as a rule, and
often have been decorated with gold
paint so thick that they are actually
encrusted; older examples also tend to
have an overall stippling of tiny gold
dots covering the 'blank' background
areas. 3/4"–2".

Satsuma buttons of any age are
highly uncommon. The buttons on the
next few pages represent an amazingly
large and diverse collection; many are
scarce and quite valuable. Others are
not of high quality workmanship, but do
represent the work prevalent during the
1950s export period.

Satsuma buttons showing women;
several are of very high quality, although
all of them are 'modern' (i.e. twentieth
century), ca. 1920 to 1950s.

Assorted immortals, gods, and Buddha
on Satsuma buttons. At lower right is an
antique button. The two designs above it
represent god masks from 'Noh'
dramas, as can be seen by the ribbons
and the shapes.

Scenic Satsuma buttons. The largest
button and the one to its left are pre-
twentieth century examples.

A combination of antique and modern Satsuma floral buttons.

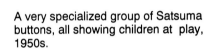

A very specialized group of Satsuma buttons, all showing children at play, 1950s.

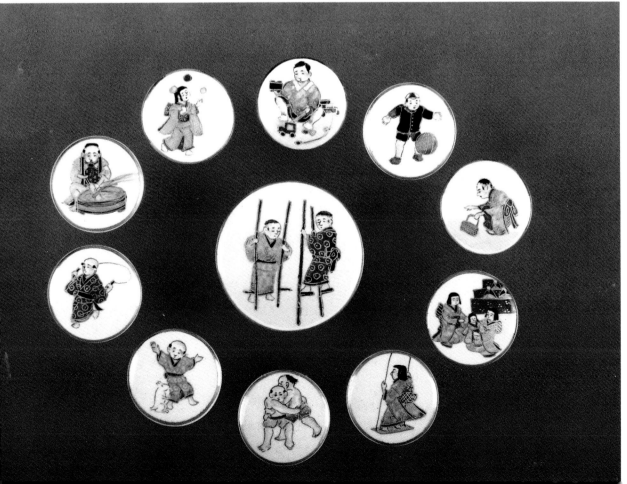

Opposite page
Birds on Satsuma buttons. Although only the gorgeous peacock at center is an antique button, many of the others here are especially fine in design and quality as well.

Assorted people on Satsuma buttons, 1920 to 1950. Collectors tend to value Satsuma buttons showing people more than any others, regardless of age.

A very broad assortment of animal life on Satsuma buttons, 1940s and 1950s.

The 1950s beatniks, the readers and writers of 'hip' rebellious literature and the habitués of smoky jazz clubs, are responsible for instigating mainstream America's attraction to pop-astrology. The interest of the 'beats' spread through the middle class as a trendy infatuation, eventually culminating in the notorious (if not always successful) 1970s singles bar pick-up line, "What's your sign?"

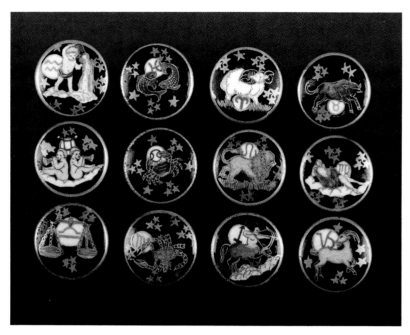

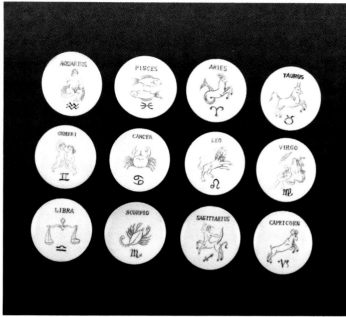

Satsuma set of Zodiac buttons, 1950s. 1 1/4" in diameter.

Ivory zodiac set from Japan, engraved and pigmented. These are deluxe buttons, signed on the back, and were probably custom-made. 1" in diameter.

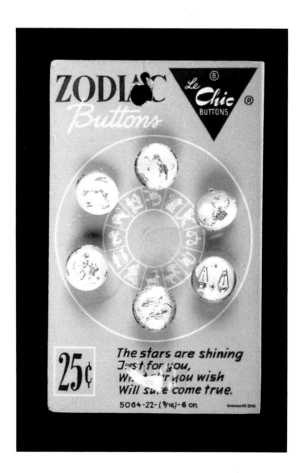

Sales card of two-piece glass buttons with zodiac designs. (Note the price!)

A pressed brass zodiac coat button and a black glass button with molded zodiac symbols, ca. 1950s.

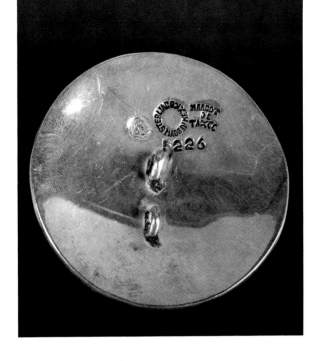

The oriental zodiac is based on the year of birth, not the month; each of the years in a twelve-year cycle is represented by an animal. These Japanese buttons, five from a set of the animals of the zodiac (the snake, rooster, ram, boar, and water buffalo) are made of pressed celluloid set in wood, 7/8", ca. 1930 to 1950s.

Backmark on a silver button, Margot de Taxco, a famed Mexican silversmith. Actual size.

During World War II, when most Western countries restricted the use of metals to war-related items, Mexican silversmiths in Taxco were able to produce fashionable sterling jewelry, much of it first-rate in design. Throughout the war, Mexican silver jewelry, including a relatively small percentage of buttons, was popular in America. This large and deluxe set of sterling zodiac buttons was made by Margot de Taxco. (The same designs were offered individually as pendants.) 2" in diameter.

Scenes of everyday life in Mexican villages—donkeys, women carrying pots, men in sombreros, cacti, adobe huts, etc—were used on linens, kitchen-wares, planters, and costume jewelry thoughout the 1940s and into the 1950s.

At the same time, Americans re-discovered their own SouthWest: Native-American Indian crafts were eagerly snapped up; silver jewelry was the most coveted, but pottery enjoyed the same vogue. Dealers and Indian traders found more than enough button collectors to buy whatever they could find in Mexican or Indian-made fasteners.

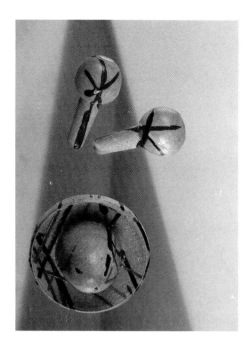

Maraccas and a sombrero, carved and painted wooden buttons. Mexico was a favorite vacation spot for middle-class America in the 1950s.

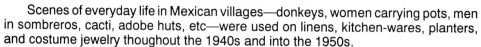
Nylon realistic button, ca. 1950

Assorted buttons with Mexican inspiration. The hand-painted scene on linoleum was made in Mexico. The rest are commercially-produced western-European glass buttons, ca. 1950s.

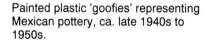
Painted plastic 'goofies' representing Mexican pottery, ca. late 1940s to 1950s.

A silly but deluxe set of plastic buttons trimmed with enameled brass, 1950s.

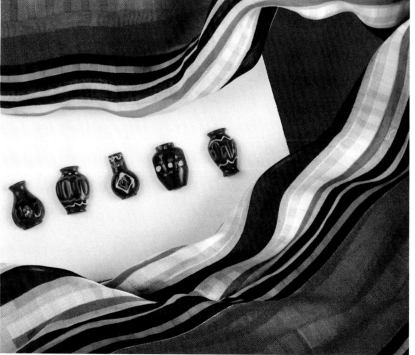

Buttons made in Mexico in the 1950s included such diverse materials as (from left, top row) onyx, copper, painted wood, filigreed silver, silver, and tortoiseshell.

The reverse of the tortoise and silver button above showing its maker's mark, William Spratling. Spratling's shop was the first and perhaps the most respected shop in Taxco, and buttons from it are quite elusive.

Mexican silver buttons, ca. 1940s to 1950s.

Silver buttons from Mexico, 1940s to 1950s.

Travelers to the American Southwest purchased Native American silver buttons, whether old or new, from traders. Buttons such as these of sand-cast silver, an unusual type, could have been made as early as the 1880s, or as late as the 1950s.

Native American silver buttons set with turquoise.

Native American cast silver buttons.

Various pueblos in the American Southwest produced pottery buttons such as these examples from the Hopi, Acoma, and Zia pueblos, ca. 1940s and 1950s.

Although Native American copper buttons were not as commonly made as silver ones were, they not as coveted today.

Buttons of beadwork on fabric and leather buttons from Native American craftsmen.

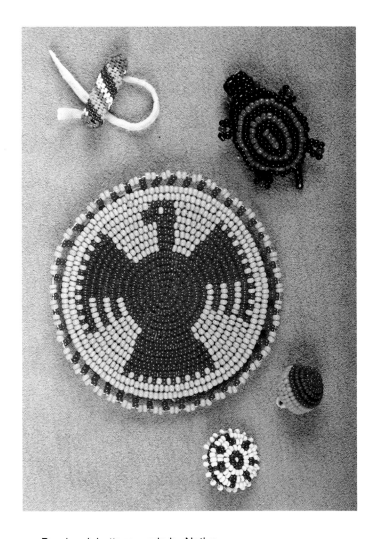

Beadwork buttons made by Native American Indians.

A Native American beaded button.

Hand-painted wooden button from a tourist store in Costa Rica, ca. 1950s.

THE 1950s

Button collectors were the only market for unique buttons during the 1950s. In the fashion world, the button had fallen from favor: between 1955 and 1980, commercial buttons grew increasingly dull, nearly disappearing on contemporary fashions in terms of impact, color, and number. But throughout these times, artisans and exporters around the world continued to sell interesting buttons to collectors.

Silver buttons from Peru, 1950s.

Purchased as tourist items in Venice in the 1950s, these mosaics set in brass with loop shanks, although handmade and very pretty, don't begin to compare with similar antique examples (see Chapter 6).

Although these pierced and engraved bone buttons may have been carved as early as the 1920s, they were brought to America for sale in the 1950s. The center button is teak, marked 'China' on the back, and was definitely made between 1910 and 1920. Although it may seem odd in view of the large numbers of carved buttons in other materials, true carved wooden buttons (as opposed to tooled, pressed, or turned ones) are actually quite rare. 1 1/8"–2".

Sterling and enamel button marked on the reverse 'Souvenir of Greece', ca. 1955 to 1965.

Queen Elizabeth's coronation inspired these buttons of glass, plastic, metal, molded horn, and fabric. Crowns, royal coaches, and various British royal and state symbols were popular jewelry motifs in America as well as in England for at least a two year period after the ceremonies, 1953 to 1954.

Commercial button manufacturers sprang up from time to time producing buttons of interest to the public, usually in connection with major historic events. These buttons of woven silk and copper-plated metal were made to celebrate the coronation of Britain's Queen Elizabeth on June 2, 1953.

Swedish buttons commemorating the coronation of Gustav VI, including , from left, sterling with enamel, enameled brass, and pewter.

Satsuma buttons commemorating the coronation of Prince Ahito (the son of the Emperor Hirohito) and Princess Michiko.

Satsuma buttons showing the Princess Michiko, and the newly-married couple, Ahito and Michiko.

Throughout the 1950s, the ever-present threat of 'The Bomb' was a sobering influence upon America's national consciousness. During President Eisenhower's terms in office, an insidious new threat developed—the Cold War. The rise of communism around the world was fast becoming a polarizing factor, and throughout the 1950s and 1960s Americans spent a good deal of their mental energy worrying about Russia and the spread of communism. The atomic bomb's disastrous potential, combined with the world's economic, miltary and ideological conflicts, eventually led nations to choose sides, to watch, wait, and worry.

A photograph print of President Dwight Eisenhower set in a red, white, and blue striped fabric button frame, 1", ca. 1956. *Courtesy of Bruce and Jane Beck*

At left, a button with a molded brass Republican elephant symbol set in polished wood. At right, a smaller version of the same button with the Democratic donkey. The center button, a transfer on ceramic, was made in Japan, all ca. 1950s.

A molded plastic composition beaurocrat's uniform button from the Soviet Union, with the Communist hammer and sickle symbol.

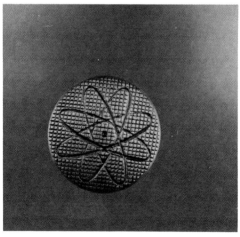

In the 1950s, the new Atomic Energy Commission set about finding peaceful uses for atomic power, and before long the atomic symbol itself was a new design motif. This two-piece brass button dates from 1955 to 1960.

Americans were enthralled with the new monument to four presidents at Mt.Rushmore. This unusual button, a glass intaglio mounted in blue nylon, celebrated its completion.

Alaska became the 49th state in 1959. The upper left sterling silver button was issued for its 25th anniversery of statehood in 1984. The rest of these buttons are scrimshaw on ivory made by Native Alaskan Eskimos during the 1950s.

Hawaii became the 50th state in 1959. All things Hawaiian were of great interest and popularity on the mainland, and buttons such as these became available. The enameled brass orchid in the center is quite lovely.

Part of the Hawaii craze, 'Gooney birds' became part of the vernacular.

A huge 'baby-boom' was under way in the conservative, Republican America of the post-war period. Millions of 1950s-era children watched television and played at being cowboys and Indians, pirates, or ballerinas.

Playing 'Pirate' was a popular pasttime for boys and girls alike. This labor-intensive button from the early 1950s is carved wood with an attached brass earring.

Buttons with a circus theme, made of plastic, hand-painted glass, and metal, ca. 1950s. In America and England, the circus was a very common theme in post-war decorative arts; clowns, big-top tents, acrobats, and performing animals appeared on many consumer items.

Pirate buttons for children's wear, of molded white metal and engraved nylon.

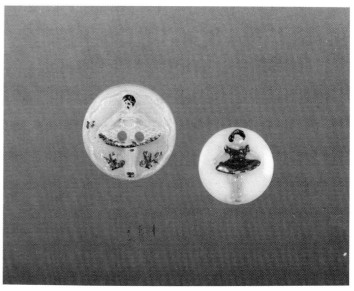

It seemed that every little girl in America in the 1950s wanted to be a ballerina, and buttons reflected it. Left, painted plastic; right, painted glass.

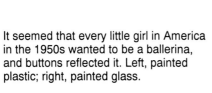

Cowboys! There may not have been an instant in the life of each 1950s boy when he did *not* want to be a cowboy. Left, two painted glass buttons, and three metal ones, including an odd sterling realistic of 'chaps'.

Without an Indian, how could there be a cowboy? The pressed brass Indian looks over a realistic metal buffalo, an electroplated plastic steer, and horse buttons of plastic, glass, metal, and plastic.

Realistic 'Western' set of metal, 1950s.

Plastic button from Hong Kong, 1960s.

Television

During the 1950s television began to have a major impact on American life. In 1947 there were 200,000 sets; by 1957 there were more than 50 million. Families gathered around the television in the evenings, as they had done through the 1930s and 40s in front of the radio. Sports fans stayed home to watch games on 'TV' in such numbers that certain teams actually changed cities in order to interest new fans. The movie industry was also affected, losing so much money that studios turned to viewing gimmicks such as '3-D' and 'Cinerama' to bring back the audiences.

The early television programs were variety and music shows, but the industry soon branched out into many types of genre programs. Situation comedies, westerns, dramas, and crime shows became the staples of evening television; Saturday mornings belonged to the kids, when youngsters were glued in front of the set watching cartoon shows.

Walt Disney was practically a genre unto itself, with animated cartoons on Saturdays, the Mickey Mouse Club, and the Walt Disney Show in the evenings. (Disney's cartoon-related buttons are explored in Chapter 10.)

"My gosh, Martha, isn't that Davy Crockett?"
Actually, it is not...the young man pictured here was the first runner-up in the *Chicago Tribune* Davy Crockett look-alike contest, 1956.The Walt Disney show found its greatest success in the 1950s five-part drama series *Davy Crockett*. The coon-skin cap, rifle, and jacket were de rigeur for virtually every boy in America. Plastic buttons (one is electro-plated) and a painted brass lapel stud, upper left, 1/2" and 2/3", ca. 1957. *Photo courtesy of Michael 'King of the Wild Frontier' VandeBerg.*

Rin-Tin-Tin, one of several dog heroes on television, was extremely popular. Here he is, captured forever on brass and white metal buttons, 1950s.

Scandal rocked the television industry when it was discovered that the producers of a game show had cheated; the hit 1956 show *The $64,000 Question* was disgraced and cancelled, but the show's title remained in the American vernacular for decades. This molded one-piece brass button commemorates these events, 1 1/4".

Rare *Cisco Kid* television show-related buttons on sales cards, from the mid-1950s. The picture is of the Kid's sidekick, 'Pancho'.

Sales card of Elroy Jetson buttons, 1960s.

The producers Hanna-Barbera began to make animated cartoons for television in the 1960s. Their first show, *The Flintstones*, was tremendously popular and was followed with the innovative *Jetsons* two years later. These small plastic clothing buttons feature characters from various Hanna-Barbera shows: Huckleberry Hound, Yogi Bear, Quick-Draw McGraw, and Elroy Jetson.

TV cartoon characters who have appeared on plastic buttons include Andy Panda©, Kwickie Koala©, and Stinger Bee©, pictured here, ca. 1980s.

The teen-agers' set, one of the most coveted realistics sets, ca. 1948.

The age of Rock & Roll began in 1955 with the hit song *Rock Around the Clock*, and by 1956, the record industry was called the "fastest growing industry" in America. The development of the 33 1/3 rpm speed record helped, for it had better sound than had 78 rpm's, but almost half of the 240 million records sold in 1956 were 45s. Elvis Presely's music hit an all-time high for record sales at 1 1/2 million copies a month.

The 'Top-40' records were religiously played by rock-and-roll DJ's (disc jockeys) at radio stations nationwide, danced to, listened to, and purchased, by what seemed to have arisen out of nowhere in the fifties: the monolithic group known as the 'teen-agers'.

The concept of teen-agers, as a specific age group and mind-set, was really completely new. In previous decades, the youth were simply seen as children and then as young adults, but now the years from 13 - 20 were seen as a time of rebellion and transition, of 'following the group', sexuality, and willfullness. Teen-agers were also a targetable new consumer group: ads in magazines, on radio, and on TV were directed to this new-found audience. To serve their varied appetites, ice-cream parlors, soda-shops, hamburger joints, and drive-in movie theatres opened by the thousands.

Teenagers were doubly stereotyped: rebellious and delinquent 'greasers' wearing black-leather jackets and riding motorcyles, versus the clean-cut kids in baggy pants, duck-tail and pony-tail hairstyles, and bobby-sox.

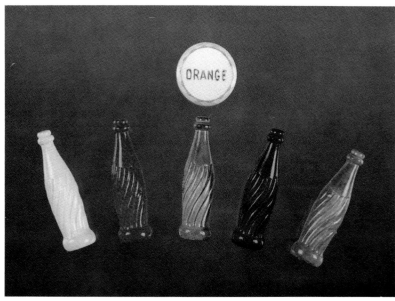

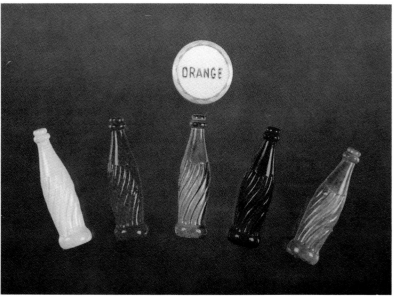

Plastic buttons designed as a bottle cap and an elusive set of 'pop'-bottle realistics, ca. 1950.

Molded plastic with a patent number on the reverse, this button has a rather surrealistic scene—a man's hand lighting a cigarette held in a woman's lips. She has a tall cocktail, he a martini. The details also indicate a 1950s home recreation room rather than a commercial lounge, 1 2/3", ca. 1951.

Along with two wooden and one glass guitar-themed buttons, one plastic music-notation button, and a small metal treble clef are five buttons that directly reflect the music industry of the 1950s. The plastic hi-fi record at the top is incised and pigmented. The set of four plastic, paper-labeled 'platters' is very rare.

The post-war ultra feminine look that Christian Dior had introduced in 1947 evolved into three different ideals in the 1950s: the wholesome girl, the elegant woman, and the sex symbol. Debbie Reynolds personified the wholesome look: a very cute, somewhat naive, marriage-minded girl in a full skirt and tight cashmere sweater, subservient but sassy. Grace Kelly was the quintessential elegant woman of the era, aloof but romantic: a stunning ice-princess beautifully attired in a full-skirted evening gown, with her hair swept up in a perfect French twist. Marilyn Monroe, of course, was the sexy 'dumb blonde,' with her hourglass figure and and tight sheath dress: bold and brassy, but somehow vulnerable.

It was this last 'blonde bombshell' ideal—the ultimate and unattainable fantasy of the 1950s male—that led Hugh Hefner to launch *Playboy* magazine in December,1953, at the age of 27. By 1957, it was a huge success.

A *Playboy* brass blazer button, made for employees of the popular men's magazine. Throughout the 1960s and 1970s, other sets of buttons—in silver or 14K gold with the 'bunny' logo in the center—were advertised in the back of the magazine; considering how many thousands of sets must have been sold, they are strangely difficult to obtain.

Extremely unusual 'cheese-cake' button, a bare-bosomed blonde with a 'come hither' look. The photograph is set under glass, mounted in brass, with a tin back. Actual size 1 1/4", 1950s. *Courtesy of Ron Cole*

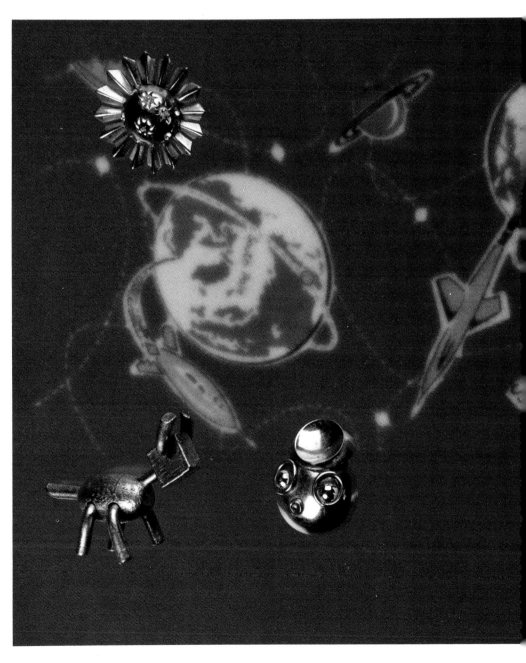

The 1950s brought robots and space-men into the forefront as never before. Japanese-made windup robots were the toys of choice for millions of households and the bottom two buttons are reminiscent of the mania. At left, a molded metal dog-like creature with pipe tube limbs and a square head. At right, a completely dimensional ball-shaped aluminum head with 'lid'. These are both very rare examples. At top, a dressy sun-symbol brass button with inset rhinestones; space travel and the planets were popular themes with adults and children alike, 1 1/2" - 1 3/4", ca. 1950s.

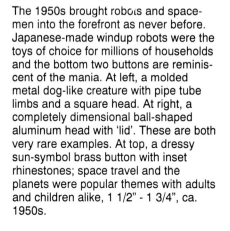

THE EARLY 1960s

In the United States, John Kennedy was elected president in 1960. He and his sophisticated, young and very stylish wife, Jacqueline, presented themselves as the equivalent of American royalty. The realities of Kennedy's time in office, however, were bleak. The Berlin Wall was constructed in Germany, the Cuban missile crisis brought the world to the brink of nuclear war, and racial strife was rampant in America.

Souvenir button from the New York World's Fair, 1964 to 1965. A beautifully designed button of quality manufacture; it is heavy brass with a glass center.

Millions toured the World's Fair in New York in 1964 and 1965 and the Montreal Expo in 1967. This pressed brass globe button, sold at stores everwhere from 1964-1968, was not a commemorative from either event but a commercial button reflecting the public's interest in the fairs

The centennial of the American Civil War in 1964 brought millions of tourists to the battlefield sites on family vacations. Manufacturers did a large business in buttons decorated with motifs, symbols, and participants of this war. Pictured are four brass buttons, and a pewter button of Abraham Lincoln. The top one, a realistic button engraved with his Gettysburg address, is the rarest.

The Space Race

The first reported sighting of a 'flying saucer' was in June of 1947, near Mt. Ranier, Washinton. The press took with delight to the description of a 'saucer-like' object skimming through the skies and stuck with the term, following the stories for years. Throughout the 1950s, designers used anything to do with space—stars, planets, rockets, robots—as decorative motifs. Early in the 1960s, the fictional spacemen and robots became reality when the real space programs got underway. President Kennedy pledged a mission to the moon as a major goal of the administration, and made the research funding available to make it a reality. He established the National Aeronautical and Space Administration (NASA) to coordinate American efforts to explore the outer atmosphere.

In May of 1961, when Alan Shepard became the first American to be shot into space, school-children across America watched the event on television in their classrooms. One month later, the Russian cosmonaut, Yuri Gagarin became the first man to actually orbit the earth. The 'Space Race' had begun.

NASA established a three-stage plan to get a manned flight to the moon. The first stage comprised of six American space flights known as 'Project Mercury'. A Mercury astronaut, John Glenn, became a national hero when he made the first orbit of earth by an American in February of 1962. The next stage included flights with two men per capsule, known as the 'Gemini missions.' The 'Apollo missions' were the third stage. These began tragically in 1967, when the three astronauts of Apollo 1 died in a fire on the launching pad, but the men of the 11th Apollo mission met the goal: Neil Armstrong became the first man to walk on the moon in July of 1969.

The Space Age began on October 4, 1957, with the launch of the Soviet satellite *Sputnik*. America launched her first satellite, Explorer I, in January of 1958. Sputnik is portrayed here in the three brass realistic buttons, and the incised blue glass button at lower right that shows the satellite orbiting a gold-colored earth. At left are brass buttons showing both satellites, ca. late 1950s.

To the moon! A one-piece pewter button at left, and another button of pressed white metal commemorate the beginning and end of President Kennedy's space dream, ca. 1960s.

John Kennedy, as shown in a large sulphide paperweight button made in the 1960s by Theresa Rarig, a glass artist from Kansas. (Shown twice actual size.) President Kennedy encouraged American participation in the 'space-race'. Determined that America would put a man on the moon by the end of the decade, he put the full support of his administration behind the U.S. effort.

Three porcelain buttons from 1960s France. A new sense of sensuality is evident in these charming designs. Skirts were getting shorter and tighter, and women's clothing in general was more revealing.

The ultra-feminine Barbie doll was new in the mid-1960s. Barbie was the first doll with an anatomically complete figure, albeit one which represented an unattainable goal for most little girls. These plastic buttons (two electro-plated and one pearlized) are extremely rare, unknown even to most dedicated Barbie collectors; they were originally sewn on a line of little girl's clothing that came out in the 1960s under the Barbie label.

Another popular toy of the 1950 to 1960 period was the Slinky, a coiled metal spring that could crawl up and down stairways. This button depicts it.

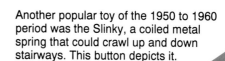

Suggestive 'sweater buttons' of brass, depicting street signs. 1960s.

In the 1960s, many changes in social mores and sexual ethics began to evolve. Sexuality was beginning to be recognized publicly and more honestly in Western society. The 'pin-up' calendars and photos of the 50s began to seem anachronistic. The entire communications industry (magazines, books, movies, and television) rebelled against censorship of any kind. There was a public shift in social attitudes as well, to a new acceptance and ease about moral questions; both behavior and clothing began to reflect this.

The beginning of a radically different era, often dark and upsetting, and always complex, began in November, 1963 with the assassination of President John Kennedy. America was becoming embroiled in the Viet Nam War, and millions of 'baby boomers' were becoming teenagers; there was trouble ahead.

Surfers were the California image known to half the world in the 1960s. This is a ceramic button with a transfer design.

Beatle-mania started in February of 1964 with the British musical group The Beatles' first American tour. To say they were a sensation is far too mild—their success was unprecedented and lasted throughout the decade; at one time the group held the first five positions on the popular music top-40 chart.

The author is unaware of any *commercially manufactured* Beatle clothing buttons that show The Beatles themselves—probably because clothing buttons were not something their management thought to license, preferring to stick with items of broader interest to their teen audience. Still, one enterprising button manufacturer found a way to 'cash in' on the mania without having to pay licensing royalties: these buttons, dating from their first American tour in 1964, have a rebus design— 'beetle music' (look closely.) They were available in the two sizes shown, in silver- or gold-finished brass.

Chapter 14. The Late 60s and The 70s

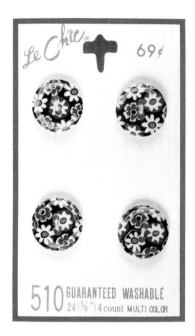

Flower Power! Another anti-war concept, in plastic buttons imitating glass millefiori work, ca. 1969.

The dove of peace, an anti-war image used everywhere throughout the late 1960s, in a two-piece plastic button with a paper insert.

In the late 1960s, inflammatory influences existed in all aspects of American society. The Vietnam War polarized society, and helped create a generational gulf; parents tended to support their government's involvement in the war, while students rejected it as un-winnable and unfounded. Drugs permeated inner cities and college campuses alike, and racial tensions were high. The assassination of John Kennedy in 1963 had been a harbinger of things to come. In 1968, assassinations again rocked the country as two prominent figures were shot: Senator Robert Kennedy in Los Angeles, and civil-rights leader Dr. Martin Luther King, Jr. in Memphis. By the time of the Democratic National Convention in August, 1968, there were riots in the streets of Chicago.

'Hippies' were determined to separate themselves from everything tradtonal. They rejected whatever standards they could: money, corporate life, manners, parents, authority, marriage, religion. They dressed 'down' in sandals and ragged jeans, wore their hair long and straight, and advocated marijuana, LSD, and free-love. Phrases like "Don't Trust Anyone Over 30," "Make Love, Not War," and "Power to the People" were their rallying cries.

Folk and rock music became the sustenance of the young. Its intensity and purpose was different from that of the music of the 1950s. The evolution of popular music was personified by the British and the Beatles, who began their careers as four clean-cut pop or soft-rock singers and ended them as full-fledged hippies.

The 'British Invasion' of popular music to America continued with the terrific popularity of the rock groups the Rolling Stones, the Dave Clark Five, and the Animals, among others. By 1968, 'soft-rock' had become 'acid-rock', which frankly acknowledged and encouraged the uses of illegal drugs (acid was a street name for the hallucinogenic drug L.S.D.). A new youth audience made groups like The Grateful Dead, The Who, Frank Zappa, Grace Slick and the Jefferson Airplane famous.

The British influence was the era's strongest in terms of fashion and design. Carnaby Street in London was the source of micro-mini skirts, short straight hair and colored tights. An Art Nouveau revival was underway in London, and its eventual melding with American psychedelia became, in the graphic arts, the definitive look of the 1960s counter-culture. Its name came from the Greek *psyche*, "soul," and *delos*, "visible." Psychedelia was abetted by LSD 'trips', tie-dyed clothes, fluorescent colors, black-lit posters, and acid-rock music. The artwork was representative of sights seen while in a drug-induced haze, whether symbolic or genuine.

The outcry for world peace was global at the height of the Vietnam war, when large groups marched in support of "Love, not War," using flowers as the symbol of their struggle. The growing numbers of 'peaceniks' believed in 'Flower Power' to end the chaos.

If San Francisco and London were the headquarters of the hippies, India was their spiritual mecca. An appreciation for Indian-style beads, sitar music, and ethnic clothing, and experimentation with the illegal drug hashish and eastern mysticism led hundreds of thousands of young westerners to dream of going to 'find themselves' in India. (Many actually did, much to the consternation of the Indian government.)

Peace and Love, the watchwords of the late 1960s, as seen on buttons. The peace sign appears in brass, copper, and silver-finished metal buttons; Love is presented in pierced brass (above), and in pressed brass.

Mary Quant was the leading young British designer who influenced the Carnaby Street fashions. The short sculpted haircut and swinging geometric earrings were the epitome of her look, as captured on a plastic button of transfer design, ca. 1967.

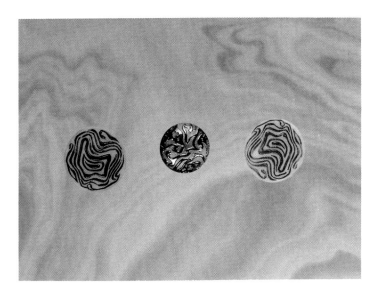

Psychedelic art is hard to find on buttons, so these iridescent, luster-coated, glass buttons from West Germany are special reflections of their cultural time, the late 1960s.

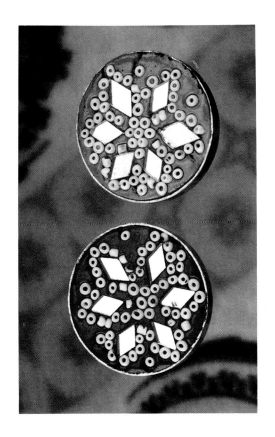

These buttons from India are bead-and-mirror craftwork typical of Rajasthan; the hippies loved this look and thousands of outfits with the same decor were exported from India in the late 1960s and early 1970s. The metal button frames are filled with glass-inlaid lacquer.

This fascinating design makes sense when you consider the influences around its period of manufacture: the Orient, Art Nouveau, and flower-power trends of the late 1960s converged to make a button that reflects its time perfectly, a nearly psychedelic image. The one-piece concave base has an attached, cast metal head.

A popular saying of the 1970s, a time of political unrest and disillusionment, was, "don't push the 'panic-button." This button is an ironic transfer on plastic.

This incised plastic button tells the story of American fashion trends for the young in the late 1960s and early 1970s.

In the middle of the 1970s, this 'happy-face' design became ubiquitous. This pin-shanked wooden button is decorated by pyrography. (The nose is the head of the 'pin-shank'.)

Few news stories inspired button designs in the 1970s as did President Nixon's historic trip to China, which is depicted on this plastic 'kiddie' button. Pandas became tremendously popular after the Chinese Premier presented a pair of the rare animals to the National Zoo in Washinton, D.C. The manufacturer of this button, JHB International, marketed it in reaction to that event.

C.B. ('Citizens' Band') radios had a flare of popularity for personal automobiles in the late 1970s, along with country music and country and western bars. Jimmy Carter, the drawling 'country-boy', had more than a little effect on the trend. This copper button dates from the late 1970s.

By 1970, a growing trend among disillusioned hippies was to move into communes in the countryside to form alternative societies. The movement spread to include many who found enlightenment in 'dropping-out of the establishment' and working for themselves. The mood was anti-industry and anti-big business; their solution to a confusing world was self-reliance—making their own clothing, crafting their own leather sandals, growing their own food. Nevertheless, a certain reality soon set in as these 'free spirits' discovered that to live, they needed to produce some income, and the most expedient way for most of them to do so was to sell their own hand-crafted work. At street fairs, art shows, antiques and crafts sales, thousands of these new entrepreneurs began to make a transition back into a capitalistic society.

There was a fashion look of simplicity and poverty peculiar to these alternativists that was aided by the newly-organized women's-liberation movement and black-activist movements. This style most of these non-conformists conformed to was characterized by cotton print peasant-style dresses or faded blue jeans, long, straight, unstyled hair (or a natural 'Afro', if black), and no make-up.

This fashion, or lack thereof, soon had an effect on the rest of society. 'Natural' was in fashion, and anything neat or studied was out. Hand-crafted and folk-related items were in demand. Macramé was very popular, as was ethnic imported jewelry and native costumes from all over the world. The skirts and co-ordinated oufits of the 1960s simply disappeared. The 'pants-suit' was the latest fashion for dress-wear and denim blue jeans were the choice for leisure. This style marked the end of not only mini-skirts, but of dresses for women in general for at least a decade, except for a short fad for 'midi-skirts', soundly hated by most men and not a few women!

Buttons continued to be quite unimportant on clothing, and the vast majority of the buttons manufactured in the 1970s were nondescript. There was, however, one trend in buttons that did reflect the cultural taste: the majority of 'normal' clothing buttons were now made of wood, horn, and other natural materials.

When President Jimmy Carter—formerly a Georgia peanut farmer—came into office in 1976, he quickly became the butt of 'peanut' jokes. This metal realistic button came out shortly after his election.

The Bicentennial of the American Revolution was celebrated in buttons, including some of cast metal, pressed brass, plastic, and enameled brass. The two pewter buttons in the center of the top row, recastings of very early U.S. military buttons, were part of a blazer set offered by Time magazine in honor of the Bicentennial celebration year.

Only the American bi-centennial celebration in 1976 occasioned more than just a few token buttons: several manufacturers produced a number of attractive, patriotically-inspired buttons.

By far the biggest trend in buttons during the 1970s was the use of natural materials, prevalent throughout the decorative arts. These buttons were all purchased at a fabric shop in the late 1970s. The majority are made from wood, but there are also natural horn buttons and two made from seed pods (a rather unusual material for a button). Two are hand-made pottery examples, one a heavy, hand-cast pewter example, two commercial pewter buttons, and one each of aluminum and brass.

In the late 1970s, the JHB Button Company designed this enameled brass button named "Ruffian" in honor of the courageous filly who caught the imagination of the American public as a contender for the Triple Crown of horse-racing, before a tragic mid-race accident resulted in her tragic death.

Just before the advent of the 1980s button boom, one company, Battersea Buttons (a division of Bergamot Brass Works, a large manufacturing and metals company) made the 1970s most beautiful buttons. Beginning in 1977, Battersea produced incredibly lovely pewter buttons.

Battersea buttons were the personal venture of the company's president, and though intended as commercial products, they were really a labor of love. He spared no expense on the buttons, much to the chagrin of some of the company accountants, and all were beautifully made. Many were copied from antique buttons, not to deceive, but for their appeal; the others were original designs. Always clearly back-marked and dated, some Battersea buttons were plated over an alloy (the copper-plated are the rarest). The rest, of solid pewter, had a unique feature: a tiny face—the bearded visage of the company president was one of them—was actually molded on the shank itself: a paragon of artistic, but certainly not thrifty, manufacture.

These wonderful buttons were a bit ahead of their time; unable to find a niche with a public then attuned to inexpensive and ordinary-looking buttons, the firm quit making them in 1979.

Battersea now does business only in the private sector, producing custom-made logo buttons for cities and many large corporations.

Although collectors usually think that Battersea went of out the button business by 1980, the company has been actively producing buttons for private industry and businesses; they simply quit manufacturing buttons for the public. During the 1990s, Battersea began to produce what are probably the most detailed cast-metal buttons ever made, known as 'City Scapes'. These pewter buttons, made for various cities, are used for offical purposes.

The reverse of various Battersea pewter buttons showing the patented 'face' shanks. The man's face on the top shank is that of the company's owner (Hi, Dan!). The next, a woman's face, was used on medium-sized examples; the face of a different gentleman appeared on the small buttons. Only the solid pewter buttons had face-shanks; Battersea's plated metal buttons (brass, copper, and pewter-plated base metal) did not. Nevertheless, all Battersea buttons were clearly marked with the company name and often were dated. (The backmark on the lower button is exclusive to a group of custom-ordered buttons.

Battersea pewter buttons, ca. late 1970s.

Bergamot Brass Works made pewter recastings like these four from antique brass or silver buttons, under the label 'Battersea' late in the 1970s.

The top three buttons are part of a gorgeous group of Art Nouveau Revival buttons that Battersa produced privately for the Calhoun Collector's Society in 1982. The lower two buttons, also in the Art Nouveau style, were stock Battersea designs from the late 1970s.

Chapter 15. Relevant Again: Buttons from 1980 to Now

Between 1955 and 1980, buttons had grown increasingly dull, nearly disappearing as significant parts of decoration and design on contemporary fashions. Major news events and cultural trends were still occasionally reflected on buttons, but they were a very small part of the fashion world. Then, quite suddenly, a button renaissance began during the mid-1980s. Buttons became the focus of high-fashion designers, followed by the dress trade, and in the decade since, this new appreciation has continued to grow in scope and spirit.

Ronald Reagan's predilection for jelly beans kicked off a jelly bean fad in America, and this little plastic button for kid's wear was one of the results.

President Ronald Reagan was the first American president since George Washington to give buttons as souvenirs to those attending his inauguration. The gilded brass blazer sets came boxed, as shown, ca. 1981.

The fairy tale wedding of Charles, the Prince of Wales (and heir to the British throne) and the Lady Diana Spencer was *the* news story of the second half of 1981. At left is a silk bookmark commemorating the event, and at right are two blazer buttons and a cheap brass button with their photograph.

During all of the excitement about the wedding, this blazer button with the three plumes of the Prince of Wales was issued by an American firm.

Although buttons were not the official gifts for Ronald Reagan's second inauguration, there were a very limited number made for the President's personal staff and for the President's own use, by the same firm as had made the first sets, the Ben Silver Company of Charleston. These are far rarer than the ones from the first inaugural.

The reverse of one of the blazer buttons above.

Also from JHB, these pro-United States plastic buttons were marketed during the Gulf War in 1991. The war brought a patriotic fervor to the country for the first time, some people think, since the late 1960s.

Dinosaurs were an enormous fad for kids in the eighties, when J.H.B. marketed this friendly trio of plastic realistics. The red stegasaurous was appropriately named 'Spike'.

These ceramic buttons, hand made and painted, were available at specialty shops in the late 1980s.

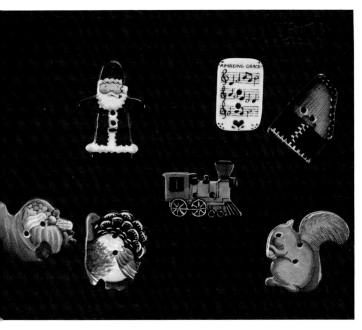

Idabelle Byers, a ceramicist from Indiana, makes extremely detailed and colorful buttons. Her work includes hundreds of designs that show both creativity and perfection of execution, a rare combination.

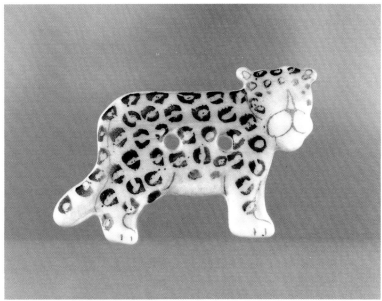

One of the wonderful glazed ceramic realistic buttons made by Idabelle Byers, this leopard is part of her big-cats series, 2", ca. 1993.

Glazed ceramic and enameled copper buttons. *Courtesy of Blue Moon Button Art*

More of Idabelle Byer's buttons: a hedgehog and an ark.

Top row: Victorian-style molded ceramic buttons with raised floral designs. Middle row: raku pottery, very unusual in buttons. Bottom row: the left two are woven fabric from Japan and the butterfly is a glazed, hand-painted ceramic. *Courtesy of Blue Moon Button Art*

This cheery transfer design on plastic tells the story of the button boom that began around 1985!

For a very short period late in the 1980s, 'treasure buttons' enjoyed quite a fad; made by various companies, they were all three-piece glass or plastic-covered metal (or metalized plastic) buttons with a variety of tiny objects enclosed.

A group of pressed metal and electroplate buttons made in Europe throughout the late 1980s. *Coutesy of Duttons For Buttons, England.*

In a quintessential case of déja vu, the impetus for the present-day button mania came from Paris, with the bold and profuse use of buttons by fashion designer Patrick Kelly. Exactly 50 years after Elsa Schiaparelli had inspired a new use of buttons in fashion (not coincidentally, she was his idol) Kelly re-juvenated the button industry with witty and wonderous use of these fasteners on his fashions. This young black American rocketed to fame when he featured huge, bright and variously colored buttons on his couturier fashions as the main design element. For Kelly, buttons were far more than utilitarian; he sewed them on his designer clothing in patterns, on unexpected places, and in odd groupings: "Kelly clothes are simply cut, sexy, and affordable—more decorated than designed."[1]

Vogue magazine commented that "Paris has exploded in buttons, bows, fruits, and festivities since America's irrepressible Patrick Kelly came to town."[2] His first button-bedecked fashion collection in the spring of 1985 caused a sensation in the press; before long, most of the major fashion houses, including Karl Lagerfield, Yves Saint Laurent, Oscar de la Renta, Bill Blass, and Anne Klein, were showing clothes laden with exciting buttons.

As had Elsa Schiaparelli, Kelly took extreme delight in the outrageous and unexpected. His sense of the absurd was first-rate: his fall collection from 1989 included buttons shaped like lipstick tubes, Eiffell Towers, straw hats, and African masks. In 1988, Kelly—whose poverty-stricken background in Mississippi could hardly be said to have prepared or exposed him to high-fashion design—became the only American ever inducted into the prestigious Chambre Syndicate du Prêt-à-Porter, the official (and very exclusive) organization of French fashion designers. Tragically, he died in 1990 at the age of 32.

As often happens in the fashion industry, this new look of button-intensive clothing spread to the ready-to-wear houses and their mass markets. The dress industry had been floundering, hit hard by pants-suits, denim blue-jeans, and the 'miracle fastener' Velcro©, but as the surge of creativity from clothing manufacturers and button companies produced increasingly eye-catching results, the public responded more than favorably. Buttons had become a sensation!

By the late 1980s, it was impossible to walk through a department store without noticing that the buttons on the racked clothes often outshone the fashions themselves. Ornate, whimsical, oddly-shaped, large, and colorful, the buttons were far more decorative than functional, and for the first time outfits often had buttons that didn't match each other at all.

In America, the big button companies have found themselves in the middle of an unprecedented consumer demand, and manufacturers worldwide have brought out an infinite variety of buttons throughout the decade. The major button companies in America, Europe, Hong Kong, and Japan now produce far more buttons than they have since the early 1950s. In addition, a large number of individual artisans are making buttons and selling them through small specialty shops, craft-shows, and catalogs.

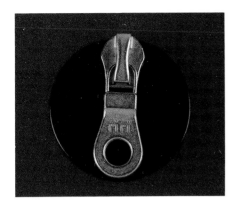

Isn't this great? The large brass zipper-pull on a thick plastic button base is attached only at the top, so it actually does lift, ca. 1990.

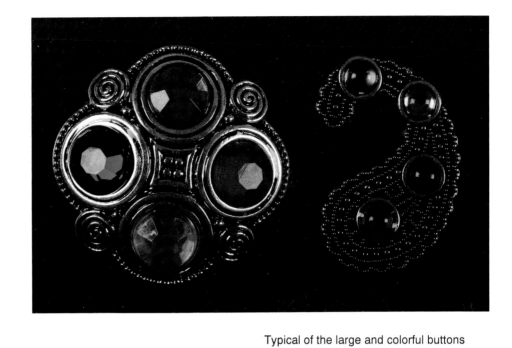

Another fun novelty button is this German import by Blue Moon Button Art, made of brass and plastic. The little plane moves through the semi-circle. The same button was also available with a moveable car.

Yin and Yang, oriental symbols of the life force combinations and harmony, came back into popularity during the 1980s. Of cast pewter, this button is backmarked "yin yang" and "pewter".

Typical of the large and colorful buttons of the late 1980s are these electro-plated plastic buttons set with plastic 'gemstones'.

A large plastic flower button with a very deep, concave body, in the style of artist Georgia O'Keefe, 1 2/3", ca. 1992.

A sign of the times for the computer generation; these sew-through buttons for men's sportscoats were simply punched out of actual circuit boards, 1" and 3/4", 1992.

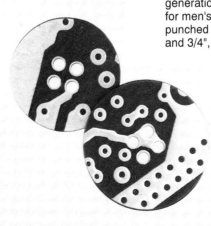

Fantastic large faces in sections; these commercially available buttons were among the unique types being manufac-tured worldwide in the early 1990s.

PATRICK KELLY

PARIS

Patrick Kelly's line of retail buttons was manufactured for him by Streamline Industries, Inc. All of the Kelly buttons shown in this photograph were part of that line. The 'Sparkles' are buttons of molded and textured electro-plated plastic, shaped like diamonds, hearts, clubs, spades, half-moons, stars, squares, circles and triangular. The one piece plastic billiard balls, gumballs, hearts, stars, treble clefs, and bows came in two sizes—large, and huge! Each was backmarked with the Kelly name.

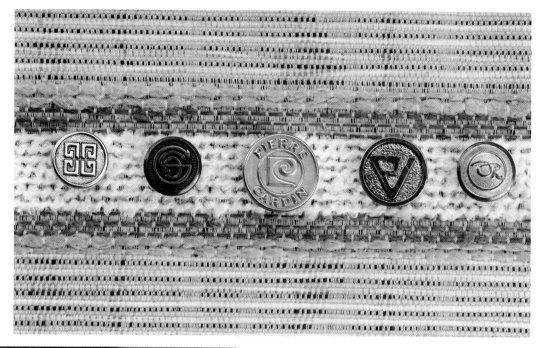

Designers' trademark brass buttons, from ready-to-wear lines by Givenchy, Giorgio Sant Angelo, Oscar de la Renta, Philippe Venet, and Pierre Cardin, 1/2" to 3/4", 1980s.

A Christian Dior signature button in molded brass and, from Coco Chanel, a button with letters of brass roping atop a brass button, 1 1/8", mid-twentieth century.

Men's brass designer sportscoat buttons from the brands of Johnny Carson, Palm Beach, and Izod, 2/3" - 3/4", 1980s.

Large and heavy brass realistic buttons of the crescent moon and the sun from designer Todd Oldham, manufactured by Streamline, 1 1/2", 1993.

Patrick Kelly's creative spirit has a sucessor in the person of Todd Oldham, a new and popular young American fashion designer. As did Kelly, Oldham has joined forces with the large American button company Streamline Industries (in early 1992) to market his creative line of buttons to consumers. Oldham's sense of whimsy certainly shows up in these sometimes tongue-in-cheek creations, which are often actually designed by his younger brother, Brad. To date, they all have been metal buttons, often realistics.

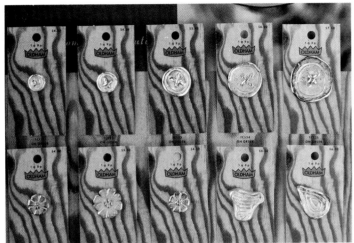

Todd Oldham sales display of metal buttons, 1992.

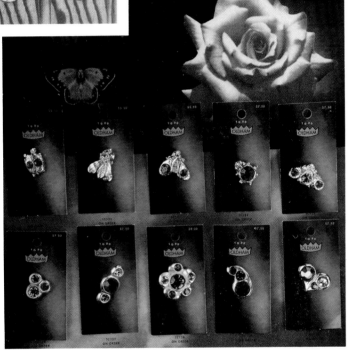

Todd Oldham's first designs included these 'jeweled' brass buttons. Note the 'bugs' in the top row.

A wonderfully whimsical set of buttons from fashion designer Todd Oldham, manufactured by the Streamline Button Company. Each dog has own private bone button! All are of heavy metal with molded shanks. Each breed of dog has a different color finish and one rhinestone for accent. The bones are 7/8", the dogs 1 1/8", 1993.

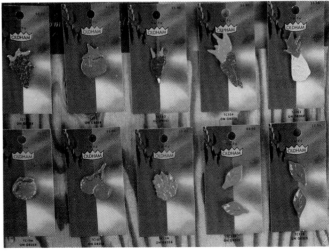

Todd Oldham buttons designed as realistic leaves, fruits and vegetables in enameled metal, ca. 1992.

From left, by row: metal mesh rolled and folded into roses; copper inlaid with silver; reflective colored-glass 'mirrors' set with rhinestones; seashells embedded in acrylic and, lower right, a transfer design, late 1980s. *Courtesy of Blue Moon Button Art*

Reflecting the world ecology movement, buttons such as these bring one's global interests up front . Made in Germany of enamel on copper, this button shows the continent of Africa, an unusual subject, 1993. *Courtesy of Blue Moon Button Art*

Fused glass buttons with foil and overlaid glass-thread trims. Some of the glass used is di-chromic (multi-colored), ca. 1990. *Courtesy of Blue Moon Button Art*

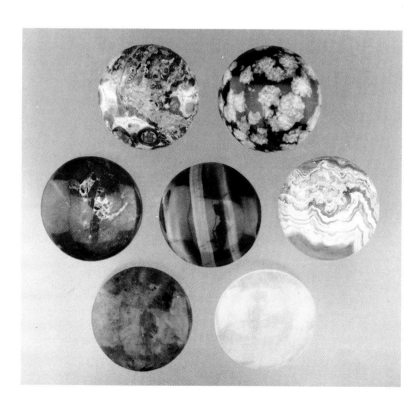

These semi-precious stone cabochon buttons were produced around the world. In the center, tigereye; upper left clockwise: sodalite, rose quartz, crazy lace, snowflake obsidian, red jasper, and leopard jasper, 3/4", ca. 1990. *Courtesy of Blue Moon Button Art.*

More now than ever since the days of the French Revolution, buttons are again reflecting social concerns and movements, especially environmental issues: ecology, the earth movement, the green movement, wild-life conservation, and animal rights.

Conservation International has targeted buttons as one of the ways it can positively influence world ecology; their goal, to blend economic development with conservation worldwide, has resulted in some interesting projects and joint ventures. In Ecuador, in an attempt to help conserve the rainforest, C.I.'s 'Tagua Initiative' encourages the harvest of tagua nuts (vegetable ivory) for use by various industries (instead of burning the trees to clear cropland) and setting up outlets throughout the west for the sale of tagua-nut products. They also enlist the help of the 'Aid to Artisans' organization, a collective of concerned American artists, to help the Ecuadoran Indians design and create interesting tagua-nut buttons and other products.

This effort is beginning to achieve the hoped-for results. Esprit Clothing, in 1992, came out with an ecologically-sound 'E' collection, in which all buttons were made from vegetable ivory. The huge button firm B.Blumenthal and Co. has not only been selling tagua nut buttons again for the first time in decades, but is also publicizing the cause by using a rainforest-specific postmark on their corporate mailings.

Danforth Pewterers, makers of wonderful (and usually realistically-shaped) butttons,[3] has marketed an 'Earth Collection' of button designs relating to the planet. The company donates a percentage of the sales to environmental groups. Other Danforth button sets feature highly detailed pewter animals—big cats, North American native wildlife, sea mammals—to appeal to people with animal-rights issues in mind.

Blue Moon Button Art has also marketed buttons with earth and animal rights themes, including many that reflect the anti-fur movement. German button producers, too, have recently marketed buttons with anti-fur themes.

Button-manufacturing projects are being set-up in various economically disadvantaged nations to help them establish self-sufficiency. Readily-available materials are used; in Ghana, for example, buttons are made from recycled, powdered glass.

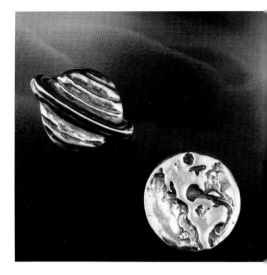

Part of the 'earth movement' of the 1990s, these two pewter buttons are backmarked 'earth' and 'Saturn' respectively, 1990s.

Blue Moon

A perfect example of the innovative new spirit of the button business in the 1990s, in its breadth, creativity, and verve, is the American firm Blue Moon Button Art. Established in California as a yarn distributorship in 1987, Blue Moon began with a tiny number of button designs, which it carried only to complement its yarns. However, it was the buttons that proved to be the most in demand, and by mid-1990 Blue Moon was concentrating on buttons alone, with over twelve hundred designs in their line.

Although they import many factory-produced buttons from Europe, the company's uniqueness stems from its large line of hand-made fasteners, fashioned for them by various American artisans, including jewelry and silversmiths, potters, ceramists, wood-carvers, and others. Its a happy marriage between custom-work and commercial availability.

Blue Moon has also been very successful in exporting buttons to outlets in Japan, Mexico, and Germany, Italy, and England.

Fimo-clay inlay button with sun and moon design, 3/4", ca. 1990.

Three dichromatic glass paperweight buttons with foil designs under the glass dome and fused gold decor, 2/3" to 7/8", 1993. *Courtesy of Blue Moon Button Art.*

Dichromatic glass paperweight button with foil under the glass and a fused gold Japanese wave design on top, 1993. *Courtesy of Blue Moon Button Art.*

A card of tagua nut (vegetable ivory) buttons from B. Blumenthal sits next to an envelope carrying their ecologically-minded postmark.

Powdered-glass buttons from Ghana, 1992. *Courtesy of Kirk Stanfield.*

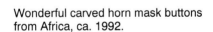

Wonderful carved horn mask buttons from Africa, ca. 1992.

Indian embroidery work on felt, ca. 1990.

From Tibet, in carved bone, a hand of Buddha. From India, rosewood inlaid with brass, ca. 1990.

Fake fur! This button was made to simulate a marten's head, resembling the marten fur stoles which were fashionable in the 1940s. This large molded plastic button from Germany has glass eyes. It is a form of editorializing on buttons while still keeping a tongue-in-cheek playfulness, ca 1990.

At left, a pair of whales made from inlaid Fimo clay, and at right, another whale pair in cast pewter, ca. 1989.

These are two of the button sets Danforth Pewter has manufactured to appeal to animal rights movements. The sea-dwellers are quite lifelike, smooth and rounded, fat but sleek; the other set, the wildlife of North America, is made in an equally detailed but rough and wooly manner. These illustrate the skills of the firm's sculptor, Judi Danforth.

Inlaid Fimo-clay buttons portraying a bighorn sheep, a rabbit, and a frog, 1" to 1 1/4", ca. 1992. *Courtesy of Blue Moon Button Art.*

A wolf made in the cane-inlay technique of Fimo-clay work. This button reflects the widespread awareness of ecology and animal rights, 1", ca. 1990s. *Courtesy of Blue Moon Button Art.*

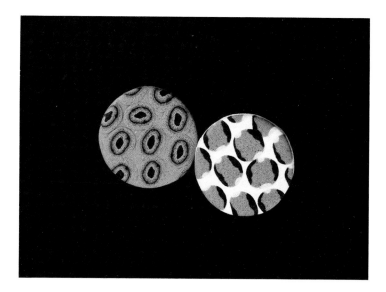

see below

A clear plastic button that has been carved and painted on the reverse to resemble animal fur. Clear buttons resembling lucite had virtually disappeared since the 1950s until German manufacturers began offering them again in the 1990s, 2".

A bevy of buttons made to look like animal skins, made from Fimo clay. These were each individually fashioned by an artist using the inlay technique, but were not 'studio' buttons made for collectors: they are commercial products sold through a button company. 1 1/4", ca. 1992. *Courtesy Blue Moon Button Art.*

Coconut-shell buttons have also been carved and painted to look like animal skins,1 1/2" and 2", ca. 1990.

PART TWO

Buttons as a Reflection of Art

Introduction

It is easy to forget that the designers of buttons are artists and that buttons are their canvas. Many button designs are excellent reflections of the artistic movements of their times.

Collectors generally focus on classifying buttons by their age, subject matter, or material. With the exceptions of Art Nouveau and Art Deco, styles which are relatively easy to determine, the connection between art styles and buttons has not yet been explored. The buttons in this section, grouped into thirty-two different styles, illustrate that connection. Each button incorporates elements indicative of its particular style and *dates from the period of the style's original popularity*.

This is a preliminary study, by no means complete. And, because art interpretation is subjective, opinions are not necessarily 'correct.' They are, however, based on research, experience, and consultations with art historians. Many button designs unquestionably match certain art styles; other designs are more obscure. There are also buttons whose designs combine elements from more than one style: these crossover examples are a challenge to categorize!

This humorous pierced brass button features an artist 'armed' with a palette shield and a paintbrush sword, 1 1/4", 1950s.

A brass button with the central cutout lined in crystalized tin to give a lake and sky effect, 1/2", ca. 1880 to 1910.

Raphael's cupid from the Sistine Chapel, an image often copied for use on decorative-arts products. Colored transfer on porcelain, 1", ca. 1895 to 1910.

Chapter 16. The Art of Buttons

History records the path of mankind; art celebrates it. The changing styles of art are the scenic rest stops along that path. Sometimes a look remains in vogue for many years, but at other times the art styles change rapidly. Frequently, the style of art presently in vogue evolves into a distinctly new form: certain elements of the original style are retained (possibly even intensified) while others are replaced, bringing about a completely different effect.

New styles of art often evolve from the past as well. Based on a popular look from decades, or even centuries earlier, these recycled styles have traditionally been known as 'Neo' or 'Revival' art; in recent years designers have used the term 'Retro' as well. An art in revival almost always shows minor modifications from the original style.

New art styles that either evolve or revive are derivative, but many other art styles emerge quite independently. The lack of connection to the past—often combined with a look so original it seems more alien than unique—makes these styles the most controversial. The art world thrives on controversy and is often quick to celebrate such styles, but among the general population, the opposite is true: the more original the style, the slower the public usually is to accept it.

Most of the new art styles that arise are transient. Only a fraction ever create a noticeable stir in the art world; even fewer actually start a trend. But when a new style inspires disciples—additional artists whose collective works share certain similarities and boundaries—it may get attention from both the art community and the *avant-garde* patron; this signals the emergence of a distinct school of art. Whether it becomes a mere footnote in art history or a major style depends on the next step.

If a new style truly has momentum, the narrow confines of the fine arts—paintings, drawings, sculpture and architecture—cannot contain it. A successful art style always spills over into the field of decorative arts, where the product designers and manufacturers, decorators, and commercial artists take over. Before long the look is everywhere; more than just an art style, it is now 'in style'.

The term 'decorative arts' refers to objects that are adorned or decorated. Furniture design, glassmaking, porcelain and pottery making, metalwork, bookbinding, graphics, and jewelry design are decorative arts; button design comes under this category as well, although some buttons, such as the French eighteenth-century miniature paintings on ivory, would also qualify as fine art.

The fine arts can be compared to the raging rapids of a river, full of unpredictable drops and sharp turns; the decorative arts are more reminiscent of a calm lake with a mirror-like surface, reflective of its surroundings. Artists navigate the one; manufacturers sail on the other. Manufacturers are not risk takers: once something is established as the *status quo*, they are not apt to fool with it. Because of this conservative bent and inherent reticence for rapid change, it is often the decor of manufactured objects that best retains and reflects the original elements of any given art style.

Many art styles are fully represented in buttons; others less so. Some styles that are rather important in terms of their impact on the fine arts were nonetheless short-lived and never really expanded into the decorative arts. They did not, therefore, trickle down into the public consciousness, nor particularly affect such things as button design. Fauvism is an example of this. There were very few buttons designed with a Fauvistic look, for the style never found general approval.

(There is a very distinct form of art known as naif or folk art which has little to do with the trends in fine arts, relying instead on tradition and individual craftsmanship. Folk artists worldwide have painted and sculpted buttons of various materials; examples are presented throughout the book.)

Chapter 17. Art Styles

These ladies are dressed in Rococo Revival style, with frills, ruffles, bows, ribbons and flowers.

1. ROCOCO (1715-1750) and ROCOCO-REVIVAL (1860-1895)

The Rococo style was a gaily romantic one, frilly and feminine, and though it was often crowded with very fussy detailing, it had a delicate elegance. First in vogue in 1715, its popularity began to wane about 1760, when the newly-developing Romantic and Neo-Classic styles took over. The Rococo-Revival came approximately a century later. There are wonderful examples of both Rococo and Rococo-Revival buttons. One judges if a button is from the original Rococo period or the revival not by any appreciable difference in the design, but by the changes in button construction between the centuries.

The Rococo style featured asymmetrical curved lines and patterns, a radically different standard when it first appeared. Other common aspects were C-shaped scrolls, curlicues, and arabesques. Multiple motifs were nearly a pre-requisite: favorites included vines, leaves, flowers (roses and orange blossoms were especially popular), feathers, be-ribboned baskets, shells, musical instruments, fans, and cherubs.

Ivory button with a very ornate, pierced silver cap. The floral decor and C-scrolls are typically Rococo.

Miniature paintings on ivory under glass, in the Rococo style, include the extraordinary button at left set entirely in gold; the girl is on a flowered swing, and the floating violin and scroll are both entwined with ribbons. The Cupids on the right button are gauzily attired amid flowers and a be-ribboned quiver, French, ca. 1770 to 1790. *Courtesy of Bruce and Jane Beck*

Rococo-Revival mother-of-pearl buttons, gilded and silvered; these are desirable types, but difficult to find in this perfect condition. At right, a shell-shaped carved cameo.

Pierced brass with c-scrolls and cut-steel trim.

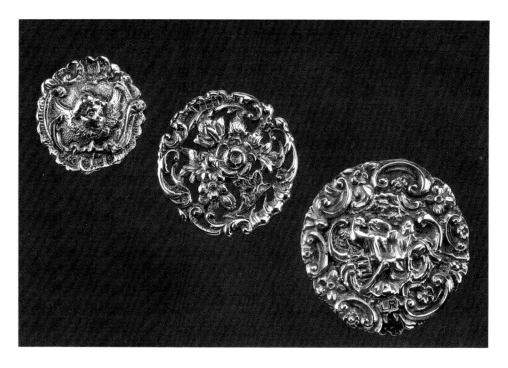

Very ornate brass with etched tin central trim. A copious floral decor surrounds cupids holding a mirror-like shield.

Beautifully Rococo, the two-piece pressed brass button at left has two birds kissing under a floral swag, over Cupid's torch and quiver; on the right, a button of pierced brass with a bird and c-scrolls.

Three English hallmarked silver buttons with floral-enhanced curlicues, shell-designs, and arabesques of Rococo style, ca 1890s.

Pierced brass button of the goddess Diana and her dog, surrounded by a florid border of shell-like c-scrolls and curlicues, ca. 1865 to 1880s.

Each of these Rococo Revival buttons employs the same motifs. At left is a two-piece, dyed brass button with a cut-out section overlaid with a blackened steel grid. At top center, a molded black glass button lustered in an unusual gun-metal finish. At bottom center, a milk glass coated button with pearlized paint. At right, a mother-of-pearl button with a gilded transfer design, all mid- to late 1800s.

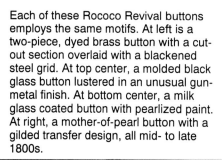

Three Rococo-Revival buttons. Left, a highly-convex one-piece repoussé button of brass with an ornate urn surrounded by heavy shell and c-scrolls: unlike urns common to Classical art, this one contains an unstructured floral display with one small group of blooms even seen unceremoniously on the floor beside it. Center, a deluxe and fragile enameled button from France with etched gold overlay of a be-ribboned flower basket; top, another be-ribboned basket of flowers on a one-piece pierced brass button.

2. ROMANTICISM (1750-1790)

Romanticism was a mid-eighteenth-century philosophy as well as an art style; its spiritual inspiration came, in part, from the French naturalist Voltaire. The Romantic Movement itself was a reaction against both conventional religion and 'science', against excessively ornate art, melodramatic allegories, and rigidly realistic portraits.

Romanticism was dedicated to nature, and to the 'everyday' human experience. As an art form, it was characterized by sentimentality, imagination, and idealism; landscapes—often idyllic views of pastoral life—were the norm. A typical Romantic affectation was to show a solitary human figure, dwarfed in importance by the magnitude of Nature, and yet at one with it.

The scenes on some Romantic-style decorative-arts items were combined with elements from the concurrent Rococo style: the combination may look rather incongruous now, but the manufacturers wanted their products to appeal to as wide a market as possible.

An enhanced version of Romanticism returned to style around 1825. (See Romantic Realism.)

This rare Romantic windmill scene is hand-painted on a late-eighteenth-century papiér-mâché button; most buttons of this material are from the mid-nineteenth century.

Two fishing scenes, French, mid-eighteenth century, in under-glass and hand-painted buttons. At the left, an ivory miniature rimmed in copper, and at right, a gouache set in silver. The smaller size is most unusual for an under-glass painted button. Both have typically Romantic scenes (man dwarfed by nature) and are painted in a dreamy, softly-blended manner.

Man in nature is the theme of these rare decorated 'colonial' metal buttons from the mid- to late eighteenth century. The left example has a reverse-painted piece of glass set over the brass base. The other is an enameled plaque set over copper. *Courtesy of M. W. Speights*

These are extremely-rare examples of eighteenth-century enameled ceramic buttons of the Battersea type. The deep rose-pink and robin's-egg blue colors of the borders are the two most associated with this era. The pastoral scenes with the lone figure are typical of Romantic Art. Classical-Art and Rococo elements (such as the pillars, and scroll borders seen here) were often seen combined with this style on the decorative arts products of the period.

A very rare example of mid-eighteenth century French Chinoiserie in an underglass button, set and rimmed in silver. The musician is hand-painted in gold and copper-colored paint on heavy vellum and the painting is signed with a cypher-type signature at lower right, two back-to-back B's topped with a crown. *Courtesy of Bruce and Jane Beck*

3. CHINOISERIE (1740-1880)

Chinoiserie was a fine and decorative art style concocted by Western designers which featured fanciful oriental scenes. Whether manufactured in European factories or made in China for export to the West, Chinoiserie items were not Chinese art: they were designed by western artists and often had a cluttered, cliché-ridden 'oriental' look. In the mid-seventeenth century, French people loved the style: Chinoiserie designs abounded on French marquetry furniture, porcelain dishes, wallpaper, and other decorations.

A century later, circa 1840, Chinoiserie came into popularity again throughout the western world. The great clipper ships that delivered goods from the west to China sailed back loaded with genuine Chinese artifacts, as well as great numbers of Chinoiserie products manufactured in China for western interests. Many Chinoiserie items were produced in European factories as well, including porcelain, pottery, jewelry, and buttons.

The most famous of the Chinoiserie designs in the western market was the symbolic, pastoral *Willow* design, used on ceramics, and even some buttons, beginning in 1780.

Chinoiserie was so popular during the mid-Victorian era that even this ordinary page from an 1885 encyclopedia, discussing mathematics, reflected the style.

A very early nineteenth-century porcelain button with Chinoiserie transfer design.

A lovely pierced, silver-plated brass button with pseudo-Chinese writing, a thunder pattern and clouds below, and birds on prunus branches above, late nineteenth century.

Willow was perhaps the most popular chinaware pattern ever made. (It is often erroneously called 'Blue Willow' for its most common, but certainly not only, coloring.) First made in England at the Salopian Works pottery in 1780, it has never since ceased being manufactured somewhere in the world. A few products other than china were decorated with the Willow pattern, including buttons, during the mid-nineteenth century. Pictured is a one-piece pressed brass button, ca. 1870s.

Although button collectors like to call this "Winken, Blinken, and Nod", it is actually a rather negative Chinoiserie design, on an impressed brass picture button of the late nineteenth century.

Willow pattern buttons in iridescent-lustered molded black glass at left, and at right, a one-piece gilded brass button, both ca. 1855 to 1870.

Chinoiserie on a crystalized tin button; the design was etched through the dark-lacquer coating to reveal the frosty-looking, shiny tin base, ca. 1860 to 1880.

4. NEO-CLASSICISM (1748-1865)

Beginning with the excavations of the ancient cities of Pompeii and Herculaneum in 1748, there was a sweeping revival of interest in the art, architecture, literature, fashions, and even the philosophies and politics of ancient Greece and Rome.

This fanatical interest fueled one of the largest art movements of all time: Neo-Classicism. Some say that the archaeological discoveries created the Neo-Classic movement; however, there had always been an interest in the ancients and their myths, lives, and arts. The impetus these archaeological finds provided was simply Europe's first exposure to examples of what ancient art actually looked like. The public was kept updated on the progress of the excavations and discoveries through various anxiously-awaited publications and illustrated news pamphlets.

The foremost art style internationally for nearly a century, Neo-Classicism's appeal was served by an additional, non-tangible factor: the widely held belief that Rome's culture was superior, its society more advanced, its citizens more noble than those of eighteenth-century Europe. (This idealistic view of the Roman Republic influenced the leaders of the French Revolution. All of the Revolution's chosen symbols were classical in origin; one legislator even proposed an official dress code featuring the toga!)[1]

The Neo-Classic style grew as artists and architects all over the western world began to incorporate classical imagery into paintings, sculptures, and monuments. Nearly every statue or public building erected from the last half of the eighteenth century through the first quarter of the nineteenth was a celebration of Neo-Classic form. Huge numbers of government buildings in cities worldwide (Washington D.C. is a perfect example) testify to this. In 1804, when "Napoleon decided to crown himself Emperor of the French, the Gothic arches of the Cathedral of Notre Dame were covered with cardboard...so that the ceremony might take place in the pseudo-classic surroundings then in vogue."[2]

Neo-Classicism prevailed in the decorative arts long after the focus of the fine arts had changed. From the mid-eighteenth century and for a hundred years following, Neo-Classical motifs and scenes dominated the design of furniture, pottery and ceramics, silverware, jewelry, and buttons. A number of elements were typically incorporated, but the hallmark was the consistent symmetry; it was detailed, balanced, and formal.

A favorite Neo-Classic motif was the idealized human figure: various Greco/Roman gods and goddesses, emperors, and other luminaries were the usual subjects. In portrait paintings and sculptures of the eighteenth and nineteenth centuries, contemporary citizens were frequently posed as ancients, wearing crowns of laurel leaves and swathed in Greek chitons or Roman togas.

Classical pillars, ruins, and assorted ancient temples decorated many Neo-Classic products. Other pervasive images were formal urns, cornucopias, amphoras, ewers, lyres, arabesques, twin torches, banner-like ribbons and carefully draped swags. Wreaths of acanthus or oak leaves, perfectly-shaped clusters of grapes, and wheat stalks were popular and realistically portrayed; other plant forms, however, were always starkly stylized.

This rare Wedgwood medallion, set on a heavy iron button disc, features figures in the Neo-Classic style. Although slightly later Wedgwood pieces were molded with colored clay bodies, this very early one has a white medallion that was slip-painted with blue; the separate molded figures were added afterwards, ca.1774 to 1775. *Courtesy of Bruce and Jane Beck*

A cast-pewter button with a lyre-playing, Neo-Classic figure. The banner is also indicitive of Neo-Classic styling.

An *en grisaille* button, painted in white and grey tones on ivory and rimmed in gold, with iron back. The Neo-Classic scene features a Roman soldier carrying a large bag with a dead boar in it, French, ca. 1770 to 1790. *Courtesy of Bruce and Jane Beck*

These 'Liverpool' transfers, invariably Neo-Classic in design, are pottery buttons named after the town where transfer-decorating was perfected. They date to the early years of the nineteenth century.

Molded black glass head set in an unusually wide brass rim, ca. 1850.

A rare, Sheffield silver (plated copper) button with a repoussé Classical head, late eighteenth century.

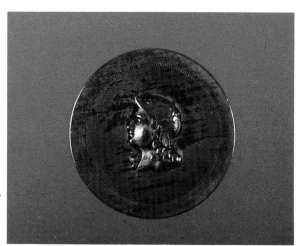

Classical heads of warriors, at left, mottled glass mounted in a heart-patterned brass rim, ca. 1880s to 1890s, and milk glass mounted in iron with a brass escutcheon head and brass rim, ca. 1830 to 1860.

Assorted heads of Classical figures including, at center, a brass button with the warrior Hector surrounded by an oak leaf and acorn border; the rest are all assorted glass buttons, ca. 1850 to 1885.

A selection of Neo-Classical heads in black glass, most ca. 1840 to 1875; in the center, mother-of-pearl with brass-escutcheon head, ca. 1860 to 1880s, and at upper right, a very early var-nished-paper lithograph set in tin, ca.1810 to 1825.

A very complex, under-glass, eighteenth-century French button with a typical Neo-Classic urn made of molded wax, reverse-painted flowers, and a foil backgound. Buttons with molded wax sculptures and figures are quite rare.

An assortment of charioteers on brass and molded black glass buttons. The cut steel, trimmed, pierced brass button at lower left features gladiators, mid-nineteenth century.

An assortment of mid-nineteenth century black glass buttons with the symmetry of design always seen in this style of art. Ewers, lyres, amphoras, urns and cornucopias—either empty or filled with formally arranged floral or wheat displays—appeared on everything from wallpaper to fine china.

Roman soldiers were a popular Neo-Classic motif; this molded brass button features a charioteer in action, with a typically classic border decoration, ca. mid-nineteenth century.

Another Classic urn on a French eighteenth-century button with a *gouache* (an opaque painting on ivory), set under glass and rimmed in brass, with an iron back. *Courtesy of Bruce and Jane Beck*

A gilded brass button with a lyre and horn surrounded by a formal wreath of oak leaves, ca. 1820s, American.

A ewer on a small, pierced brass button with a border of grapes and leaves, mid-nineteenth century.

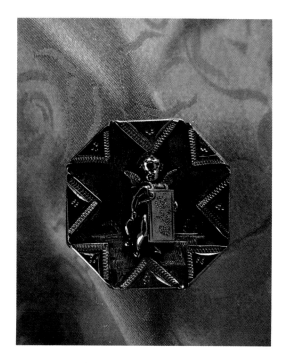

A gorgeous, very heavy, one-piece brass button of the type collectors call a 'handkerchief-corner', because of the folded-over edges. (All handkerchief-corner buttons are quite coveted.) The Cupid design, the general balance, and the hand-punched patterns on this early-nineteenth-century button are Neo-Classic in style.

Assorted conventional (as opposed to pictorial) designs on early nineteenth-century buttons. At upper left is a pierced, steel-trimmed, mother-of-pearl button; opposite, a transfer-decorated pearl. The button at center is a known as a steel cup (a concave steel body with a separate center piece). At bottom left, a faceted black glass button is set in brass and surrounded with a wreath-like cut-steel border. At bottom right is a wooden button with a steel medallion, brass escutcheon, and a cut steel star.

Early to mid-nineteenth century buttons of brass, black glass, mother-of-pearl, camphor glass, and pewter. The symmetry, wreaths, and geometric treatments are typically Neo-Classic.

5. ARCHAEOLOGICAL (PSEUDO-ETRUSCAN, ASSYRIAN (1850-1880)

Archaeologically-styled decorative-arts products were made to copy the look of Etruscan and Hellenic jewelry from the 7th to 3rd centuries B.C.. Sun signs, animal-heads, wreathes, and broad, flat leaves were among the usual motifs.

In ancient times, the goldsmiths of Etruria (now western Tuscany, Italy) were greatly admired for their technical mastery and artistry in gold-work, especially the technique known as granulation—the affixing of decorative trim made up of tiny gold beads to a gold surface. The archaeological digs of the early nineteenth century yielded examples of this work, which had until then never been seen by modern metalsmiths. The gold-granulation decorative process had been lost, but Roman dealer and jeweler Fortunato Castellani sought to revive the styles, motifs, and artistry of such pieces. He did indeed discover the long-lost methods, and his copies became world-famous, the definitive modern reproductions of this ancient technique; the process is now often just referred to as 'Castellani-style'.

A large and beautiful mother-of-pearl button with a Neo-Etruscan brass trim. The lines of the arabesques are molded to give the appearance of hundreds of tiny balls, like the much-admired granulation on original Etruscan hand-worked gold jewelry.

Etruscan jewelry often had filigree and granulation trim. This method of goldsmithing was lost until rediscovered in Italy in the early nineteenth century. These buttons of steel-trimmed brass and of silver in the Etruscan style date to the mid-nineteenth century.

The steel-bodied button at lower right has an Etruscan escutcheon over a wooden backdrop, although the central motif is Neo-Classic style. There are also a few important additions typical of the Etruscan style: the balls at the base of each radiating brass strip, this particular leaf shape, and the zig-zag pattern on the flat brass strips. The lower left button, pierced brass with a cut-steel center, features a fanned palm leaf and curved square-within-a-square border often found in Etruscan metal-work. Both of the brass buttons at the top are decorated with animal motifs, ca. early nineteenth century.

A Gothic cross of tortoiseshell inlaid with gold in a method known as picqué, 3/4", ca. 1850 to 1880.

The Gothic cross motif, portrayed in nineteenth-century buttons of various materials. The button at the top, a one-piece brass with riveted cut steels, is the classic Gothic cross design; the rest show variations. The upper left is of bone. To the right of it, and below it, center, and left, are black glass buttons. In the center is a brass with an acid-etched, reverse-painted glass center. To its right is a camphor glass button with a transfer design. In the next row is a painted milk glass button and one of pierced brass. The bottom row contains a silver lustered pierced black glass at left, a black glass inlaid 'tile' button at the right, and a brass button with a milk glass cross.

THE TWO STYLES OF ROMANTIC-MEDIEVALISM (1825-1875)

Romantic-Medievalism flourished in two simultaneous variations: Gothic-revival (Section 6), and Renaissance-revival (Section 7). European manufacturers (including button-makers) were influenced by Medieval and Renaissance jewels, architecture, and statuary, as was reported in 1839 in *World of Fashion* magazine : "The forms of our *bijous* are now entirely borrowed from the style of the Middle Ages..."[3]

6. GOTHIC-REVIVAL (Romantic-Medievalism variant) (1825-75)

The Gothic-Revival style of art was part of the general mid-nineteenth-century interest in the history and mythology of the Middle Ages. It gained impetus through the renewed public enthusiasm for Sir Walter Scott's romantic tales, the then-current popularity of Victor Hugo (*The Hunchback of Notre Dame*, etc.) and other Gothic-themed novelists.

The major art of the Gothic period (1100-1400) was church architecture. All of the other arts of the era—paintings, sculptures, stained glass, and jewelry—followed the shapes and motifs of the architecture. These same shapes, taken from the great old cathedrals of France—pointed arches, gables above window and doors, heavy iron hinges, pointed finials—were the basis of nineteenth-century Gothic-Revival art. Many mid-Victorian jewelry items, including buttons, feature such motifs.

Important elements in original Gothic architecture and art, liberally plagiarized during this revival period, were the pagan-based grotesques: ghoulish masks, devil's-heads, mythic creatures, fabled beasts, and gargoyles.

Other aspects of Gothic-Revival art were heraldic designs and ecclesiastical symbols—most commonly Gothic crosses. In France, these cross-shaped designs were often comprised of fleur-de-lis representations. Other typical decorative elements were serpents, grapes with vines and tendrils, and other lush, stylized foliage designs.

The medieval Gothic period, which had virtually ignored the human figure, ended with the advent of the Renaissance, which relied on the human figure for basic proportions in both art and science.

Dragons crafted in the Gothic manner; many fabulous animals are found on buttons, and they split rather well into those of classic mythology and those of the Medieval fantasies. The smaller button shown here is luster-finished, molded black glass; all the others are brass.

A grotesque mask, typically Gothic., on a brass button, 1870s.

The grotesque was an important feature of Gothic design, in which mask-like images, demonic figures, and frightening fantasy creatures abound. These examples from the first half of the nineteenth century include, from left to right, a steel button with a brass escutcheon, a heavy brass mask, and a demonic mask with faceted steel eyes riveted to a steel base.

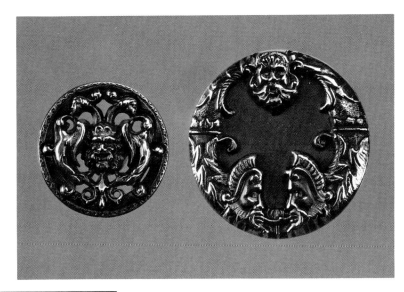

Gothic brass buttons featuring demonic images. The one at left is flanked by angels.

The brass button at the center features a design similar to ornate iron door-hinges of the Middle Ages. Each of the others has cut steel trim forming a cross design. The heavy look of the ornamentation on these mid-nineteenth century buttons is typical of Gothic style.

A lithographed button that looks like a Renaissance stained-glass rose window. This is an unusual button: its design is conventional, not pictorial, and there is no protective cover over the paper lithography, mid-1800s.

7. RENAISSANCE-REVIVAL (Romantic-Medievalism variant) (1830-75)

Through the middle decades of the nineteenth century, there was a vogue for the themes, designs, and colors found in the arts of the Renaissance period (1400-1600). The Renaissance was the apogee of stained-glass craftsmanship, and the colors common to that glass, dark blue, red and yellow, were those that the nineteenth-century romantics used in their own enamels and mosaics.

Renaissance artists were concerned with harmony, balance, the geometric precision of complex but never superfluous details, and the technical mastery of representational art, whether in paintings or sculptures; Renaissance-Revival artists delighted in copying some of the more famous works of Renaissance artists like Leonardo da Vinci, Michaelangelo, and Raphael. Buttons in the Renaissance-Revival style were designed with scenes from some of these same works.

Other buttons from the Renaissance-revivalism movement include examples with rose-window designs and assorted cherubs.

A lovely pierced silver mid-nineteenth-century button in a fine Renaissance-Revival design. The multi-pointed star, the complex but symmetrical curvilinear pattern, and the delicate overall effect are typical.

Variations of the Renaissance Revival star and rose window patterns appear on these buttons of brass, center; milk glass, upper right; and black glass. The black glass examples include an inlaid 'tile' at upper left, an engraved and gilded button at bottom left, a gold and silver-lustered button at lower right, and, above it, a molded black glass button with an iridescent luster.

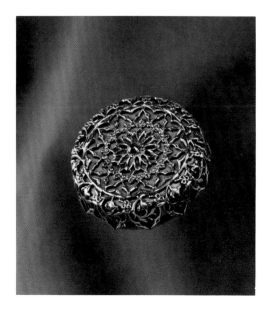

A side of the center button above, showing its unusual sheathed construction.

A lovely large iridescent pearl button, engraved with a Renaissance Revival pattern.

A deluxe painted enamel button of high quality, with foil trim and a Renaissance putti.

Glass buttons inlaid with a centerpiece of differently-colored glass with decorative foil or gilding behind it. These are highly collectible and favorites of button collectors, who call them Tingues (after a Senator who encouraged young ladies in the late nineteenth century to collect buttons). They are examples of the influence of Renaissance coloring and geometric precision on the decorative arts of that period. One tingue button is considered a prize: this whole collection is an extremely rare sight.

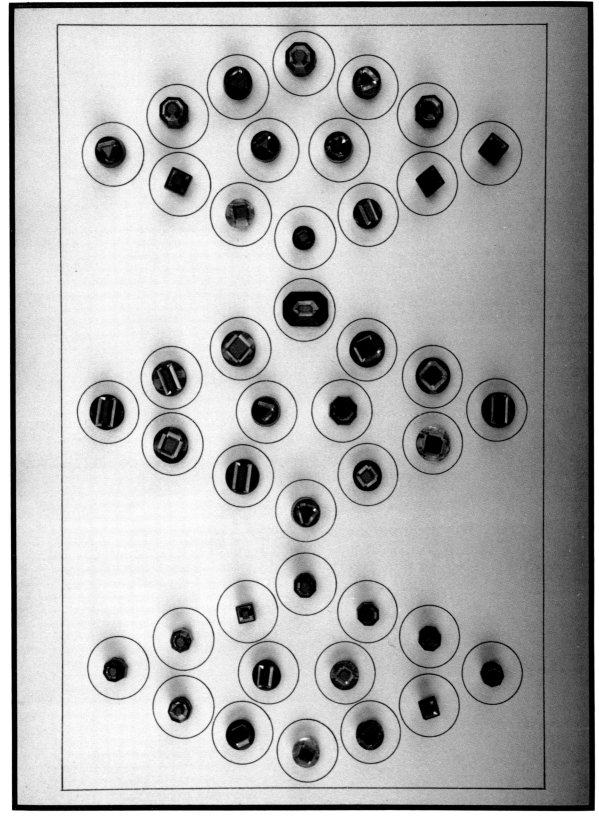

This two-piece brass button has a Gothic animal form with a lavish scroll effect.

8. HIGH VICTORIAN (1845-1880)

High Victorian was a flamboyant combination of art styles, in which elements of Baroque, Classic, and Gothic art were frequently combined in one design. Excessive, often heavy in appearance, and and rarely balanced, the High Victorian style was confined to the decorative-arts field, and mercifully rare even there. It can be argued that High Victorian was the low point of nineteenth-century design. Nevertheless, some quite attractive decorative-arts products did result from the odd juxtaposition of styles.

A really odd-looking design, this High Victorian two-piece pressed brass button has a Cupid astride a Queen Victoria-faced sphynx, surrounded with Rococo scrollwork, 1860 to 1880.

The central theme of these High Victorian buttons is a fabulous animal in Gothic style; each is surrounded by Rococo scrolls and/or shell forms. Dating from the final quarter of the nineteenth century, this group includes a milk glass at the bottom, molded black glass in the center, silver-lustered openwork-mold black glass at the upper right, and, at the lower right, an incised and pigmented grey pearl button.

Three High Victorian one-piece brass buttons of the 1850 to 1880 period. The Gothic lion's head at left has a Rococo garland of cameo-carved mother-of-pearl roses bordered with raised brass circles centered with cut steel rivets. The other two feature fabulous dragon creatures, both Gothic in appearance but with Rococo lines. The basic Neo-Classic style of the center button contrasts with the ornamented creature on it.

9. THE PRE-RAPHAELITE BROTHERHOOD (1848-1855)

Just as much a philosophical movement as an art style, led by a small group of writers, artists, and poets in England known as the Pre-Raphaelite Brotherhood, this was a reactionary art. They hated the scientific precision of the Renaissance revival and were aghast at the beginnings of the industrial revolution, seeking a return to what they thought of as pre-Renaissance Medieval simplicity. The Pre-Raphaelites were a limited group, both in size and in public acceptance; they did not appeal to the masses, nor did they want to. Within a decade, the British Arts and Crafts movement developed from the vestiges of this movement.

A painted enamel button with a Pre-Raphaelite-style lady surrounded by tendrils and flowers.

This large brass button features a Limoges-style raised enamel plaque with an Etrusacan-style inner border and a floral vine- design around the outer border. The lady is painted in Pre-Raphaelite style, almost 1 3/4". *Courtesy of Bruce and Jane Beck*

10. THE ARTS AND CRAFTS STYLE (1861-1925)

The participants in the Arts and Crafts Movement agreed philosophically with some of the romantic viewpoints and art ideals of the Romantic Medievalists, but focused their energies on craftsmanship instead.

One of the most influential members of this very lengthy art movement was England's William Morris, who founded Morris & Co. This company produced and distributed his own works along with creations of other artists who adhered to the same tenets of workmanship and design. Morris and Co.'s output included carpets, enameled objects, furniture, wallpaper, fabrics, ceramics, and jewelry. He also published beautifully-bound books.

Morris encouraged the use of a Medieval palette of deep blues, dark reds, umbres, and assorted tans and browns, along with dark woods. He also encouraged depictions of the idealized Medieval lady, usually a dark-haired and serious-looking beauty, clothed in the style of the Middle Ages.

A *champlevé* enamel button featuring a woman in Middle Age dress to create a typical Arts and Crafts style appearance.

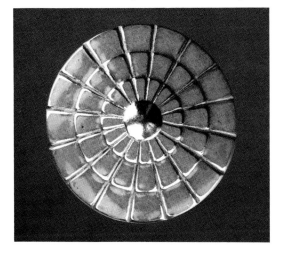

A large coat button of pewter-like metal with enamel.

Two small tin buttons with Arts and Crafts style designs. The floral design on the left has screwhead flowers, and on the right, an interpretive view of a Medieval door-hinge, ca. 1880 to 1890s.

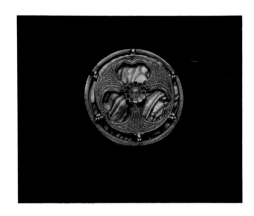

A brass, drum-shaped button with a lovely abalone shell background. The brass is molded in a manner that is reminiscent of hand-hammered Arts and Crafts metalwork. 1 1/3" in diameter.

There were other groups of like-minded artists who banded together worldwide and formed coalitions or workshops to encourage the new Arts and Crafts standard. In Germany and Austria, similar societies included the Vereinigten Werkstatte in Munich,1897; the Viennese Sezession,1897; and the Wiener Werkstatte,1903. In England and America, the Arts and Crafts movement re-established the Medieval system of guilds. The Guild of the Handicraft was started in 1887 in England by John Ruskin; a small number of button collectors have been lucky enough to find signed Ruskin Pottery buttons. The English Guild of Craftsman, 1888, and the Arts and Crafts Exhibiton Society,1888, were joined by a number of American guilds, including Tiffany's Workshop and the Associated Artists in 1879 and the Art Workers' Guild in 1880. Arts and Crafts Societies in Boston, Chicago, and Minneapolis were all established in 1897.

The Arts and Crafts ideal rejected the use of valuable materials for jewelry, intending their work to be judged for its finesse, design, artistry, originality, and craftsmanship. Silver jewelry had been out of fashion before this time, but suddenly became the metal of choice.

For centuries, jewelry and metalwork worldwide had been the sole province of masters of the trade. The Arts and Crafts Movement opened doors for a new type of jewelry designer—the craftsman or artist with little or no training in metalwork or gems who used non-traditional materials and new methods to create ornaments; Celtic-based designs were among the most frequently employed. Morris's intention was to bring art to 'the people' by surrounding them with good design in every facet of their daily existence. Ironically, however, his works were too expensive for most of the public because he refused to mechanize any of his processes.

One of best known of the Arts and Crafts design firms was Liberty and Co., founded in London in 1875 as a retail store specializing in oriental imports. Founder Arthur Liberty created an outlet for oriental-style work, including his own designs—fabrics, metalwork, and jewelry. His business grew extremely successful.

Liberty-style jewelry was of two types: first, imported Japanese metalwork and East Indian enamels set into jewelry mounts by his designers in England, and second, the store's own line of crafted sterling and enamel pieces. Liberty jewelry items marketed under the *Cymric* trademark were fine art-metal enamels produced for commercial purposes, from 1899 to around 1915.

This superb set of English silver and enamel buttons has been preserved in it's original presentation case. *Courtesy of Tadema Gallery, London*

A perfectly wonderful set of Liberty &
Co. enamel and silver buttons in their
case. The red enamel is rather unusual.
Courtesy of Tadema Gallery, London

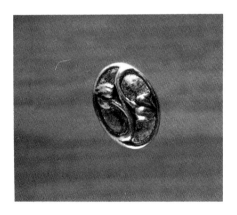

A Liberty & Co. silver and enamel
button.

Liberty & Co. silver and enamel hallmarked buttons, late nineteenth century.
The blue/green coloring of the enamel
work is typical of Liberty & Co.; the
larger button is centered with a baroque
pearl.

The back of a Liberty & Co. silver button
showing the hallmarks, the L&C logo in
diamond-shaped depressions, and the
soldered shank attachment (it resembles
a strap handle) always used by Liberty's
silversmiths. Liberty buttons are greatly
sought; they are now quite expensive
when offered for sale but if you learn the
indicators— the coloring of the enamel
work, the design motifs, the unique
backmark, and the shank attachment—
you may find a 'sleeper'.

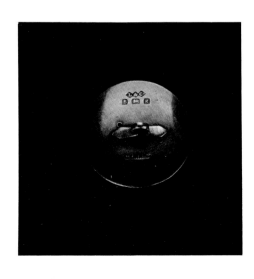

A hand-painted porcelain stud from the early twentieth century in a superb Arts and Crafts style design.

Five American Arts and Crafts style buttons seem to float above an embroidered Arts and Crafts-style linen. The two larger metal buttons are copper, one with brass overlay, and the smaller ones are brass. The most unusual one in the picture is the embroidered button, a simply marvelous interpretation of the Arts and Crafts style, ca. 1915 to 1935.

A hand-crafted, commercial, art pottery button with a crackled green glaze, this is reminiscent of work from Tulane University's Newcomb Pottery in New Orleans, almost 2", ca. 1895 to 1920.

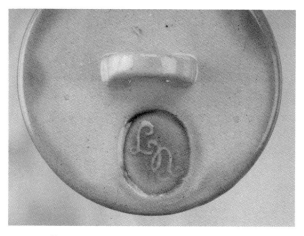

Reverse of the previous button, showing the artist's initials.

Shown with an Arts and Crafts style workshop-bound book from the 1890s are two buttons with very similar designs ,made of Bakelite with silver plated and pewter attachments, 1 1/2" each, ca. late 1920s.

These two buttons are in the Czech version of the Arts and Crafts style; at left, camphor glass, incised and colored, and at right, brass with a sheet-celluloid background, both ca. 1900 to 1920.

Also in the 'Jugend-stile', the German/ Austrian/Czech Arts and Crafts style, the patterned glass button at left and the brass one at right date from ca. 1897 to 1920.

This huge pierced, carved mother-of-pearl cape button still retains its paper label "made in France" on the reverse. Centered with a mottled blue enameled disc, it has 2 large metal shanks to help distribute its weight when sewn on. Ca. 1900. 3 1/2".

11. JAPONISME (1851-1899 and 1919-1929)

Japonisme is the name given to the occidental use of oriental motifs, lines, and styles, initially those of Japanese art. Following the Crystal Palace Exhibition in 1851 in London, at which Japanese goods were displayed for the first time in well over a century, the public wanted more of this exotic style than could be imported.

After Japan's long years of isolationism, trade with the west slowly began. The "sweeping reforms of the Meiji Resoration in 1867-68, led not only to the rapid westernization of Japan but to the export of Japanese art and artifacts to Europe and America in vast quantities in the late nineteenth century, stimulating a craze for Japonisme from 1875 onwards. Initially this was satisfied by the genuine article, but as the supply began to dry up, entrepreneurs in America, France, Germany, and Britain began to develop decorative styles which often loosely imitated (and sometimes parodied) Japanese originals."[4]

European porcelains had long been designed in imitation of Chinese potteries but many other Asian arts—the cloisonne enamels, the lacquer-work, the fancy Shakudo metal-work—were excitingly new to western eyes, and inspired direct copies as well as modified versions; western manufacturers of every kind geared up to supply Japonisme-styled articles, including many buttons.

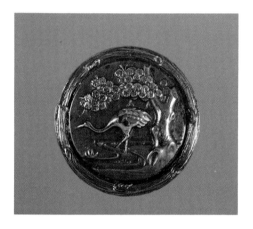

Natural blonde horn with a hand-painted Japanese scene, this button may actually be Japanese, but it may also have been painted by a European artisit imitating Japanese techniques. It is, regardless, a lovely little button, actual size, 3/4".

This little brass button is a nearly perfect blend of a Japanese block print and European impressionism.

A stunning Japonisme-styled brass picture button from the late nineteenth century.

Japanese design had significant influence on products manufactured in Europe during the last quarter of the nineteenth century. One interesting aspect of this was the use of Japanese family *mons*, or crests, not for the heraldic or identification purposes for which they were traditionally used in Japan but strictly as decorative elements. In Japan, use of these *mons* was tightly restricted to the families who had earned the right to them, but the western world used even the crest of the Japanese Imperial family with abandon: the large brass button features the Imperial mon. At the top left is a blue and white glass button; all the rest are black glass with various decorative lustered and painted finishes.

These are rare examples of true Japanese lacquer work on buttons, two with black lacquer on wood, and one with silver-lacquered fish on an ivory lapel-stud.

Many buttons made in Europe at the end of the nineteenth century were inspired by Japanese craft techniques; even more of them were influenced by the art style. These are Japonisme-styled buttons, and although two of them imitate mixed-metal work, the rest reflect only the art and not the craft tradition of Japan. The upper left example is mother-of-pearl with a brass escutcheon and below it is a painted milk glass button. The steel-bodied button at the top has a brass center decorated with gilt and copper overlays, and with steel. The three on the right are underwater scenes; two are brass and the third is iridescent-lustered black glass. Below is a highly convex, silver-plated brass button, and finally, a tiny pictorial of Madame Butterfly in silver, trimmed with enamel.

These are lithographed-celluloid buttons in imitation of Japanese lacquer work, ca. 1896 to 1905.

Celluloid buttons imitating Japanese lacquer work. Although we might think of dismissing them as 'just plastic', these two buttons actually were hand-painted with thick gilt, making them rather deluxe, ca. 1890 to 1910.

A gorgeous Aesthetic-styled, pierced silver button set with a white sapphire and two aquamarines. The leaves are overlaid in gilt. Both the design and technique of this button were inspired by Japanese metalwork, but the styling is too ornate to be faithful to Japanese art.

This *Shakudo* (Japanese metalwork in brass, gold, and silver on a silver base) button clearly shows the simplicity and elegance of line which surprised and enchanted European artists late in the nineteenth century and influenced the trend toward Aesthetic Art, followed by Art Nouveau. The Impressionists also found inspiration in the romantic, but interpretive, look of Japanese art. Darkened silver button with silver moon, copper stems, gold leaves and engraved signature, 1 1/4". *Courtesy of Bruce and Jane Beck*

Japanese *Shakudo* buttons, and a lapel stud at bottom. The metalwork is just outstanding, with copper, silver, gold, and iron used to advantage, mid-nineteenth century.

The exotic look and high level of craftsmanship in Japanese metalwork inspired the artists and the commercial designers of Europe. Many lovely buttons imitating the *Shakudo* work were made in Europe, mainly in France, from about 1880 to 1900. These French buttons in Aesthetic and Art Nouveau styles are imitations of Japanese mixed-metal workmanship, from the late nineteenth century.

The manufacturers of metal buttons were not the only ones interested in indulging the public's interest in Japonisme: these black glass buttons are each designed in complementary imitation of their mixed-metal work. The lower right example has steel and brass set into it, and the others are etched, then highlighted, with silver and gold lusters.

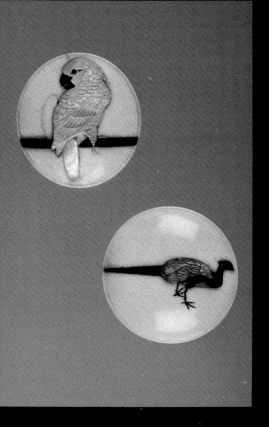

The Japanese have a traditional style of inlay, done in ivory or wood, called *Shibayama*, after the man who first used the technique. *Shibayama* inlays use mother-of-pearl, ivory, coral, horn, and other materials.

Shibayama birds in ivory.

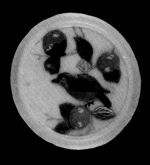

A superb and rare example of a *Shibayama* button.

Two more breathtaking inlays in ivory showing the sophistication of good *Shibayama* work. These are quite rare.

This tiny fly is amber and coral inlaid in ivory.

A grey pearl butterfly, two cranes made of mother-of-pearl, and tiny coral beads inlaid in ivory; this piece is later than the others shown and not as fine. It is not entirely inlaid; some of the design is etched and pigmented.

A painted metal button with an Impressionistic scene of a mountain, sunrise, and birds, and a cut-out center revealing embroidered fabric. Buttons like this were made in the Czech region around 1900 to 1915.

12. IMPRESSIONISM (1872-1890)

This art style began in about 1872 in France, among such now-famous artists as Claude Monet, Edouard Manet, Paul Cézanne, Hilaire Degas and Pierre Auguste Renoir. The Impressionists, as these painters were known, believed in painting not the detailed reality of a scene, but their 'first impression' of it—in other words, their emotional reaction, how they felt about a particular view. To do this, they used color and light in a brand new way: only the colors found in the natural spectrum were used, with no blacks or dark browns, and, because light itself is a determining factor in the impression of a scene (e.g., mood combined with both the actuality and the perception of a given sight), the many effects and degrees of lighting became an integral part of Impressionistic paintings.

Impressionism was the first style of modern art, the first total break with past tenets of art, and it caused a huge rift between the artists and the general public; rather than a mere progression in taste, this new art was a radical departure. The public was not alone in its dismay: art critics hated it as well. Galleries refused to even consider hanging Impressionistic works, and established artists of the old order refused to admit the 'rebels' to their salons.

Impressionistic designs featuring the sun, on a variety of buttons. The largest one is engraved celluloid, ca.1900; at the top center is a dyed brass, and to its left is a larger pressed brass example. The others are black glass buttons decorated with various lusters. A definite Japanese influence is evident in some of these.

Another blend of Impressionism and Japonisme is this celluloid wafer button with a raised design of a mountain in the moonlight, with a pine tree in the foreground. This has a Japanese appearance and conveys only the most basic emotional impression of a mountain, ca. 1900.

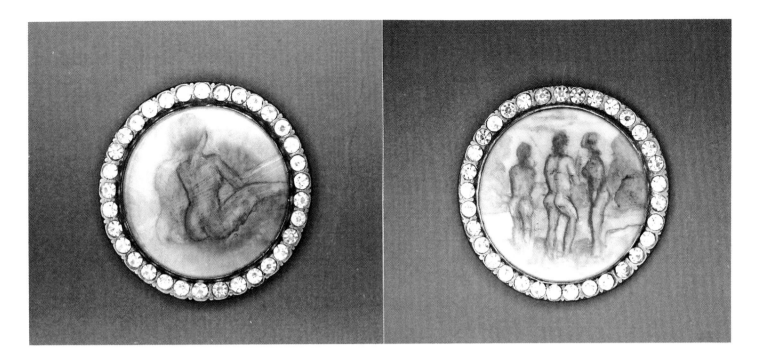

Two exceedingly unusual buttons from the last quarter of the nineteenth century, painted nudes on ivory, set under glass in brass frames, and rimmed with paste jewels. The technique is the same as that used for deluxe French buttons of the late eighteenth century. The nudes are complelety Impressionistic in style, and are nearly copies of some in the series of paintings by Paul Cezanne collectively known as "The Bathers," painted during the 1880s and 1890s. *Courtesy of Lucille Weingarten, photographed by M. W. Speights.*

13. POINTILLISM (1885-90)

Pointillism, also known as Divisionism or Neo-Impressionism, was a minor art style which grew out of Impressionism. Its basic theory contends that by closely mingling small dots of primary colors, the blending necessary to form the secondary colors will take place in the eye of the viewer, from an appropriate distance, resulting in a far more natural view of color than could be accomplished by blending them together on the artist's palette. Pointillistic paintings, therefore, are made up of thousands of little patches of paint.

Georges Seurat was the best known devotee to its theory. Pointillism flourished only for about five years, and buttons designed in this style are very rare finds.

These two buttons were intended to capture the appearance of Pointillistic art, a derivation of Impressionism. The floral design on the left button is lithographed on a sheet of celluloid set in an ornate brass frame. The sheet was textured to give the impression that each dot was individually placed. Next to it is a black glass button of a bird in flight, ca. 1895 to 1900.

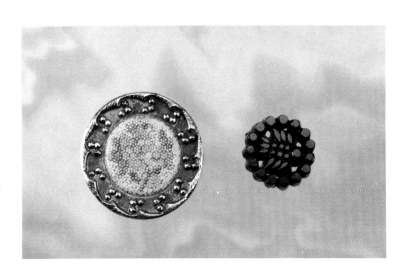

14. AESTHETIC ART (1875-1890)

The Aesthetic Art movement was as much dedicated to a particular lifestyle and mood as it was to art. Its members, an influential group of artistic and literate men—including Oscar Wilde—were known for their extreme sensitivity and their espousal of a particular standard of beauty and elegance. Their stated philosophy was "art for art's sake". This was mainly a British based art, though Aestheticism flourished for a short while in France as well.

The Aesthetics preferred very fluid lines, accompanied by graceful asymmetry. A few motifs were so well-favored that they are now strongly associated with this movement: sunflowers, long-stemmed lilies, lilies-of-the-valley, water-lilies and the moon. The semi-precious moonstone was their gem of choice.

Elements from this movement led into the Art Nouveau style. Aesthetic-style buttons are always quite lovely.

Late-nineteenth-century mother-of-pearl button, etched, gilded, and painted in the Aesthetic style.

Three sunflower designs from the late nineteenth century. At the bottom of the picture are two mother-of-pearl buttons, one cameo-carved and the other with a brass escutcheon; the delicate open-work brass button on top features a border of riveted cut steel beads and includes a moon—another motif dear to the Aesthetic movement.

A stunning large button of blackened silver with an engraved silver overlay and an inset paste 'diamond'. It is hard to imagine a more elegant button than this.

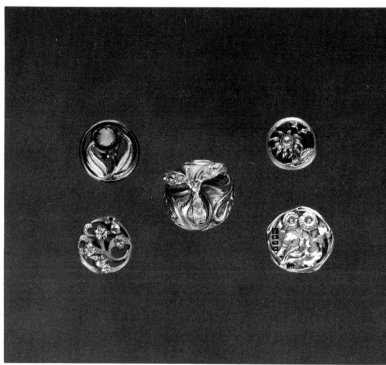

Five small buttons typifying the Aesthetic style in design and motifs; the sunflower (seen on the two buttons at the far right) was the favorite flower, and the semi-precious moonstone (upper left) the gem of choice.

15. ART NOUVEAU (1890-1912)

Art Nouveau, or "new art," swept the European and American continents beginning in 1890; by 1912 it was no longer stylish, but the effect it had on architecture, graphic arts, and decorative arts was enormous. Its designs are distinguished by entwined, sinuous lines, and by curved, flowing images—a languid, romanticized view of nature. Art Nouveau was among the most feminine of art styles.

The artists and designers of the Art Nouveau era used precious stones and gold, but also worked with less valuable metals, natural materials, and inexpensive semi-precious gemstones. For the artists who espoused Art Nouveau, the use of materials was an artistic choice, an experiment, so they used any material that suited their purposes, common or dear. This flexible attitude towards materials was part of the reason that Continental artisans—particularly jewelers—preferred Art Nouveau to the Arts and Crafts movement. "The craft ethic, so enthusiastically embraced in Britian and the United States [by the Arts and Crafts movement], was quite alien to continental taste. Almost without exception, French and Belgian jewelry designers connected with the Art Nouveau movement." [5]

Among the motifs commonly found in this style are plants and flowers, especially irises and lilies, reeds, and cattails. Swans, dragonflies, and butterflies were among other favorite natural motifs used by the designers.

Peacocks were tremendously appreciated by this style's artists. The national bird of India, peacocks had been popularized as a motif through the influence of Arthur Liberty's imported oriental fabrics and objects. The previous use of the peacock motif in the decorative arts was a head-on view, with a fully arrayed, perfectly symmetrical tail. Art Nouveau peacock-based designs took advantage of the birds' curves and colors instead.

Beautiful ladies with long, flowing hair are the most romantic and memorable of Art Nouveau images. The curving, swirling hair itself was an important element of the design.

Art Nouveau buttons abound and more than a few collectors specialize in this type alone.

Brass buttons with *plique-à-jour* (light of day) enameling, excellent examples of Art Nouveau styling. Enamels done in this technique, which resembles a stained-glass window, are the rarest type. Although these two are not deluxe compared with many enamel buttons, all *plique-a-jour* buttons are highly valued by collectors.

Art Nouveau buttons most commonly have floral motifs; the small ones shown here are all from the early years of the twentieth century. Starting with the hand-carved ivory iris at the left of the photo, the materials include brass with enamel, pewter, painted enamel, painted brass (3), tin, and plain brass.

Art Nouveau brass and enamel buttons, two with floral motifs and two with conventional (non-pictorial) designs. The square button has *émaux-peint* (painted enamel) flowers and brass wheat stalks.

These three fine Art Nouveau buttons are undoubtedly French, from the late nineteenth century. At left, a pierced silver iris is attached to the center of a large, smoky pearl; the mother-of-pearl base of the bottom button provides a beautifully shimmery setting for the convex pierced-brass waterlily; and the upper right example features an iridescent-pearl disc decorated with a dramatic black transfer design set in brass.

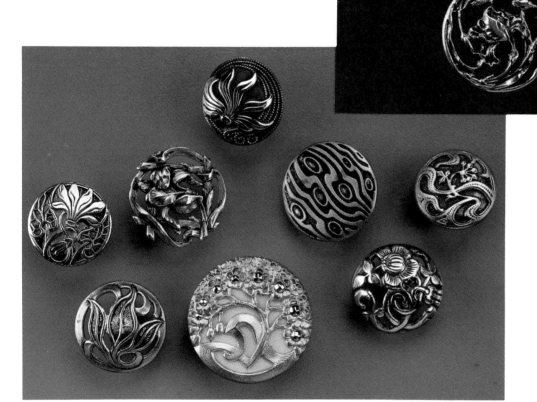

Four beautiful pierced or openwork buttons in the Art Nouveau style, including three with an iris, a favorite design of artists of this period. The two sterling silver buttons at the bottom have English hallmarks; the others are brass.

Art Nouveau floral buttons in a variety of clear, colored, and black glass. The designs were either molded or etched before being trimmed with lusters and/or paints. This type of button was made in the last decade of the nineteenth century.

Six brass and two white metal Art Nouveau floral designs that are slightly cruder than earlier examples; the buttons themselves are not deluxe, though still quite collectible. The earliest and finest one of this group is the largest, a two-piece brass button trimmed with facet-cut steels that has an imitation mother-of-pearl background made from a sheet of celluloid, ca. 1890s. The rest probably are from the end of the period, ca. 1920, judging by their cheaper construction and an overall heaviness of design.

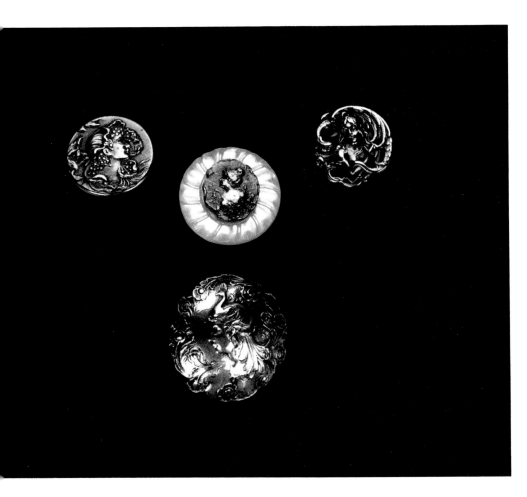

An ornately detailed molded brass head with flowing hair, typical of Art Nouveau style, attached to an extra-large celluloid wafer button.

Four Art Nouveau ladies' heads, two of brass, the bottom of plated brass, and the center of mother-of-pearl with a brass medallion in the center. The left button is 'Summer', one of the four seasons from a popular graphic of the period. Many Art Nouveau artists did sets of the Four Seasons, either as paintings, stained glass murals, sculptures, or prints.

For many collectors, the most desirable Art Nouveau buttons are those featuring the heads of beautiful ladies. Although many were made, they are rather hard to find—collectors of both buttons and Art Nouveau objects seek them with enthusiasm. The pictured examples include a silver-plated button at upper left; silver, trimmed with cut steel rivets, upper right; white metal at center; pierced brass at bottom left; an etched and dyed mother-of-pearl with a silver plated medallion set into it; and a partially gilded silver. The bat-like lady seen on the unusual button at upper right is surrounded by inlaid cut-steels to resemble a starry night sky. 1"–1 2/3".

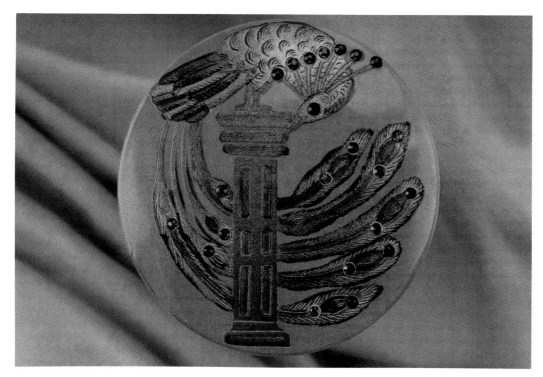

A simply fabulous, large, celluloid wafer button with an engraved and painted peacock set with paste 'gemstones', shown actual size, ca. 1895 to 1900.

Animal life on Art Nouveau buttons is far more unusual than conventional or floral designs. These very pretty period examples include two butterflies, mother-of-pearl at upper left, and molded brass at right, and a brass snake with a mother-of-pearl background.

This Art Nouveau silver-plated brass design is rare because it pictures a man, not a woman, playing a lute.

Expressionism: Fauvism and Synthesism

Expressionism refers to a stylistic departure from reality-based art, towards an emotionally-based outlook. The artists who developed this style were searching for new ways to express their feelings through their art, hence the term 'Expressionism'. Expressionistic art featured scenes with "exaggerations and distortions of line and color; a deliberate abandon of the naturalism implicit in Impressionism in favor of a simplified style which should carry far more emotional impact."[6]

Expressionists were interested in color, line, and form, but not in the Impressionists' view that light and color were inseparable and equally important. Expressionists reduced colors to the basics—intense and primal, never toned or shaded. The Dutch artist Vincent van Gogh's later works were Expressionistic, as were those of French artists Henri de Toulouse-Lautrec and Paul Gauguin, and of the Norwegian Edvard Munch. The work of the Expressionists is sometimes referred to in today's art world (where it is greatly admired) as 'Degenerate Art'. Two varieties of Expressionistic art have evolved: Fauvism (Section 16) and Synthesism (Section 17).

16. FAUVISM (Expressionism variation) (1905-1908)

Fauve, "wild beasts" in French, was the name used quite negatively to describe a small number of French artists (including Henri Matisse) and their work, beginning in 1905. It was a short-lived style, featuring an uninhibited and sometimes inappropriate use of garishly brilliant colors in scenes that are otherwise basically Impressionistic in style. The scenes were painted in a realistic 'first impression' sense, but the artist's own free-ranging, mood-centered perception of the scene was not only expressed but was greatly emphasized by means of color.

Fauvism is unusual in the decorative arts, for it never gained general public acceptance and manufacturers of consumer goods were loathe to produce items in this style. These two buttons, therefore, are quite strange. Although at first glance they may seem to be standard, late-nineteenth-century iridescent-lustered black glass, they are far more garish. The colors are shocking and discordant and the overall effect is exactly that of a scene painted by a Fauvist.

A lithographed celluloid button, classically Synthetic in its odd coloring and segmented floral pattern, ca. 1900 to 1910.

17. SYNTHESISM (Expressionism variation, Czech/German) (1899-1905 and 1915-1935)

The alternate name for Synthesism is 'Cloisonnism,' from the word *cloison*, "small cell," which explains the main aspect of this style—images sectioned into small, self-contained planes of color. (Cloisonné enamels and stained-glass pieces are much the same in concept.) The object was "the expression of ideas, mood, and emotion and the complete rejection of naturalistic representation. Their pictures were painted in brilliant colors, separated by black lines, and sought to be both decorative and the abstractions, or syntheses, of the ideas which inspired them."[7]

The Synthetists were inspired by the flat, non-shaded coloring and spatial design of Japanese wood-block prints, and by the intense, primal colors of the West Indies, Tahiti, and South America. Paul Gauguin, a French artist who was raised in Peru, and later lived in the South Seas and the Caribbean, was the most famous member of this art movement.

The original movement died out by 1905, but the Synthetic aesthetic returned to popularity between 1915 and 1935, somewhat more controlled and less garishly colored. The majority of the era's German and Czech graphic arts, and many of their decorative-art products were Synthetic in style. In fact, although many of the contemporary French and Japanese ceramics were similarly styled with bold, segmented designs, Czech ceramic products from this period are so identified with the Synthetic look that many people now refer to the whole style (innaccurately) as Czech Deco. (Deco was a Cubistic, not Expressionistic art style.)

There were Synthetic-styled buttons manufactured during both the original period of popularity and the revival. Those from the turn of the century are quite rare. The hand-painted glass or wooden examples from the 1930s—the vast majority of which were made in Czechoslovakia—are far easier for today's collectors to find.

Lithography applied directly on metal was an unusual technique, done only between 1897 and 1915. This cat, set in brass, is Expressionistic in design, exhibiting the color segmentation typical of Synthesism.

Burned and painted wooden buttons, with Synthetic colors and patterns, made in Czechoslovakia , 1930s.

These molded and/or engraved Czechoslovakian glass buttons with hand-painted details show the typical bold coloring, simplistic floral patterns, and geometric sectioning that distinguish the Czech Synthetic style, ca. 1930s.

Art Moderne

Each of the art styles specifically described in Sections 18 through 24 is part of the twentieth-century art movement known collectively by the French term *Art Moderne*.

18. CUBISM (1907-1950)

Cubism began in the first decade of the twentieth century. Though a rebellion against Impressionistic art, it was not Expressionistic either; these artists were less concerned with expressing the emotion they felt about a scene than they were in explaining it in terms of its basic makeup: shapes, planes and form. The name Cubism was first used, derogatorily, by a prominent art critic.

Artists in the Cubist movement, including Georges Braque, Pablo Picasso, and Juan Gris, attempted to paint the 'pure form' of an object. They emphasized the angles and other geometric basics in the dissected elements which, taken together, made up the movement and structure of a given subject. Cubists showed that anything that could be depicted on canvas or in sculpture (whether an object, a person, or a scene) could be broken into fundamental shapes and planes.

Not concerned with the tactile surface or the dimensional effects of shadow and contour, Cubists did not seek to effect a three-dimensional look at all. They used a certain color disonance, a remnant of Fauvism. The Cubists were also quite influenced by the forms and colors of African and Pacific/Oceanic native art. Native paintings, sculptures, and other cultural objects had never before been considered other than as archaelogical oddities or icons, but during the early decades of the twentieth century, both artists and the socially avant-garde began collecting these native artifacts as works of art.

Cubism lost favor by the early 1920s, but did lead into several off-shoot categories. (See Futuristic Streamlining (Section 19), Machine Art (Section 20), Art Deco (Section 21), and Surrealism (Section 22).)

A sterling silver button with a marvelously jagged cat .

A black and white, realistically-shaped, celluloid elephant.

An extraordinary wooden button, carved and hand-painted to look exactly like a framed picture. The Aztec head is so stylized that it is only apparent with careful study: in fact, it was purchased from a dealer who had displayed it upside down, making it seem to be just a modernistic design. The face, headdress, and feathers are broken down in basic geometric components typical of Cubism, ca. 1930.

A carved Bakelite head reminiscent of idols from the South Sea islands. The Cubistic planes and geometric treatment of oridinary forms are obvious, ca. 1930.

19. FUTURISTIC STREAMLINING (1910-1918 and 1919-1933)

Beginning around 1910 in Italy, a group of artists known as the Futurists developed a *streamlined* style symbolic of speed and electricity. Lightening bolts and zigzags, for example, were often used on a flat surface to represent power.

Eventually, the center of their philosophical and practical art would be the Bauhaus in Germany. Founded by Walter Gropius in 1919, the Bauhaus was a loosely knit, diverse group of artists. The Bauhaus building, their headquarters in Germany, was a manifestation of the Futurists' philosophies of structure and functionalism, exemplifying (and housing) their work.

These artists worked in many fields, but were united by a pledge to design art that was just as functional as it was visually pleasing. Rejecting the art styles of the past, they espoused an ethic known as 'form equals function' and strove to produce an art that, instead of being anti-mechanization, was compatible with machines, even to the point of mass-production.

A mounted grouping of celluloid buttons, all trimmed with chrome, ca. 1910 to 1920. Chrome was then a new product and not common in jewelry, including buttons, for it cost as much or more than silver-plate. These were stylish buttons. The simplicity and the chrome are part of the Futuristic stylization, with close connections to Art Deco, but more attuned to a 'machine aesthetic'. Many of the best examples of the more modern art styles are found in celluloid buttons, ca. 1910 to 1915.

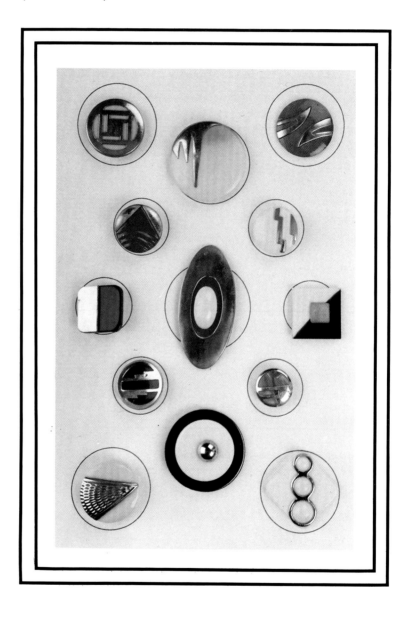

20. MACHINE ART (NEW REALISM) (1917-1935)

Machine Art was "a form of curvilinear Cubism, dependant on the dynamic shapes of machinery and their geometric bases: cones, cylinders, cogged wheels, pistons, and brilliant metallic surfaces."[8] It celebrated industry and mechanization with motifs inspired by machine parts, gears, chains, tooling, valves, nuts and bolts. The major proponent was Fernand Leger.

The large, chunky jewelry so popular in the early 1930s reflected a widespread obsession with machinery: exposed screw-heads, chrome ball-bearings, jagged-toothed cogs, and so on, were used to trim jewelry. Buttons of the era also showed the same pre-occupation with metal-trim, machinery, and heavy, solid shapes. Wood, Bakelite, and celluloid, sometimes trimmed with chrome, were the usual materials for these Machine-Art inspired buttons.

Wood, Bakelite, and black glass buttons from the 1930s and 1940s, all with the industrial Machine Art look. The assorted cog designs, wheels and notches are typical of this style.

21. ART DECO (1910-1939)

Art Deco was a nickname first used in 1925, taken from the title of a large exposition in Paris, *L'Exposition Internationale des Art Decoratifs et Industriels Modernes*, which showcased arts, crafts, manufactured products, and furnishings in the latest style. It presented a modern approach which artists, graphic designers, architects, jewelers, and manufacturers alike incorporated into their subsequent work.

The Art Deco style used "stylized abstract and geometrical forms derived from Cubist art which in turn borrowed freely from primitive art. Stepped architectural forms and motifs were drawn from Mayan, Aztec, and Egyptian cultures."[9]

The arts of Africa, and of Native-American Indians were enormously influential on the geometric patterns and pictorial designs of the style. Common motifs included the scarab, snakes, symbols of the sun, jets of water, parrots, waterfalls, and women with hair streaming straight out to the side, as though in a high wind. This was part of the artists' pre-occupation with speed: symbols of speed included diesel train engines, planes, gazelles, airplanes, greyhounds, and very fit young women.

Art Deco is distinguished more by its form and line, however, than by its motifs. The lines are angular; curves, when used, are for definition as opposed to emotion. Colors are clear and always in sharp contrast. Many colors were associated with this style: black and white, red and black, silver and kelly green were the most prevalant. The color silver was often called for in designs, and was provided by the metals platinum, chrome, aluminum, silver, and steel.

Art Deco buttons are sought as much by aficionados of the style in general as they are by button collectors. There were probably more buttons designed in the Art Deco manner than in any other art style except the Neo-Classic.

Pewter button with a fabric background and an attached pewter, Deco-styled snake.

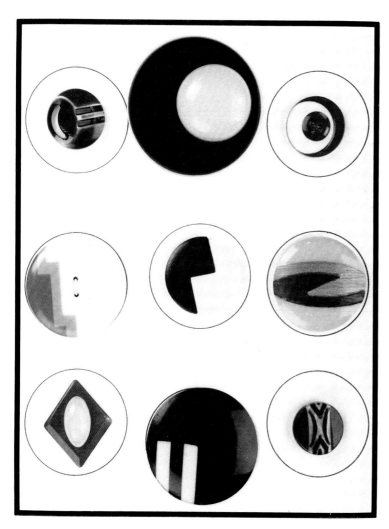

Deco-styled celluloid buttons from 1910
to 1920.

These are unique buttons! Plaster Art
Deco Chinese heads with body-like silk
tassels dangling from them, ca. 1930s.

Enameled Art Deco buttons in a Deco-
styled frame.

This group of typical Art Deco buttons includes celluloid, Bakelite, painted brass, and tooled leather.

Overleaf:
A mounted collector's card of celluloid wafer overlay buttons; these were made by layering various colors of celluloid and cutting down through the layers on an angle, thus showing all of the colors. They were copied with plenty of artisitic license from Native American Indian designs, ca. 1915 to 1930.

The jester's head is gold plastic, made by the Diamond Co. in 1938; there is a patent number on the reverse of the button.

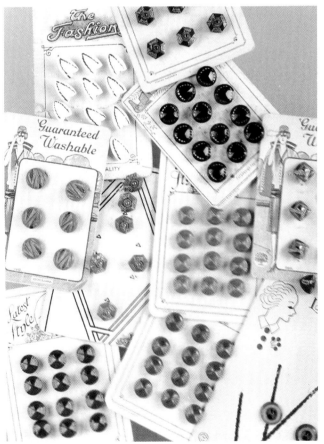

Sales cards of small dress buttons from the heydays of Art Deco.

Glass buttons with Deco-inspired designs.

This large, two-piece, brass button has a wonderfully angular design of belts and buckles.

Any pictorial button in the Art Deco style is a collector's delight. This glazed head was first sold as a molded celluloid button, then was re-issued in pottery in various colors.

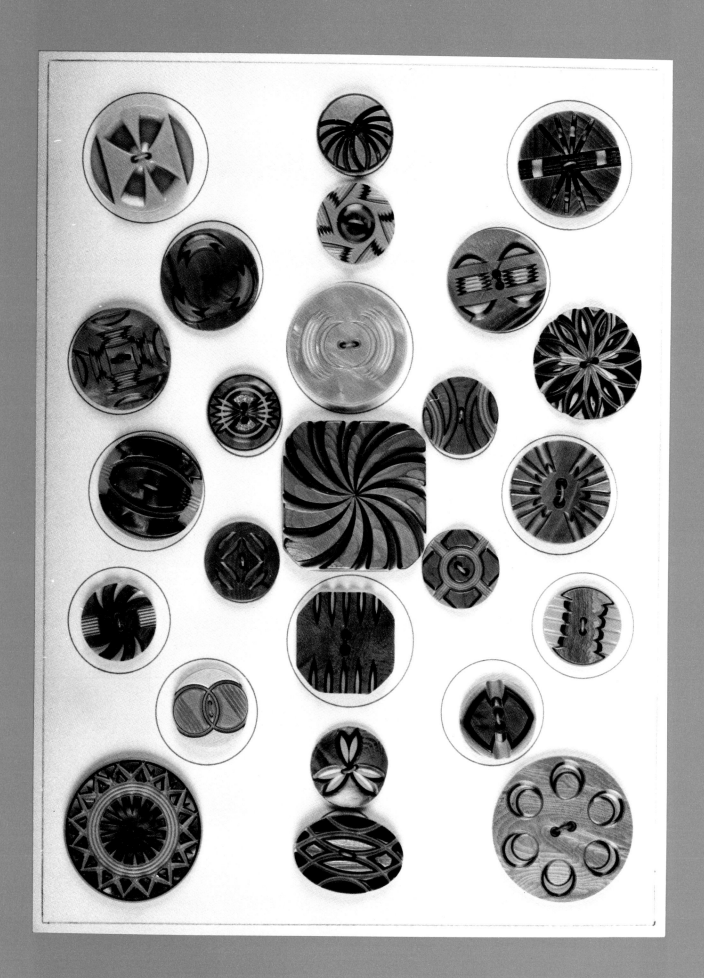

22. SURREALISM (1922-1955)

Surrealism is an elemental art style, derived from Cubism but relying on fantasy, including the absurd, the incongruous, the wierd, and occasionally the morbid. It never had the impact on the decorative arts that it's fame since would imply. Surrealism was almost entirely limited to the most radical element of the fine arts community; thus buttons with motifs that can be called Surreal are very rarely found.

Surrealism was as much an exercise of intellectual freedom as it was a fine art. Its philosophical leaders, such as Germany's Max Ernst and Spain's Salvador Dali and Pablo Picasso, intended it to be free of every normal aesthetic and moral limitation. "The object was to free artists from all accepted means of expression, so that they might create according to the irrational dictates of their subconscious mind and vision."[10]

It is difficult to fit Picasso into any one style of art because of his forays into many styles, including Expressionism and Cubism as well as Surrealism, but there are buttons that very closely resemble his work.

A rare, thoroughly Surreal button from a set of brass realistics with colored deal transfers of the covers of the era's major magazines

One of the themes common to Surrealistic art was the disembodied hand. Unlike the hand images prevalent in the Victorian era, the Surrealistic hand was mystical, quite unconnected to even an unseen body, and vaguely disconcerting or threatening. This small West German glass button with stylized hands was made during the mid-1950s.

Images of impossible happenings were one of the essentials of Surrealism. This white metal, imitation sew-through button is tranformed from ordinary to Surreal by the totally unexpected and completely misplaced leaves sprouting through the fake button holes. This design is reminiscent of Maz Ernst's works.

A high-quality carved Bakelite button with a most unusual design—a detailed, feathered wing that appears to be attached to a hose! Very Surrealistic in this odd juxtaposition, ca. 1930s.

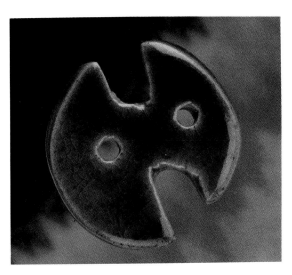

A cast ceramic material, deeply incised with a Picasso-like horse under the blazing sun, is Surreal in design.

Very suggestive of a face, this glazed ceramic button features one of Surrealism's often-encountered themes: a face, and especially the eyes, in a distorted, dream-like manner.

Engraved wooden button with a design reminiscent of Pablo Picasso's early Surrealistic works. The near-face effect also shows in this design.

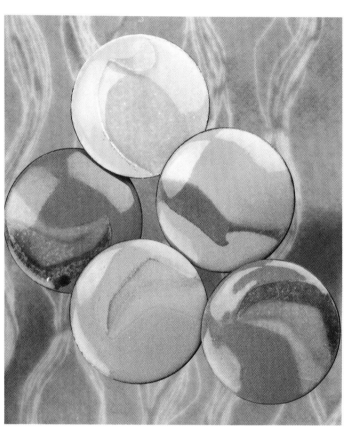

Wooden tubular beads dangle from a hole in this wooden button to create a simple, abstract design.

23. ABSTRACT ART (1912-1960)

Abstract Art is based on the belief that the only artistic values are those that "reside in forms and colors and are entirely independant of the subject of the painting or sculpture."[11] Therefore, Abstract Art is not representational (pictorial or scenic) in appearance, though it may be in the artist's mind.

Abstract Art buttons are striking designs able to stand alone as tiny works of art. See also Geometric Abstract Art (Section 24) and Fifties Style (Section 26).

Bakelite and chrome abstract button, 1 1/2", late 1920s to 1930s.

Abstract art buttons, very large and enameled on heavy copper; these were custom made by an artist for a woman's coat, 2", 1950s.

These sew-through buttons would have been ideal for a lady of the 1950s who was not only stylish but artistically avant-garde. The two white plastic buttons at the top were overlaid with a layer of colored plastic and cut on the bevel. The abstract design of the mottled ceramic button stems from the judicious application of shiny red glaze.

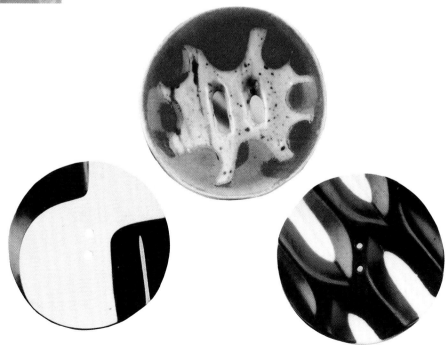

24. GEOMETRIC ABSTRACT ART (MONDRIAN) (1920s-1940s)

The Geometric Abstract style of painting is so associated with artist Piet Mondrian from Holland that it is sometimes simply called 'the Mondrian style'.

Mondrian's Geometric works represent complete Abstractionism. He limited himself to the most abstract of all techniques, using only straight lines and blocks of color in balance, though not necessarily symmetrical. Mondrian used only the three primary colors (yellow, blue, and red) and the non-colors (black and white) in his paintings in the Geometric Abstract style.

Piet Mondrian's work was widely copied in the fine and decorative arts. These buttons, Bakelite on the left and glass on the right, dating from the 1930s and 1940s, show this basic look of neo-Plastic design.

Another 1950s glass button with a Mondrian-style pattern.

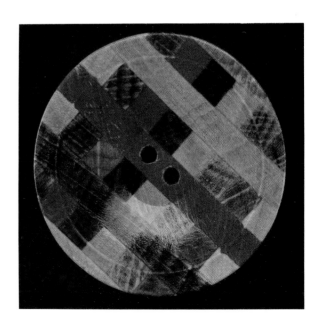

A large, laminated wood button with different strips of colored woods forming a Mondrian-style pattern.

The horse in Swedish Modern forms; buttons of ceramic, pottery, white metal, pewter, and white glass from the 1960s.

25. SWEDISH-MODERN (1957-1968)

Swedish-Modern was primarily a decorative-arts style—only to a much smaller degree a fine-arts style—which is associated with Swedish furniture design. It epitomized minimalistic sophistication, and for several years the entire home-decor industry was under its influence. Various graphic arts were also widely involved.

Representational art from this period was drawn in a simple, clean-lined, almost child-like manner and color was kept to a minimum. But whether a conventional design, or pictorial theme, the look was rather stark.

During the late 1950s and early 60s, when the influence of this style monopolized the decorative arts, buttons were not in fashion and manufacturers produced few of interest. Nevertheless, a dedicated collector will be able to find buttons from this era that reflect the Swedish-Modern style.

Two Modernistic button designs, of aluminum at left and of brass at right, ca. 1965.

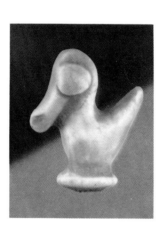

A modern art duck of blue-glazed pottery with a metal loop shank embedded in the reverse, 7/8", 1950s.

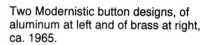

Opposite page right:
A black wire 'fifties-style' frame is the setting for an assortment of typical motifs, including the dart, the boomerang, and faux-Formica©. All are glass buttons except for the upper-right plastic one, and the orange one at center.

Opposite page, far right:
West German glass factories supplied the Western world with a huge quantity and variety of buttons throughout the 1950s and into the early 1960s. All of these buttons are molded and/or painted glass with 'fifties' designs, except for the large engine-turned wooden button. The polka dots, radiating lines, and intersecting circles are typical of this style.

A thin, cut-out brass button with tulip design, ca. 1960.

26. FIFTIES STYLE (1952-1960)

What we now call the Fifties Style is a variety of abstract decorative art, defined by color, material, shape, and pattern. The most prevalent colors of the era were orange and turquoise, followed by pink, gray, black, and red, all used with great exuberance. Polka-dots in bright primary colors were commonly used on all types of items, from housewares and curtains to clothing; buttons were no exception.

Among the important new materials associated with the Fifties Style is plastic laminate, or Formica. It was invented in the mid-1950s, and it created a sensation that is difficult to imagine today. Formica was such a hit with the public that many other consumer products—shoes, handbags, kitchenwares, jewelry, and buttons—were manufactured in faux-laminate materials. Laminates, originally conceived as substitutes for costlier materials, were themselves copied, in glass or various other plastics.

The shape that typified the Fifties-Look was the boomerang. Said to have stemmed directly from World War II camouflage designs (called 'disruptured patterning' in British War Department doublespeak!) the boomerang design was also known as free-form, or the amoeba pattern; it certainly owes part of its development to the Abstract Art movement as well, and to the then-trendy artist's-palette motif. The boomerang was ubiquitous; coffee tables, ashtrays, and swimming pools in this shape typify Fifties-style design.

Other important patterns were randomly scattered dart-like shapes, and intersecting, asymmetrical triangles. The cherry-on-a-stick remains one of the most instantly recognizable elements of the Fifties Style; derived from models of atomic and molecular structure—a quite new and exciting image in the 1950s—it formed the basic design of countless wall-clocks, lamps and furnishings. The 'H' shape of television aerials, in many variations, was also adapted as a decorative-arts motif, one exclusive to Fifties-Style art.

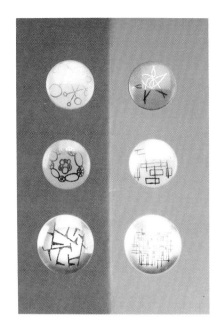

Medium-sized glass buttons with gold-colored transfer designs, extremely indicitive of 'fifties' design. At upper left is the 'cherry-on-a-stick' motif; the other two blue buttons plus the bottom right one are based on the 'H' shape that evolved from the new look of television antennas. 1"–1 1/4".

Plastic button with a red transfer of lips. Though there is no instrinsic value in this button, it is unusual in subject matter and therefore collectible, ca. 1960s.

Wooden button with hand-painted cartoon-like figure reminiscent of the style of *Terry and the Pirates* and other strips. These 1930s and 1940s characters became design motifs under Pop Artists, ca. 1964.

Glass buttons from West Germany showing the look of 'super-graphics' usually found on walls!

1960s

There were three distinct new art styles in the 1960s: Pop, Op, and Psychedelic. Aside from the rhyming names of the first two, there was no other similarity between them. All three of these styles were commercially employed. The Psychedelic art of the nineteen-sixties was as much a function of culture as of art, and is discussed in Chapter 14, The Late 1960s and 1970s.

27. POP ART (1966-1975)

Pop Art set the standard for commercial art success in the 1960s. No other style of art has been quite so exploited or exploitive. The appelation 'Pop' stood for popular, and indeed it was.

Pop Art celebrated the mundane, in an urban, and urbane, way; it was stark, blatant, and brightly colored. The high priest of pop kitsch, painter Andy Warhol, elevated the tomato soup can to icon level when he made it the theme of a famous series of paintings. His images of Marilyn Monroe and multiple photo-lithographs of other celebrities peered out from framed works of art. Warhol and other artists mass-marketed countless reproductions, as 'limited edition' fine art. This element of Pop Art never had any great impact on the decorative arts, and buttons along these lines are particularly rare.

A second major theme for Pop artists was the comic art of the 1930s and 1940s. Roy Lichtenstein was the champion of this style. His works re-popularized the comic strip style and re-introduced Depression-era comic-book heroes to a whole new generation. Lichtenstein's work became a favorite theme of graphic artists, television and print advertisements. Still, buttons with this sort of image are rare.

The Pop Art style included one more important variation, the 'super graphic'. Super graphics began in the fine arts field as simple and stark paintings that featured a single bold, exacting ribbon of color traveling across a huge canvas, or even across several canvases hung in a row. These paintings became popular with decorators. Artists specializing in super graphics also found commercial success painting huge, simple lines or great, broad strokes of color directly on white walls, as seen in corporate lobbies, airport hallways, large modern apartments, and so on. Sometimes the graphic went up or down, across, and even around corners, onto the next wall.

Super graphics were copied by industry designers for wallpaper applications, furnishing and housewares. Before long, platters were adorned with nothing more than a bright streak of color leading off the edge, and linens featured plain-colored backgrounds with just a slash of contrasting color as the focal point.

Jewelry and button designers found ways to apply the super-graphic effect to their small 'canvases' as well; without the added dimension of impressive size, however, the look had limited appeal. Examples of super-graphic Pop Art jewelry or buttons are already scarce.

28. OP ART (1966-1975)

Op Art came into style around 1966 and lasted into the early 1970s. It found great acceptance in the fine-arts field as artists worldwide—working in all mediums—embraced it and experimented with it. The decorative arts never became so saturated with it as did the fine arts, but some manufacturers did produce Op Art products, buttons among them.

'Op' stands for optical, and is a succinct expression of the intents of artists working in this visually stimulating style. Op artists were creating optical illusions, art that would seem to move and pulse while you gazed steadily at it. One of the tenets of Op is that the eye of the viewer is a part of the artwork itself; the eye actually activates the design. And as in many optical illusions, the retinal memory, or after-image, added extra lines, movement, and dimension to the picture.

Good examples of Op Art are difficult to look at; they force your eyes to see movement that is not there, lines that do not exist, and patterns that seem to jump out. A classic work of Op Art does not let the eye rest; unless you glance away, you are drawn around and around within the picture. Other designs effect your depth of vision, pulling your focus in and out. Some people actually get dizzy when confronted with a work of Op Art. Even a muted, less intense work of Op Art must induce at least a mild degree of disconcertion and eye involvement.

Op Art is not pictorial, but rigidly controlled, exacting design. Whether made from many closely spaced lines, tightly cocentric rings, tiny intersecting squares, or grids of endless dots, it is repetitious and usually symmetrical. The artist had to pre-plan and carefully execute his conception; if a line was the tiniest fraction of a space off, or an element misplaced, the illusion was broken. The eye would not be compelled to move continually about, but would instead land on the error and take refuge.

"Typical 'Op' of the 1960s used hard-edged black/white patterns with moiré dazzle effects which, being easily reproducible, became commercially popular."[12] ("Easily reproducible") means well-suited to machine-copying, for there was nothing easy about the exacting execution of the original!

When colors other than black and white were used, it was not for their beauty but for increased optical effect. Certain colors, when spaced closely in narrow lines, added an overall shimmer to the work, or, used in blocks, forced the vision to switch back and forth between them.

Op Art worked better as a fine art than as a decorative art. Its use had to be tempered for general consumption; Op was best appreciated in small doses. It was far easier to deal with the disconcerting optics of an oil painting on the wall than it was to try to live within a room lined with Op-Art wallpaper. Decorators and manufacturers soon found that people had to be able to get away from the art style, to let their eyes escape—immediately—to a peaceful view. So, even though it was commercially popular, Op designs were used as decorative accents or focal points only.

This limitation was perfectly suited to both jewelry and clothing buttons, and there were many wonderful Op Art buttons produced, the best by German designers. The iridescent glass buttons made by the West German glass industry in the 1960s (collectors call these 'auroras') were quite often patterned with outstanding optical designs.

An Op Art painting is the backdrop for two sets of Op Art buttons, The left group of white metal and the others of plastic composition set in brass, ca. 1965 to 1969.

Iridescent modern glass buttons from West Germany of the type collectors call 'Auroras'. An amazing number of these, popular in the mid-1960s, are in perfect Op Art patterns; the iridescence actually adds to the effect in many cases. Also included are metal and plastic buttons.

29. THE COUNTRY STYLE (1976-1990)

The cow is modelled from polymer clay and is typical of the friendly, almost anthropormorphized images of cattle that flooded the decorative arts field during the late 1980s and early 1990s.

During the late 1970s, the Country Style came into vogue. Its impetus came from the return-to-the-land lifestyle of the ex-hippies and their new crafts-based economy, but before long, the nostalgic view of the simpler life of the rural folk began to hold great appeal for the discouraged middle-class population of the United States. The nation was undergoing a general re-apprasisal of its values and goals, struggling to regain its sense of peace following the Vietnam War and the social unrest of the late 1960s. A vogue for Country-Styled clothes, crafts, and home decor quickly spread through the general population and blossomed into a huge decorative trend. Country-Style remained one of the premier influences on the decorative arts throughout the 1980s, but with continually evolving variations: French Country, English Country Garden, and American Country West.

The Country Look was strictly a decorative art, with no fine arts adjunct. Laura Ashley's™ floral prints, and white geese with blue neck ribbons, ruffled curtains, cows (cows and more cows), dried herbs and flowers, hearts, Pennsylvania-Dutch symbols, crazy-quilts, and the old wooden toys and teddy bears of childhood reign as the most pervasive of the Country motifs. Buttons with these themes have been produced by button companies worldwide.

The Country Look has made a minor impact on button design during the last two decades. Popular Country motifs include those shown here—barns, covered bridges, farm animals; Pennsylvania Dutch themes include the five lower buttons along the left of the photo: the milkmaid, the double flower in a heart, the distelfink birds, and the horse and buggy. In addition, at least one manufacturer and several individual artisans have produced buttons featuring classic quilt patterns. The quilting buttons by Danforth Pewterers were part of an extensive line of Country-inspired designs produced during the late 1980s and into the 1990s. The wooden marquetry, quilt-patterned button at the lower right was made by an individual craftsman.

30. THE SOUTHWEST STYLE (1930-1950 and 1983-Present)

The Southwest Style had its roots in the 1930s, when such artists as Ted de Grazia and Georgia O'Keefe took up residence in Santa Fe, New Mexico and began painting and living according to the traditional local style. Before long, the Southwest Style began to travel back east. The impressions Native American crafts made on the public were not lost on commercial manufacturers. By the 1940s, these motifs were being featured on a wide range of commercial products.

It was during the early 1980s, however, that Southwest Style became a major decorative and fine-art trend. It began with a renewal of interest in the artists who had been inspired by the American Southwest's muted, sun-drenched colors, its flora, fauna, landscapes, sky, and people. This resurgence was quickly combined with a renewed interest in Native American tribal arts.

The Southwest Style evolved throughout the decade, and by 1990 had become more vibrant and less precisely wedded to the past: a refreshing sense of humor had begun to show up within the framework of the newer designs. In addition, though long noted for tan, turquoise and pastel sunset colors, the Southwest Style has expanded its palette to include earthy browns, burnt umber, bright orange/reds, tangerine, deep yellow, black and white, plum, dark green, and a much more intense turquoise.

Favorite motifs and patterns include those taken from woven Native American blankets and throws, as well as their painted pottery, stick-figure art, sterling jewelry designs and symbolic drawings. In addition, stylized versions of local flora and fauna appear on many Southwest-Style decorative-arts products.

Recent buttons with Southwest motifs and colors have been manufactured not only by American firms, but by German and Japanese button companies as well.

An iguana on iridescent gold-foil, fused to glass. A beautiful button that fits right in with the mania for Southwest-style decor. 7/8", ca. 1990s,.

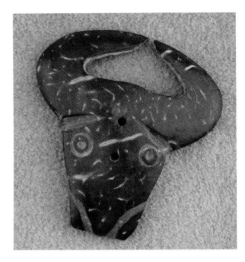

A coconut-shell steer's head. 1 1/3", ca. 1980s.

An overlaid plastic button from Germany with a design reminiscent of Native American Indian art, and Danforth pewter buttons shown at the right with Southwest interpretive designs.

White metal blazer buttons in three sizes, with Southwest-style designs based on Native American patterns; and a very simple, yet striking, design in a copper button with copper wire woven through holes along the edge, ca. 1992.

Plastic button molded in relief with a long-horned steer and cattle brand design. Buttons styled with the look of the American Southwest were in popular use throughout Europe and Japan, ca. 1990.

A Raku-pottery button with a gorgeous multi-iridescent glaze. The Seguaro cactus shown was a most popular theme with the Southwest-style designers, 1 1/2", ca. 1990. *Courtesy of Blue Moon Button Art.*

31. MEMPHIS-STYLE (NEW-WAVE) 1984-1990

New Wave (or Memphis-Style) design made quite an entrance in the 1980s. Though its appeal was far from universal, it quickly took the decorative-arts field by storm, dominating design for much of the decade. It was hard to miss; jarring, vivid, exuberant, playful, outrageous, and eccentric, the overall intent was to impart a sense of fun into functional design. The colors, shapes, motifs, and patterns were purposely mismatched; at its best, the New Wave style was completely unpredictable.

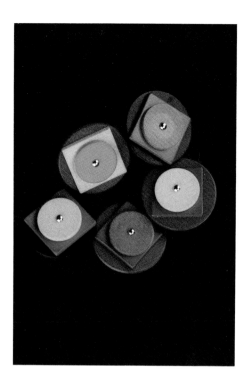

Following on the heels of the earth-toned 1970s, when quiet, natural, muted, monotone, clean-lined, and minimal were watchwords, the new look was absolutely shocking. It first appeared in 1981, in the odd furniture and colorful housewares of the Italian design collaborative Memphis/Milano. Other artists and design firms worldwide began to create furnishings and sculptures in the same mode. In America, the Philadelphia-based architecture firm of Venturi, Rauch and Scott Brown was at the forefront with a line of uniquely patterned and colored furniture.

Originally christened 'New Wave', by the mid-1980s the style was known simply as 'Memphis', acknowledging the undisputed leaders of the field, the design team from Milan.

According to Richard Horn, Senior Editor of *House Beautiful*, Memphis-Style designs can be distinguished in three ways.

Memphis style buttons of plastic in three layers, each with a pin shank through center. The discordant juxtapostion of colors was a dominant feature of Memphis or New Wave design, 7/8", 1985 to 1990.

"First, they are usually not 'period'—that is, they are not based on earlier traditional patterns [but] spring afresh from the designer's head...If any other models are used, they are obscure ones...from various parts of the world [or from industrial] elements of the urban...environment that we don't [usually consider] decorative.

"Secondly, the 80s patterns tend to be very colorful. Sometimes they resound with primaries: red, yellow, and blue. Other times, the tones are more unusual: candy-colored pastels, grayish pastels, or ultra-bright, intentionally synthetic-looking Day-Glo tones.

"Thirdly, the patterns themselves...tend to be hard-edged. There are no fuzzy outlines or blurry forms here. Instead the lines jump and pulse, and the shapes are strongly defined. Together, they create what some call a visual equivalent of rock music."[13]

The exuberant motifs and various shapes were often juxtaposed in odd combinations quite unlike any seen before in the mainstream of decorative arts. Memphis was not a look for the faint of heart.

Clear plastic round and triangular Memphis-style buttons. The Memphis look of these single-colored buttons comes only by combining a group of these in various color combinations on one outfit. Seen individually, they are not particularly New Wave in effect, except for their peculiarly fluourescent-looking colors, 1", 1985 to 1990.

Opposite page:
With a Memphis-print scarf as a background, an assortment of Memphis buttons from the late 1980s; From left, top row: plastic triangles, one with faux granite, a pink and blue fused glass button, two oddly colored boomerang-shapes in pearlized plastic. At bottom left, a group of three plastic buttons with cut down and painted areas, an interesting set from Japan with assymetrical holes and geometric shapes, and a tooled and painted leather example, at right. Large triangle top left. *Courtesy of Debra Hill*

A column in *Metropolitan Home* magazine (1986) begins: "A houseful of Memphis furniture is more than anyone should have to endure...," referring to the 1986 movie *Ruthless People* with Danny DeVito and Bette Midler, where the set designers filled the couple's screen mansion with Memphis furniture, accessories, art, and sculpture. The production designer "...wanted Midler and DeVito's home to have a threatening, obnoxious quality."[14]

This is typical of the love-hate relationship Memphis-Style design had with the press and the public. Calling it playful, zingy, zany, zesty, lively, vibrant, shocking, exciting, stimulating, energetic, etc., the design critics and fashion mavens sang its praises, but also saw its limitations. The decorating magazines of the mid-1980s were suggesting the judicious use of just one piece of Memphis art or furniture in a room, for impact; no one pushed a unified Memphis look!

Furniture design was where Memphis was at its most outrageous. The general public simply never took to the furniture, but by the time the style filtered into the decorative arts, it softened slightly; the out-of-the-ordinary housewares and Memphis-look fabrics became quite popular. Ready-to-wear clothing, linens and domestics, jewelry and buttons, electronic products, wallpaper, floor rugs, commercial art and advertising, toys, and graphic design all showed the Memphis influence.

Memphis as an art form died out late in the 1980s, but its impact on the clothing and jewelry industries continued into the 1990s.

Memphis-Style buttons were never produced in great numbers, but some of the major button firms worldwide did make wonderful examples. Seen individually, many of the Memphis-Style buttons would appear to be simply geometric or brightly colored, but used in a variety of colors on one outfit, and sewn so that each slants differently, the effect is typically Memphis.

The European public was more appreciative of Memphis designs than Americans were; many of the buttons in this category were made and used there. Others were manufactured in Japan. Very few were put out by American button firms.

No metal object made during the Neo-Stone Age mania was safe from this fake verdigris! Here it has been applied to a copper electro-plated plastic button, ca. 1990.

Electro-plated plastic buttons with the multi-textured surface look common to items decorated in Neo-Geo manner, 1 1/4", ca. 1990.

The Neo-Geo look of peeling wall surfaces and layered granite, slate, and so on, is copied in these examples. The bottom two are ceramic buttons with layered glazes; the top is plastic with a rough, pebbly top coating, ca. 1990.

32. NEO-STONE AGE (LIFE AMIDST THE RUINS) (1980s)

A small but significant style of design began early in the 1980s and faded away before the end of the decade. Although it was international, it was a fragmented movement without leadership, appealing only to a sophisticated audience of decorators, commercial artists, and upwardly mobile, young urbanites. It was sometimes called the 'Venetian' look; others termed it 'Neo-Stone Age'. I like to call it 'So Faux'.

This style was a reaction to the minimalist modernism of the 1970s. Designers wanted to return to basics, so they re-invented the classics, but with a decidedly '80s spin: illusion. The *effect* was far more important than reality.

The look was old. Very old. Ancient, in fact. Walls were purposefully faded and distressed, cracked and broken marble pillars were preferred to new ones, and metal without verdigris was worse than no metal at all.

Artists learned to use new finishes, paints and lacquers to reproduce the look of crumbling stone walls, corinthian columns, and faded *trompe l'oeil* friezes on walls of high-rise apartments.

The term *faux,* "fake" or "false," was spoken with religious reverence: faux marble floors, faux granite countertops, faux furniture finishes, faux stone walls featuring fragments of faux frescoes. The fake marble furniture and cast-plaster Corinthian columns were often more costly than the genuine article. Another new phrase that entered the vocabulary—'frankly fake', meaning that a piece was not done well enough to be truly *faux* and was an obvious fraud—was always stated as if it were a positive.

Faux verdigris was the most ubiquitous of all. A dusty, distressed green coating was added to almost anything metal: vases, bookends, bird cages, lamps, candlesticks, even buttons. This green became the dominant color of the movement. Glass items were also invariably green; cloudy and pale, they were encrusted so that they would look as though they had been excavated.

The other colors that set the mood for Neo Stone-Age were deep gray tones, white, and various stone, granite or marble-colored basics.

The man-made archaeology—ruins and relics, painted friezes, oxidized iron—the textures, and colors all contributed to the desired goal: escape into a fantasy of faded grandeur.

Relatively few personal articles were designed in the Neo Stone-Age style. It was not a look with wide public appeal and the vast majority of commercial designers and manufacturers ignored it. Nevertheless, some buttons from Europe and the U.S. did reflect the spirit of this short-lived style.

The look of the Neo-Stone Age is apparant in this small group of buttons that were commercially available in the early 1990s: Roman pillars in electro-plated plastic and a faux-marble plastic button with an attached metal strip engraved with Roman numerals.

Footnotes

Chapter 1 : none

Chapter 2:

1. Cobb, Richard, General Editor, and Jones, Colin, Editor, *Voices of the French Revolution*, Salem House Publishers, Topsfield, MA,1988, p.139. An excellent book for those who find history too dry; its spirited chronological account of the Revolution is laden with intriguing information.

2. Simon, Schama, *Citizens, A Chronicle of the French Revolution,* Alfred Knopf, New York, NY, 1989, p.604.

3. Schama, Simon, ibid. p.414. The full story of Palloy is quite astounding, very funny, and far to involved to tell here. I encourage readers to enjoy this, and other stories in Schama's wonderfully detailed narrative with a cultural/social view of the Revolution.

4. Schama, Simon, ibid., p.416.

5. Schama, Simon, ibid., p.557.

6. Schama, Simon, ibid,. p.557.

7. Schama, Simon ibid., p. 846-47.

8. Cobb and Jones, op.cit., p.229.

9. Cobb and Jones, ibid., p.229.

Chapter 3:

1. Schama, Simon, op.cit., p.24.
2. Cobb and Jones, op.cit., p.242
3. Halliday, Richard, "I Lift My Lamp Beside the Golden Door", *American Heritage* Magazine, Feb.1966, p.37.

Chapter 4:

1. Sullivan, Edmund, *Collecting Political Americana*, Crown Publishers, Inc., New York, NY, 1980, p.3.

Chapter 5: None

Chapter 6:

1. Spencer, Robin, *The Aesthetic Movement*, Studio Vista, London, and E.P.Dutton & Co., New York, NY, 1972, pp.132,135

2. Phillpotts, Beatrice, "Victorian Fairy Painting", *Antique Collector* Magazine, 7/78, p.81.

3. Phillpotts, Beatrice, ibid., p.81.

4. Phillpotts, Beatrice, *The Book of Fairies*, Ballantine Books, New York, NY, 1979, p.4.

5. Schama, Simon, op.cit., pp.97-98.

6. Sutton, Denys, *Fads and Fancies*, Wittenborn & Company, New York, NY, 1979, p.132.

7. Sutton, Dennis, ibid., p.132.

8. Gere, Charlotte, *Victorian Jewellery Design* (sic), Henry Regnery Company, Chicago, IL, 1972, p.225.
9. Ashdown, Marie, "Opera Momentos", *The Encyclopedia of Collectibles*, Volume O-P, Time-Life Books, Inc., 1979, p.43.

Chapter 7:

1. Covales, Virginia, *1913; An End and a Beginning*, Harper & Row, New York, NY, p.225.

2. Kennett, Frances, *The Collector's Book of Fashion*, Crown Publishers, New York, NY, 1983, p.34.

3. Frye, Helen, "The Automobile and American Fashion", a chapter from the book *The Automobile and American Culture*, Lewis and Goldstein, Eds., The University of Michigan Press, Ann Arbor, MI, 1983, p. 54.

4. For further information, refer to an excellent article on Peary buttons in the July, 1985 *National Button Bulletin*.

Chapter 8: none

Chapter 9:

1. Baker, Lillian, *One Hundred Years of Collectible Jewelry*, Collector Books, Paducah, KY, 1978 (updated 1986), p.6.

2. Bomar, Edna, from her lecture "Forget Me Not", quoted in the "Antique Review Preview" of the October 1, 1989 *Antique Review* Magazine, Worthington, Ohio, p.19.

3. Gere, Charlotte, *American & European Jewelry, 1830-1914*, Crown Publishers, Inc., New York, NY, 1975, p.56.

4. Bomar, Edna, op.cit., p.16.

5. Flower, Margaret, *Victorian Jewellery*, A.S. Barnes and Company, Inc., South Brunswick, NJ, p.22.

Chapter 10:

1. Hillier, Bevis, *The Decorative Arts of the 40's and 50's; Austerity/Binge*, Clarkson N. Potter, Inc., New York, NY, 1975, p.50.

2. *Our Century, 1920-30*, David S. Lake Publishers, Belmont, CA, 1989, p.8.

3. White, Palmer, *Elsa Schiaparelli: Empress of Paris Fashion*, Rizzoli International Publications, Inc., New York, NY, 1986. p.53.

4. Kennett, Frances, op.cit., p.156.

5. Mulvagh, Jane, *Costume Jewelry in Vogue*, Thames and Hudson, London, 1988, p.52.

6. Ibid., p.52.

7. Kennett, op.cit., p.27.

8. Battersby, Martin, *The Decorative Thirties*, Walker and Company, New York, NY, 1971, p.185.

9. Robinson, Julian, *Fashion in the Forties*, Academy Editions, London, St Martin's Press, New York, NY, 1976, p.44.

10. Glassner, Lester, *Dime-Store Days*, Hardmondsworth, NY: Penguin, 1976, p.111.

11. Glassner, ibid., p.111.

12. Glassner, ibid., p.30.

Chapter 11:

1. See an excellent, in depth article, "Chinese Toggles", by M.W.Speights, in the *National Button Bulletin*, Nov/Dec.,1978.

2. White, op.cit., p.143.

3. Kennett, op.cit., p.148.

4. Dekin, Albert R., "Sealed in Time", *National Geographic* Magazine, June 1987, p.835.

5. Petein, Theodor A., *Oriental Motifs for Creative People*, Charles E. Tuttle Company Inc., Rutland, Vermont and Tokyo, Japan, 1965, p.10.

6. Although button literature always refers to a 1960s date for manufacture of Arita buttons, there are, for instance, nine Arita buttons pictured (though not named as such) in the 1949 book, *The Complete Button Book*. Aritas were made before World War II (and, perhaps, some were indeed made after), but were *imported to the United States* in the 1960s.

Chapter 12:

1. Baker, Lillian, *Fifty Years of Collectible Fashion Jewelry, 1925-1975*, Collector's Books, Paducah, KY, 1986, p.8.

2. Sulzberger, C.L., *The American Heritage Picture History of World War II*, American Heritage Publishing Co., Inc., New York, NY, 1966, p.401.

Chapter 13:

1. Hillier, Bevis, op.cit., p.80.

Chapter 14: none

Chapter 15:

1. Conant, Janet, "Buttons and Billiard Balls—A Designer From Deep South Captures Paris", *Newsweek*, June 27,1988, p.67.

2. Reed, Julia, "Talking Fashion",*Vogue*, September,1989, p.778.

3. See Realistics, Chapter 11, for further Danforth information.

Chapter 16: none

Chapter 17:

1. See The French Revolution, Chapter 2

2. Elliott, Huger, *Fashions in Art*, Books for Libraries Press, Freeport, NY, 1971, p.2.

3. Gere, Charlotte, *Victorian Jewellery Design*, p.40.

4. Mackay, James, *An Encyclopedia of Small Antiques*, Harper & Row, New York, NY, 1975, p.136.

5. Gere, Charlotte, *American & European Jewelry, 1830-1914*, pp.76-77.

6. For further information, see a wonderful article by Mildred Combs and M.W. Speights on Art Nouveau buttons, illustrated with a tremendous number of examples, in the December 1988 *National Button Bulletin*, pp.216-236.

7. Murray, Peter and Linda, *A Dictionary of Art and Artists*, p.103.

8. Murray, Peter and Linda, ibid., p.312.

9. Murray, Peter and Linda, ibid., p. 175.

10. DiNoto, Andrea, *Art Plastic: Designed For Living*, Abbeville Press, New York, NY, 1984, p.28.

11. Murray, Peter and Linda, op.cit., p.311.

12. Murray, Peter and Linda, ibid., p.1.

Bibliography

Aesthetic Movement, The, Robin Spencer. Studio Vista, London, and E.P. Dutton and Co., Inc., New York, NY, 1972.

American & European Jewelry, 1830-1914, Charlotte Gere. Crown Publishers, Inc., New York, NY, 1975.

American Heritage Magazine, Feb.1966, p.97, "I Lift My Lamp Beside the Golden Door", E.M. Halliday. American Heritage Publishing Co., Inc., New York, NY, 1966.

American Heritage Picture History of World War II, The, C.L. Sulzberger. American Heritage Publishing Co., Inc., New York, NY, 1966.

Antique Review Magazine, October 1, 1989, "Antique Review Preview" Section, "Forget Me Not", a lecture by Edna Bomar. Antique Review Publications, Worthington, Ohio, 1989.

Art Plastic: Designed For Living, Andrea DiNoto. Abbeville Press, New York, NY, 1984.

Automobile and American Culture, The, David L. Lewis and Laurence Goldstein, Editors, for Chapter: *The Automobile and American Fashion, 1900-1930*, Helen Frye. The University of Michigan Press, Ann Arbor, MI, 1983.

Big Book of Buttons, The, Elizabeth Hughes and Marion Lester. Boyertown Publishing Co., PA

Book of Fairies, The, Beatrice Phillpotts. Ballantine Books, New York, NY, 1979.

Button, Button, Peggy Ann Osborne. Schiffer Publishing, Ltd., Atglen, PA, 1993.

Button Lover's Book, The, Marilyn V. Green. Creative Machine Arts Series, Chilton Book Company, Radnor, PA, 1991.

Buttons, Diana Epstein and Millicent Safro. Harry N. Abrams, Inc., New York, NY, 1991.

Citizens; A Chronicle of the French Revolution, Simon Schama. Alfred A. Knopf, New York, NY, 1989.

Collecting Political Americana, Edmund B. Sullivan. Crown Publishers, Inc., New York, NY, 1980.

Collector's Book of Fashion, The, Frances Kennett. Crown Publishers, Inc., New York, NY, 1983.

Collector's Book of Jade, The, Arthur and Grace Chu. Crown Publishers, Inc., New York, NY, 1978.

Collector's Encyclopedia of Buttons, The, Sally Luscomb. Crown Publishers, Inc., New York, NY,1967, reprinted by Schiffer Publishing Ltd., Atglen, Pa, 1993.

Complete Button Book, The, Lillian Smith Albert and Kathryn Kent. Doubleday & Company, Garden City, NY, 1949.

Costume Jewelry in Vogue, Jane Mulvagh. Thames and Hudson, London, 1988.

Decorative Arts of the Forties and Fifties, The; Austerity/Binge, Bevis Hillier. Clarkson N. Potter, Inc., New York, NY, 1975.

Decorative Thirties, The, Martin Battersby. Walker and Company, New York, NY, 1971.

Dictionary of Art and Artists, A, Peter and Linda Murray. Hardmondsworth, NY: Penguin, 1976.

Dime-Store Days, Lester Glassner. Hardmondsworth, NY: Penguin, 1976.

Elsa Schiaparelli: Empress of Paris Fashion, Palmer White. Rizzoli International Publications, Inc., New York, NY, 1986.

Encyclopedia of Collectibles, The; O-P, pp. 34-47, "Opera Momentos", Marie M. Ashdown. Time-Life Books, Inc., Chicago, IL, 1979.

Encyclopedia of Small Antiques, An. James Mackay, Harper & Row, New York, NY, 1975.

Fads & Fancies, Denys Sutton. Wittenborn & Company, New York, NY, 1979, compilation of articles from the issues of *Apollo* Magazine. Chapters: The Paradoxes of Neo-Classicism, pp.96-107, and The Incomparable Josephine, pp.130-143.

Fashion in the Forties, Julian Robinson. Academy Editions, London, and St. Martin's Press, New York, NY, 1976.

Fashions in Art, Huger Elliott. Books for Libraries Press, Freeport, NY, 1971 (reprinted from 1937).

Fifty Years of Collectible Fashion Jewelry, 1925-1975, Lillian Baker. Collector's Books, Paducah, KY, 1986.

House Beautiful's Home Decorating Magazine, Vol.25, No.2, Summer 1986, pp.97-99, "New Wave Designs-Patterns for the Eighties", Richard Horn.

Illustrated Dictionary of Jewellery, An, Anita Mason and Diane Packer. Harper & Row, New York, NY, 1974.

Just Buttons Magazine, all issues. Published by Sally Luscomb, from Oct.1942 to Dec.1979.

Metropolitan Home Magazine, Vol.XVIII, No.8, August, 1986, p. 6, "Hot Properties", Arlene Hirst and Michael Walker.

National Button Bulletin, The, all issues. The National Button Society, Canton, Ohio; editor: M.W.Speights, Houston, Texas.

National Geographic Magazine, pp.824-836, June 1987, Vol.171, No.6, "Sealed in Time—Ice Entombs an Eskimo Family for Five Centuries", Albert A. Dekin, Jr. The National Geographic Society, Wash.D.C., 1987.

Newsweek Magazine, p.67, June 27,1988, "Buttons and Billiard Balls-A Designer From Deep South Captures Paris", Janet Conant with Meggan Dissly (Paris). Newsweek, NY, 1988.

1913; An End and a Beginning, Virginia Covales. Harper & Row, New York, NY, 1967.

One Hundred Years of American Theatre; 1860-1960, Daniel Blum. Chilton Company (Book Division), Philadelphia, PA, 1960.

One Hundred Years of Collectible Jewelry, Lillian Baker. Collector Books, Paducah, KY, 1978, updated 1986.

Oriental Motifs for Creative People, Theodor A. Peteln. Charles E. Tuttle Company, Inc., Rutland, Vermont and Tokyo, Japan, 1965.

Our Century. David S. Lake Publishers, Belmont, CA, 1989.

Those Fascinating Paper Dolls, Marion Howard. Dover Publications, Inc., New York, NY, 1981.

Twenties, The, Alan Jenkins. Universe Books, New York, New York, 1974.

Victorian Jewellery, Margaret Flower. A.S. Barnes and Company, Inc., South Brunswick, NJ, 1967.

Victorian Jewellery Design, Charlotte Gere. Henry Regnery Company, Chicago, IL, 1972.

Visual Dictionary of Art, A, Ann Hill, General Editor. The New York Graphic Society Ltd., Greenwich, CN, 1974.

Vogue Magazine, September, 1989, pp. 778 & 786, "Talking Fashion", Julia Reed.

Price Guide

The following guide is intended only as a point of reference for new collectors to enable them to judge the relative desirability or rarity of the various types of buttons. It is in no way intended as a price list.

Prices in the button world are fluctuating greatly at this time. Experienced collectors and specialized button dealers have been shocked at the recent rise in the prices of many types of buttons. The extraordinary present popularity of buttons in the collectibles and antiques fields has changed what was once a rather private community of knowledgeable collectors into an explosive seller's market. The public is buying buttons in droves, and from dealers who, new to the field, have no basis of knowledge on how to price buttons. These new customers and dealers have contributed to the rapid price increases. The price ranges suggested in this book are based on an average of what I think specialized dealers would charge.

Pricing also will vary by location: in the U.S., East Coast prices are usually higher. Certain buttons are more valued in England and will cost more there than they do in the U.S. Fine old French historicals are greatly valued in France but may be a relative bargain elsewhere. Japanese collectors are presently paying premium prices for Satsumas, which are already far from inexpensive in the U.S.

Particular types of buttons that fit into other collectible fields are often worth far more as collectibles in those specialties than they are as buttons: Disney collectors value early Disney buttons and pay far more for them than button collectors would imagine, sports collectors pay more for sporting-related buttons, etc.

Values are in U.S. dollars. Positions of photographs on a page are indicated by the letter codes L (left), R (right), C (center), T (top), and B (bottom).

9	Set	500-600	15	BR	200-300	21	T	1000-1100 the pair
10	Set	600-1000	16	TL	650-850	21	CR	200-250
10	CL	400-500	16	TR	80-125	21	CL	350-450
11	Set	7,000-10,000	16	CL	20-24	21	BR	350-450
12	TL	150-250	16	BL	650-750	22	TL	200-225
12	TR	300-400	17	TL	100-125	22	TR	50-80
12	C	400-500	17	TR	150-400 (square)	22	BL	600-650
12	BL	600-750	17	BR	30-40	22	BR	350-400
12	BR	225-275	18	TL	350-450	23		Too Rare to Price
13	TL	450-550	18	TR	350-500	24	TL	75-100
13	TR	125-175	18	C	500-650	24	CL	250-275
13	CL	400-500	18	BL	600-700	24	C	80-100
13	CR	75-100	18	BR	650-750	24	CR	90-110
13	BL	500-700	19	TL	Too Rare to Price	24	BL	50-55
13	BR	Too Rare to Price	19	TR	30-35	24	BR	225-275
14	TL	15-25	19	C	200-250	25	TL	100-125
14	TC	10-14	19	CR	125-150	25	TR	100-125
14	TR	20-40	19	BL	75-100	25	C	over 700
14	B	20-70	19	BR	100-125	25	B	75-80
15	T	35-50	20	TL	300-375	26	TL	100-125
15	CR	100-140	20	CL	350-400	26	TR	600-650
15	C	70-100	20	BL	200-225	26	BL	2000-2500 the set
15	BL	30-100	20	BR	500-600	26	BR	150-175

Pg	Pos	Price	Pg	Pos	Price	Pg	Pos	Price
27	TR	500-600	55	TR	15-18	74	BR	8-12
27	CR	12-22	55	CL	rare	75	TL	150-175
27	BL	200-275	55	C	18-22	75	TR	90-110
27	BR	20-30 ea	55	CR	12-18	75	C	4-9
28	TL	10-16	55	B	30-45	75	B	10-20
28	TR	12-18	56	TL	20-30	76	TL	140-180
28	CR	18-24	56	CR	30-50	76	TR	25-40
28	B	3-6	56	CL	8-15	76	BL	8-18
29	TR	18-30	56	BR	12-15	76	BR	10-12
29	CL	10-20	57	TR	10-12	77	TL	24-40
29	CR	18-24	57	CL	30-45	77	TR	100-120
29	B	55-75	57	CR	25-35	77	BL	35-50
30		15-150 (enamel w/steel highest)	57	BL	5-9	77	BR	5-12
31	TR	225-275	57	BR	7-15	78	T	2-22
31	TL	100-125	58	T	10-12	78	CL	15-20
31	BL	8-10	58	C	15-20	78	CR	15-18
31	BR	2-15	58	BL	12-18	78	BL	15-20
32	TL	14-18	58	BR	15-18	78	BR	12-18
32		900-1000 the set	59	TL	8-20	79	TL	2-10
33	TL	150-180	59	CL	6-10	79	TR	20-30
33	TC	150-175	59	BL	10-12	79	B	5-22
33	TR	200-250	59	BR	10-20	80	TL	18-24
33	CL	7-20	60	TL	12-20	80	TR	20-22
33	BL	150-175	60	CL	15-20	80	CL	12-18
33	BR	65-85	60	TR	18-24	80	CR	24-30
35	TL	10-15	60	BL	18-22	80	BL	12-16
35	CR	3-8	61	T	3-55 (silver)	80	BC	20-24
35	BL	5-35 (enamels highest)	61	B	6-40 (bottom celluloid)	80	BR	7-9
36	TL	1800-2000	62	TL	22-30	81	TL	25-30
36	B	300-2000	62	TC	15-20	81	TR	30-35
37	TR	150-175	62	TR	12-15	81	C	12-18
37	CL	60-75	62	BL	3-35 (Saturn)	81	BL	14-18
37	CR	45-55	62	BR	4-24	81	BR	10-12
37	BL	40-50	63	T	3-22	82		6-12
37	BR	200-225	63	B	8-28 (paste border)	83		10-22
38	TL	150-175	64	T	2-24	84		6-12
38	TR	60-75	64	B	8-14	85	T	5 (bottom) -75 (top)
38	CL	300-400	65	TR	25-32	85	B	5-30
38	BR	100-125	65	TL	75-80	86		2-15
38	BL	35-45	65	CR	14-16	87	TL	12-30
39	TR	350 and up	65	BL	7-20	87	R	6-11
39	BR	100-125	65	BR	20-25	87	CL	4-12
40		3-60 (ladies head escutcheon)	66	TL	400-450	87	BR	2-10
41	T	75-100	66	BL	350-375	88	T	8-15
41	B	35-45	66	BR	15 (flowers) - 80	88	B	50-120
42	T	250-275	67	TL	45-80	89	T	7-45 (bottom)
42	L	35-175	67	TR	20-25	89	B	3-20
42	R	600 the pair	67	B	3-25 (pique)	90	TL	18-22
43	TR	8-22	68	TL	10-20	90	CR	8-30
43	BL	10-15	68	TR	85-200 (ladies walking)	90	CL	7-10
43	BR	100-125	68	CL	130-140	90	BL	30-40
44	L	2-18	68	BL	100-150 (stud)	90	BR	8-25
44	R	4-25 (silver)	68	BR	150-175 lava; 125-150 carnelian; 75-85 shell	91	T	7-25
45	T	2-15	69	T	225 tiger; 700-800 the set	91	B	18-35
45	BL	3-7	69	B	1700-2000 the set	92		5-25
45	BR	12-15	70	T	12-20	93	TR	18-24
46		2-14	70	L	Too Unique to Price	93	C	5-22
47	T	5-22 (enamel)	71	T	10-90	93	BL	14-18
47	BL	Too Rare to Price	71	B	20-100	93	BC	35-45
48,49		7-20	72	TL	very rare	93	BR	7-12
50	TL	15-20	72	TR	30-40	94	TL	4-14
50	BL	20-25	72	CR	7-25	94	CR	10-25 (ivory)
50	BR	8 (florals) - 45	72	BL	25-45	94	BL	6-24
51	TL	2-12	72	BR	30-40	95		10-32
51	TR	12-20	73	TL	5-10	96	TL	24-50 (tortoise)
51	B	5-22	73	TR	45-60	96	TR	25 ea
52	T	2-20	73	BR	4-7 gold: 24-26	96	BL	8-12
52	BL	2-25	74	TL	20-25	96	C	15-24
53	T	15-24	74	TC	12-15	96	BR	8-12
53	B	10-50 (Madonna)	74	TR	60-80	97	T	300-400
54	T	20-40	74	L	10-40	97	TR	4-7
54	B	5-15	74	C	20-24	97	CL	30-45
55	TL	18-24	74	CR	7-12	97	CR	25-35
			74	BC	5-10	97	BL	75-80
						97	BR	25-35

Page	Pos	Price
98		8 (black glass) - 45
99		15-30
100		7-25
101	TR	18-24
101	CR	18-22
101	BL	10-35
102		7-28
103		10-25
104	TL	175-250
104	BL	8-10
104	BR	10-14
105	T	5-14
105	B	12-35
106		3-30 (for the larger and the enameled)
107		8-15
108		5-14
109		4-14
110		5-12
111	T	7-18
111	B	4-37 (enameled)
112		5-20
113		5-18
114		5-12 (sheet glass 25-35)
115		5-20
116	TL	4-8
116	TR	4-12
116	CL	4-9
116	BR	75-125
117	T	3-18 (Satsuma 100-150)
117	B	10-24
118		6-35
119		5-18
120	TL	6-8
120	TR	35-50
120	BL	22-36
120	BR	5-22
121	T	5-20
121	BL	5-40 (porcelain)
121	BR	150-175
122	T	8-23
122	C	8-20
122	BL	18-22
122	BR	From left: 20, 160, 15
123		5-25
124	TL	5-24
124	TR	3-12
124	C	8-20
124	BL	10-20
125	TL	6-15
125	TR	5-10
125	CL	5-14
125	CR	55-70
125	BL	5-25
126	TL	8-28
126	TR	5-50 (Tortoise)
126	CL	5-24
126	BL	2-10
127	T	3-18
127	B	4-20 (Enamel-40)
128	TL	12-50
128	TR	150-180 the set
128	B	10-30
129	TL	5-12
129	CL	24-30
129	CR	20-25
129	BL	200-225
129	BR	6 (small) - 24
130	Left Side	8-50 (pianist and organist highest)
130	BR	2-15
131	TL	10-32
131	TR	15-18
131	BL	3-8
131	BR	6-18
132		15-30
133	TR	18-25
133	C	100-125 the set
133	BL	10-20
134		15-24
135		18-34
136		10-26
137		10-24
138		20-25
139	T	15-20
139	C	15-18
139	B	20-30
140	TL	12-20
140	CR	100-150
140	BR	5-7 ea
141		25-40
142	TL	15-20
142	TR	8-20
142	CR	50-75
142	BL	7-18
143		100-110 the set
144	TL	5-18
144	TR	3-18
144	BL	5-14
144	BR	8-12
145	TL	6-12
145	TC	15-25
145	TR	36-55 set
145	CR	10-14
145	BL	25-35
145	BR	10-15
146	TL	8-12
146	CL	15-20
146	BL	40-65
146	R	5-25
146	B	3-5
147	TL	15-125 (large pearl)
147	TR	20-28
147	BL	150-175
147	BR	18-22
148	TL	75-100
148	CL	10-15
148	BL	6-10
148	BR	7-12
149	TL	12-20
149	TC	4-6
149	TR	40-60
149	CL	100-125
149	C	25-35
149	CR	12-18
149	BL	8-22
149	BR	55-75
150	TL	50-65
150	CL	10-12
150	CR	12-22
150	BL	1-12 (soldier)
150	BR	12-25 (tanks)
151	T	150-175
151	C	300-400
151	B	250-275
152	TL	600-750
152	CL	350-450
152	R	Too Rare (as a button) to Price
152	B	350-400
153	TR	1-4
153	CR	25-35
153	L	1-4 (cuffs)
153	BR	15-20
154	T	20-24 for postcard
154	C	6-9
154	B	10-30 (buttons only)
155	TL	30-35
155	TR	7-12
155	CR	15-20
155	B	12-18
156		5-35 (center)
157		1-3
158	T	1-12
158	B	5-8
159	TR	4-7
159	CL	7-10
159	CR	6-10
159	BL	25-30
159	BR	15-25
160	TL	100-150
160	TR	25
160	BL	15-22
160	C	12-18
160	BR	15-18
161	TL	8-15
161	TR	5-12
161	C	4-6 Set 20-25
161	B	125-175 the set
162	TL	25-35 ea
162	TR	6-10
162	CL	3-6
162	C	8-10
162	CR	12-18
162	BL	top set-50, others 6-10
163	TR	8-12
163	CR	7-10
163	L	5-7
163	BR	3-5
164		Large set-200, carded 55-65, small 8-12
165	TR	set-10, others 5-9 ea, the square 22-25
165	CL	3-12
165	CR	15-20 carded
165	B	12-22
166	TL	20-24
166	CL	12-20
166	CR	3-6
166	BL	8-12 set
166	BR	5-10
167	T	8-12
167	TR	5-14
167	CL	3-7
167	Box	4-7
168	TL	3-5
168	CL	2-12
168	CR	5-8
168	BL	125-175 the set
168	BR	4-6
169	T	2-10
169	CL	3-9
169	CR	1-9
169	BL	2-5
169	BR	1-4
170	T	30-40
170	CL	2-3
170	BL	35-45
170	BR	2-18 (photo)
171	TR	clockwise from left, 12-15, 5-8, 2, 20-22 ea
171	BL	1-4; Bakelite boot and wood head, 10-20
171	BR	3-6
174	T	
174	CL	20-25
174	BL	125-150
174	BR	6-18
175	TL	40-50 set
175	TR	7-14 per card
175	B	8-12 per card
176	TL	8-10
176	CL	10-16
176	B	1-6
177		8-20 per set

178	T	4-6	197	BR	3-7	223	BL	3-25 (the center one)
178	C	20-30 card	198	TL	15-24	223	BR	7-10
178	B	5-8 ea	198	CL	10-14	224	TL	4-6
179	T	3-5 per card	198	Set	20-30	224	TR	6-20
179	BL	40-50	198	BL	4-12	224	CL	5-8
179	BR	40-45	199	TL	18-22	224	BL	5-8
180	TL	125-150	199	TR	10-20	224	BR	7-22
180	BR	8-15	199	CL	5-10	225	TL	8-18
181	TL	20-22	199	Bread Set 50-65		225	TR	2-14
181	TR	15-20	199	Pie Set 40-55		225	CL	5-10
181	CL	4-12	200	TL	5-7	225	BL	20-30 ea
181	BL	8-15 ea; carded 50-65	200	CL	5-20	225	BR	20-40 ea
181	BR	set of 4, left 40-50; carded	200	CR	25-40 each	226	TL	15-24
		set 40-50	200		70-85 the set	226	TR	8-15
182	L	Bakelite set 80-125;	201	TL	4-6	226	L	6-10
	set of 4:	40-50;	201	TC	8-12	226	C	6-8
	others	8-15	201	TR	3-5	226	BR	17-20
182	TR	8-15	201	Sets	9-22	227	TL	8-30
183	TL or TR	35-40	201	BR	5-9	227	BL	6-10 as a card
183	CL	8-12	202		6-12	227	R	2-8
183	CR	8-12	203	Set of Gods 150-180; the rest		229	T	2-6
183	BL	12-20			from 65 lowest	229	C	1-3
183	BR	6-10			to 200 highest	229	B	15-20 the set
184	T	5-7				230	TL	7-10
184	CL	90-120 set	204	L	1-2	230	CR	5-15
184	CR	5-7	204	R	3-8	230	BL	8-16
184	BL	3-8	206	TL	10-12	230	BR	4-7
184	BR	3-5	206	BL	15-20 Set	231	TL	22-28 per card
185	T	24-30	206	R	2-7	231	CR	5-12
185	TL	8-20	207	T	3-5	231	BL	20-22 card
185	R	75-110	207	L	1-3	231	BR	2-4
185	B	1-2	207	R	5-8	232	TL	18-25 card
186	Set of 6, 50-60:		208	TL	2	232	CL	15 Set
	carded 60-75;		208	BL	1-4 ; 50-65 Satsuma	232	CR	2-12 ea
	Bakelite set 60-75;		208	B	Set 100	232	BL	18-24
	others singly 5-12		209	TL	15-20	233	TR	8-10
187	T	Set 15-24	209	TR	3-5 ea	233	TL	20-30
187	CR	3-6	210		5-15	233	B	8-24
187	CL	6-8	211	CL	5-10	234	T	5-10
187	BC	8-15	211	CR	3-8	234	C	1-3
188	TL	10-20	211	BL	50-100	234	B	5-10
188	TR	65-85	212	TL	10-18 ea, set 200	235	T	7-15 (glass)
188	BL	4-10; the insect 75-80	212	TR	50-160	235	C	5-9
188	BR	10-35	212	B	25-210	235	B	35-50
189		8-12	213	TR	35-150	236	L	24-30 the set
190	Glass set 15-20		214	T	25-125 (Buddha)	236	TR	10-15
190	Baseball set 50-75		214	B	25-100	236	CR	20-25
191	All sets 6-25 (Pantry)		215	T	25-60	236	BR	4-7
192	Coconut 2-8		215	B	50-125	237	T	5-9
192	Footballs 2-5		216	T	50-80	237	B	10-15
192	Dog	20-25	216	B	40-60	238	TL	8-10 card
192	BL	3-10	217		25-125	238	CL	3-6
192	BR	5-10	218	TL	500-600 the set	238	BL	5-8
193	TL	8-15	218	TR	500-700 the set	238	BR	4-6
193	TC	7-12	218	BL	12-18 Set	239	TL	5-7
193	TR	7-12	218	BR	5-8	239	TR	8-12
193	CR	10-16	219	TL	8-12 ea	239	CL	7-12
193	Fan	8-16	219	BR	Margot de Taxco Set 1500-	239	BR	1-3
193	BL	10-15			2000	239	BL	1-2
193	BR	4-7	220	TL	4-7	240	TL	1-3
194	L	5-15	220	TR	5-7	240	CL	1-2
194	R	10-20	220	CL	5-8	240	CR	3-4
195	TR	30-35	220	BL	15-18 Set	240	BL	1-3
195	CL	60-85	220	BR	10-15 Set	240	BR	1-8
195	CR	5-8	221	T	3-12 (The tortoise	241	TR	1-7
195	BL	5-8			Spratling is listed below)	241	BR	7-10
195	CR	18-30	221	CL	Signed Spratling 35-45	242	TL	5-14
195	BR	35-50 the set	221	CR	8-18	242	C	5-12
196	TL	8-12	221	BL	8-18	242	BL	7-16
196	SET	60-85	222	TL	7-15	243	TR	2-3
196	BL	4-11	222	TR	7-14	243	CL	40-50
196	BR	3-14	222	BL	8-16	243	C	5-7
197	T	4-8	222	BR	8-15	243	CR	4-6
197	CL	4-8	223	TL	2-7	243	BL	No value available
197	CR	4-10	223	TR	7-20	244	T	2-4

Page	Type	Price
244	B	4-6 ea
245	TL	5-8
245	TR	5-8
245	CL	3-7
245	CR	4-7
245	BL	3-7
246	T	1
246	C	2-3
246	B	1-5
247	TL	5-10
247	TR	3-6
247	CL	3-4
247	C	3-4
247	CR	4-8
247	BL	7-9
247	BR	3-5
248-249		7-25
250	T	1-3
250	C	1-3
250	BL	.50-1
250	BR	10-12
251	TR	10-12
251	BL	5-10
252	TL	4-7
252	TR	6
252	BL	7-10
252	BR	5-8
253	TR	3-5
253	CR	5
253	BL	8-10
253	BR	8-10
254	C	7-10
254	BR	6-8
254	BL	6-8
255	TL	7-12
255	TR	4-8
255	CL	5 per card
255	BL	5-8
255	BR	4-8
256	TL	3-4
256	TR	5-7
256	CR	5-8
256	BL	3-5
259	L	12-18
259	R	450-650
259	B	15-22
260	Silver	45;
	enamel	30-40;
	pearl	22-26;
	others	8-20
261	T	65-80
261	CL	350 and up
261	BR	200-300
262	TL	500-650
262	CL	12-18
262	C	75-80
262	Others	7-18
263	TR	350-375
263	CR	70-80
263	BL	450-550
263	BR	25-40
264	TR	75-85
264	Others	8-22
265	TR	400-475 if perfect
265	TL	8-20
265	C	12-15
265	CR	325-350
265	Others	5-8
266	TL	75-90
266	Others	5-15
267		10-22
268	TL	22-35
268	BL	5-18
268	BR	8-15
269		7-20
270		7-25 (silver)
271	TL	275-325
271	B	35-55
272		5-22
273	TR	75-80
273	TL	150-200
273	CR	50-70
273	BL	12-14
273	BR	4-7
274	T	35-45
274	B	Too volatile for pricing info
275		Too volatile for pricing info
276	TL	18-22
276	TR	7-35 (Fabric)
276	B	25-30
277	TL	20-25
277	TR	4-7
277	B	7-10
278	TL	15-20
278	CL	20-24
278	CR	7-9
278	B	6-17
279	TL	8-24
279	TR	15-24
279	C	18-22
279	B	20-30
280	TL	85-100
280	TR	50-70
280	CR	60-100
280	CL	25-35
280	BR	4-7
281	Inlay	25 (small) - 80
281	B	7-10
282		6-20
283	T	300-400 each
283	B	10-15
284	TL	15-22
284	C	55-70
284	BL	8-20
284	BR	4-9
285	TR	Too volatile to suggest a price
285	C	3-24 (Ivory)
285	BR	15-24
286	TL	24-30
286	CR	25-45
286	CL	6-14
286	BR	8-14
287	TL	12-24
287	TR	35-45
287	B	15-32
288	T	65-75
288	C	25-60 (snake)
288	BL	18-22
289	B	10-12
290	TL	20-22
290	CL	22-26
290	BL	7-10
290	BR	6-10
291	TR	25-28
291	CR	18-20
291	BL	24-30
291	BR	24-30
292		4-18
293	T	2-8
293	BR	14-20
294	T	2-12
294	BL	22-26
294	BR	7-15
295	Cards	10-12
295	Others	3-18
297	TR	10-14
297	Others	5-20
298		2-8
299		4-9
300		3-12
301	TR	7-10
301	B	1-5
302	T	10-12
302	C	10-14
302	B	3-6
303		3-8 ea
304		2-3
304	Cards	4-6
305	TR	18
305	B	12
305	Others	1-4
306	T	3
306	B	1
307		2-12
308		2-6

Index